The Good New

The Good New

A Tuscan Villa • Shakespeare and Death

John Glavin

Washington, DC

Library of Congress Control Number: 2017953764
ISBN 978-0-9986433-7-3 hardcover (alk. paper)

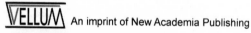 An imprint of New Academia Publishing

 NEW ACADEMIA
PUBLISHING

New Academia Publishing
4401-A Connecticut Ave. NW, #236, Washington DC 20008
info@newacademia.com - www.newacademia.com

Cover image: "Villa Le Balze, Fiesole" by Annibale Niccolai, 1994,
Charles A. Strong Center, Georgetown University.
Gift of Marquesa Margaret Rockefeller de Larain.
Reproduced by permission of Georgetown University.
Photo, Philip Humnicky, 2017

For

Cecilia and Thaddeus
i ragazzi della Villa

and

Carole Sargent
la madrina del Libro

Table of Contents

SEPTEMBER   1

Week One, September 3-9
Sunday morning; Mid-day; Le Balze; San Gimignano; Monday:
the First Class; Lucca, Up in a Loggia; Shots; A picnic.   3

Week Two, September 10-16
The Celle, Morning; Mid-day; Evening; Class/Gaps; Urgent;
Midweek: An Alumna Calls; Edging Gender; A Call from Rome;
Other Edges; A Cena.   35

Week Three, September 17-26
Sunday un dramma italiano; First Encounters; A Garden Walk;
Kissing; 222; Dora calls and a star comes calling; Volpaia.   58

Week Four, September 24-30
A Dark Drive; Preposterous; Pericoloso; Going Like Lynn; Dora;
Loggia and Lecture; Basta così.   80

OCTOBER   105

Week Five, October 1-7
"Educating in Paradise"; Siena; Much Ado Part One; Drying
Out; Rotgut; Detection; Maggie Ritornata.   107

Week Six, October 8-14
Up at the Castello, Down at the Villa; Grooving in the Grove;
Rotgut; Taddeo; Blithe and Bonny; Montepulciano; The Interpo-
lated Tale of Enrico Schnauzer; Friday, October 13, Ominous date;
Freud's nephew.   128

Week Seven, October 15-21
Cip; Getting to the Ort; Frutta; A bust beneath the jasmine; Jazz-ing the Ort; The Detective's Theory; Remembering Mark Gillen.

156

Week Eight, October 22-28
Archery; Interpellations; Rotgut's crisis; Our Belmont; Mercy; Worsening Conditions; Rome; Assisi.

178

Week Nine, October 29-31
Sant'Antimo; Away; Rome; Dora's Account of the Detective's Discoveries.

213

NOVEMBER

215

Week Ten, November 5-11
Reversals; Race Matters; Paradise; Othello Reclaimed; The Elec-tion; Ventuno; Verona; Return.

217

Week Eleven, November 12-18
Purgatorio; Lagniappe; The Bright at their Best; Marcello's Star Turn; Becoming Othellos; Waldo; The Slaves; Cecilia Returns.

238

Week Twelve, November 19-25
Closing In; Last Classes; Ventuno è arrivato; Thanksgiving, Try the First; Thanksgiving, Try the Second; An unexpected call; Too late.

261

Week Thirteen, November 26-December 2
The Sense of an Ending; I Tatti; All's Well That Ends Well; Rome; Corridoio; Veschi G. e Figli.

282

Finale Ultimo, December 6-7

302

Afterword 2017

306

Toward the end of this book you will find this story told again, in its proper place in time.

A pilot in his mid-twenties, amateur but experienced, is flying his own small plane. He is traveling north from Rome. An hour or so into the flight, he seems to hear a voice, a voice he knows well, speaking to him, though he is alone in the cockpit. This voice warns him to turn round at once.

Because he knows the voice, indeed because he trusts and deeply loves the person whose voice he hears, instinctively he turns around and heads back toward Rome.

Approaching the airport, suddenly all the instruments fail. He panics. He tries everything he knows. Nothing works. The instruments stay blank. Outside the sun is setting. Flying blind, in the dark, he knows he will crash when he tries to land.

And then he hears the voice again. The first time it was stern, this time it is amused.

It says: *dispone di un telefonino.* "You have a cell phone."

The pilot fishes the cell phone from his pocket. He calls an emergency number. He is connected to the tower of the airport where he houses the plane. The tower talks him into a perfect landing.

He later learns that traveling north he was flying directly into an unexpected storm, one that would surely have overwhelmed his small plane.

The stories that follow in this book turn out to be, in one way or another, versions of this story. And that is because of something they all share. They are all, despite their many differences, stories from Italy, stories of Italy. More specifically, they are stories from Tuscany in the year 2000.

SEPTEMBER

WEEK ONE
September 3-9

Sunday morning

Two nights ago, over our upgrade-to-Business Scotches, my wife Maggie and I were assuring each other how right our friend Stefano had been when he e-mailed last spring, "Oh what a good *new.*" He'd just heard we were coming back here to Fiesole, this bijou of a Tuscan town cresting the high hill north of Florence. (Even Italians who speak excellent English say *new* not *news; novità*, the Italian word for news, is singular.) Stefano's an expert on the Hittites, more reliable on the far past, on the very far past, than on the present. But a good new is precisely what we've come here for. What we both need. Let Stefano the scholar this time also prove himself a prophet.

Here's why we pretty badly need a good new.

On my birthday three years ago, Maggie and I met after work for a celebratory drink. Without thinking the answer would matter, I asked something like "How'd your day go?"

"Not so good. I had a bad mammogram."

And then began the toughest year of our lives, infinitely tougher for Maggie, of course, than for me. Surgery. Chemotherapy. Radiation. Since then all signs point to a complete recovery. The oncologists are unanimously optimistic. Tests and the numbers couldn't be better, they insist. But that year pushing back against death just about finished us. Up until that rainy late October afternoon we not only thought we had it made, we thought we had it made for good. One sweet year would fold smoothly into the next until some unimaginably remote, hardly perceptible twilight would bring us to a close we'd barely notice. It didn't take many gruelling sessions of chemo and radiation to teach us both how foolish we had been. How unreliable life not only can be, but, inevitably, will be.

And that is why we've come back to Italy, to Fiesole and the Villa Le Balze, Georgetown University's outpost in Tuscany, to find Stefano's elusive, much needed, *new.* We've lived here before, from January through May in 1987. That winter into spring transformed our lives. At that point we'd been married for fifteen years. We had two children: Thaddeus, 14, and Cecilia 11. We had a heavy mortgage, and we were struggling to meet two private school tuitions. Money was so tight that we'd begun paying for our groceries in cash—including coins—to make sure we didn't write a bad check. Vacations, if there were vacations, meant a week, in a good year two weeks, in a tiny bungalow at the tip of the Jersey shore. Each of us had been doing the same job for 20 years, Maggie at the Department of Agriculture, me at Georgetown. We loved each other; we adored our children. But our lives somehow, year by year, had just kept getting thinner, duller, dimmer. Boredom, we could both sense it, was building up toward backlash.

And then I got the chance to come for the first time to teach at Le Balze, where Georgetown runs a small study abroad program for juniors. Taking the chance was entirely Maggie's idea. She's always been the bolder of the two of us, the one more open to risk. But when she first suggested I apply, I didn't pay much attention. I thought she'd never get leave from Agriculture. And besides how could we live without her salary? But when her bosses heard she had a chance to live for five months in Italy, they not only said *Of course*, they practically shouted *Grab it*. So we did.

We took Thaddeus and Cecilia out of school, to the dismay of their teachers and the disgust of their friends. We told them they didn't have to do anything in Italy but try to pick up some Italian and sit in on Art History lectures. We emptied our paltry savings to buy the plane tickets. And hoped that my salary would keep us fed and clothed and afloat for five months. We even managed, just before we left DC, to sublet our house (which made up a bit for the loss of one salary). On the day we flew out from Dulles, a blizzard socked the city, crippling it for the better part of a week. In Fiesole we found everyone in shirt sleeves.

It began well, and with each week it got better.

Years later, when it came time to select a topic for his college admissions essay, Thaddeus wrote about Florence. He said that on his first solo trip into the city he had the sensation that comes when you taste something for the first time and know that from now on this is going to be your favorite food. Even after a few weeks each of us would have said the same thing. But Maggie and I also learned something more, something far more valuable than anything I was teaching my students. Living in Italy taught us to upscale our demands. The Italians around us were doing just that, daily, hourly setting the bar beyond high. (Florentine Stefano, when I told him we were invited to see the palazzo of a Principessa with a famous name and title, lamented: "But, Gian, she is only a *Roman* princess.") Tuscany quickly taught us not to settle for a merely good life. Life worth having, we learned, wants demands placed on it. It turns out that the more you ask from Life, the more you are likely to receive in return. Our increasingly settled routines had asked for too little, and as a result, inevitably, each year we got even less. Italy that year made us see Life's fundamental, maybe even its secret, irony. *To him who has more shall be given. To him who has not even that shall be taken away.*

Once we began to learn that, we lapped up our Italian lessons. And life kept getting better well beyond our stay here. For the next dozen or so years after our Italian sojourn, Maggie and I kept asking for lots from life, and life kept on giving us more than we could have ever hoped, more than we could even have imagined. Until that October evening, when we, without warning, topped out.

So now we've returned, same job, same place, but from the start demanding even more than we ever have asked before. After our brush with catastrophe, when the chance to live and teach here again unexpectedly opened up, Maggie insisted we grab it. I was even more surprised this time by her eagerness. After all she was enjoying the biggest job in her increasingly distinguished career. Leaving it now would probably bring that career to a complete and premature end. But she didn't care. Whatever her post-chemo tests and numbers say, she knows even better than I that she's not her old self, not even anything like that self. Italian has a haunting word *ombra*—it means both shade and shadow. When I look at Maggie now, really look at her, I see that she has become *un'ombra*, a shadow of what she was, physically, emotionally, spiritually. But she's also what the Ancients called a shade, someone caught between life and death, subdued, paled, an echo. And often when we talk I hear underneath our conversation, unsaid, the aching unforgettable lament from Gluck's opera *Orfeo ed Euridice*, when Orfeo realizes that his beloved wife Euridice will not ever come back to life. *Che farò senza Euridice?* What will I do without Eurydice?

Maggie is exhausted; I'm terrified.

But on the plane, over those Scotches, we told ourselves that Stefano's got to be right. The first time at the Villa we started off knowing nothing about Italy, knowing no one. This time it already feels like a homecoming. We have friends, dear friends, eager to welcome us back into their lives. We know the places, some famous, many not, that were special for us. We understand how the Villa works, and how to make it work when it frustrates. We've even managed to sublet the house again, another house. So this time how can things not be even better than they were? We've got a running start, and we've promised ourselves we won't allow a missed turn, a foolish choice, a wasted minute.

We can't.

Mid-day

After lunch I walk from our apartment, in what is called the villino, to the villa itself. For the first time I am going to meet my students, always referred to by Le Balze as *gli studenti*. If you ask Maggie and me why I'm here, the answer is: to help Maggie recover, to help both of us recover, to grab that good new. If you ask Georgetown, my employer, why I'm here: it's to teach. Sooner rather than later I know I've got to figure out how to make those two quite different, and I already sense, potentially opposing goals, rhyme. Because if it were up to me, I'd never leave Maggie alone.

This meeting isn't a first class. That's scheduled for tomorrow, Monday. But our astute and diplomatic program director, Marcello, has suggested a little get-acquainted orientation after lunch, *pranzo*, in Italy the major meal of the day. *Gli studenti* have already been in Italy for a week, on home stays with Italian families in Urbino, 70 miles due east of Florence, across the Apennines. Marcello tells me this has been a big success. They have already bonded with each other and with Marcello, and so I start off as something of an interloper. Not only do Maggie and I not live in the villa with them, we don't take our meals together except on special occasions. I am literally an outsider. Marcello hopes this informal meeting will serve as a kind of transition, to enable me, as it were, to slip smoothly into their world.

Gli studenti, perhaps twenty-five in all, have stayed on after the meal in the small stuffy dining room, a room designed to seat no more than twelve. Crowded between tables, collapsed on benches and chairs, they sprawl, a blur of apparently interchangeable t-shirts and shorts. The food at Le Balze has always been memorable with a treasury of favorite recipes developed by the first cook, the one we knew fourteen years ago, Clara Fransoni. She's retired now, the kitchen is managed by two new cooks, but the recipes remain pretty much hers. Today it's been a Tuscan bean soup, followed by ravioli with sausage and walnuts, completed by Clara's truly remarkable tiramisu. And of course wine. As much as you want for as long as you care to linger at table. This may be Georgetown but it is Georgetown in Italy. With that menu and as many helpings of each course as they chose, and the wine, on this airless afternoon, no wonder they all seem on the verge of stupor. At this point I could probably announce that I am here to teach nuclear physics and hear no objection.

In the flat silence that greets my appearance Marcello delicately suggests that I tell *gli studenti* something of the course I propose. He professes himself delighted by everything he has already heard about it, and is eager to hear more. Eager is not what the students seem.

The course, I explain, is called "Shakespeare in Italy." I explain that I am not a Shakespeare scholar; my writing and teaching focus on issues of adaptation, from stage to page, and from page to stage and screen. That means I work a lot with Shakespeare's texts, but primarily as they influence or as they are reshaped by writers like Charles Dickens or Anthony Trollope or Oscar Wilde. Scripts fascinate me, how they suggest performance, how they are released and revised and even repressed through performance. I once published an article entitled "The Problem of the Playwright's Authority," in which I demonstrated, convincingly in my clearly prejudiced judgment, that playwrights have no authority at all over their texts. Certainly not the authority of novelists or poets.

In this course, I continue, we will read Shakespeare's seven and a half "Italian" plays, plays that are either set in Italy or, like *The Tempest*, are about Italians. The half is *All's Well That Ends Well* which ends well because, though it starts in France, it ends right down below the villa in Florence. The others are: *The Two Gentle-*

men of Verona, *The Taming of the Shrew*, *Romeo and Juliet*, *Much Ado About Nothing*, *The Merchant of Venice*, *Othello*, and *The Tempest*. After a somewhat wobbly start, Italy turns out to produce a wow of a play list. The last three certainly in anyone's judgment among the greatest of the master's master works.

Gli studenti, however, do not seem wowed.

I press on. We are going to group these plays together by asking whether their shared setting in Italy should actually make a difference to how we read them, separately and as a group. It doesn't seem to matter that *Measure for Measure* takes place in Vienna. Or that *Love's Labours Lost* is set in Navarre. Navarre? So does it matter that these plays are set here? Do we gain anything by hypothesizing some idea we can call Italy working within and behind the individual plots? After all, I point out, there was really no state called Italy until the 1860s. Before that, the peninsula was a hodgepodge of diverse and independent territories: kingdoms, dukedoms, principalities, independent republics, and of course the Papal States. (And it remains true that there are at least two different Italies, the north, the *Settentrione*, and the south, the *Mezzogiorno*, with almost nothing in common except corrupt government pretty much everywhere.) What's even more telling: we know that it's highly unlikely that Shakespeare ever set foot in Italy. And for significant parts of his time in London most Italian merchants had withdrawn from the island. So does it count that one play takes place in Verona and another in Padua? Does it matter that none of these plays is set in Rome? Are all the place names merely nominal? Or, if they do matter, is it only to suggest something generically foreign, exotic, other, a sort of Renaissance version of a galaxy far, far away?

The continued silence in the room suggests general consensus that these questions do not matter at all, for any reason, to anyone.

I try to up the ante. And does it matter that we will be reading the plays not in classrooms in Georgetown but in our own villa, in Fiesole, in Italy? Can reading them here, should reading them here, show us things about them and about Italy we wouldn't see if we were doing this course on the banks of the Potomac rather than the Arno? Come December, when we've had three months of shared experience, shared texts, shared travel, will Shakespeare have told us something about Italy, something that will be particularly relevant to us?

Will our Italy shed light on Shakespeare's "Italy"? Will Shakespeare's "Italy" shed light on ours? Does *where* we read something alter *how* we read it?

No one says a word, but I seem to hear them thinking: this is Sunday; classes begin tomorrow. This is our final day of freedom. It's not fair today even to talk about work.

Sensing that indifference having turned into boredom is now verging on resentment, Marcello suggests I tell them about the performance.

In lieu of a final exam, I explain, we will try to stage at least an abridged version of *All's Well*. Marcello adds that he is already looking into theater rentals down in the city.

Despite Marcello's enthusiasm, even this does not thrill.

I murmur my goodbyes, chalking up their benumbed silence to the wine and the tiramisu, and head back to the villino. After all, they are right: classes don't begin until tomorrow, either for them or for me. But has Marcello's little overture boomeranged, I can't help but wonder? Have I, inadvertently, edged apathy to the verge of hostility?

Le Balze

Heading back to our place, I take a few moments to reconnoiter.

Maggie and I live in a self-contained, three-storied apartment just outside Le Balze's front gate in what's called the villino, attached to the wall but outside the Villa proper. It's reserved for the faculty member who comes each term from the main campus in DC. The rest of the staff, academic and curatorial, are all Florentines with their own places in and around the city. We alone live up here—and of course also not here.

The villino is older by several centuries than the villa, which was built in 1911-12. It's also a great deal more rustic than the big place. Five, narrow, rough-plastered rooms, and fairly primitive plumbing. The original owners of Le Balze housed extra staff here, the chauffeur, folks of that sort. And of course, in a real though never mentioned way, despite grand titles like *dottore* and *professore*, I am staff too. Which is certainly the impression left on me by my just concluded encounter in the dining room.

Le Balze was built by an American named Charles Augustus

Strong and donated to Georgetown by his only child, Margaret, by her first marriage the Marquesa de Cuevas, and by her second, the Marquesa de Larrain. In 1889 Strong, the star of his Harvard class, later a Columbia professor of philosophy, married Bessie Rockefeller, the oldest of John D. Sr's daughters. She was 23, a recent Vassar graduate. He was 27, a prize-winner, a soon-and-sure-to-be major figure in America philosophy. Their families were close friends. In fact, Charles' father, a Baptist minister, more or less functioned as the senior Rockefeller's spiritual advisor. Nevertheless, it was, by every account, a love match. So it should have worked out well for all concerned. But it didn't.

First, and with an odd abruptness, Charles lost his faith. That made him literally anathema to his father, and certainly unwelcome to his strictly observant father-in-law. And then Bessie had a mysterious but close to total breakdown, both physical and emotional. Charles surrendered his Columbia professorship. The couple went to live in Europe, ostensibly to seek better medical care for her, but also because Strong increasingly felt he needed to live in a world with no claims but those of thought. By 1906 Bessie was dead, leaving Strong at 38 with their only child, Margaret, born in 1897.

Despite pressure from the Rockefellers, Strong never returned to the States. Instead, in 1911, he was persuaded by two close friends, the literary philosopher George Santayana and the art connoisseur Bernard Berenson, to build for himself a villa in Fiesole, the hill town nearest to the north side of Florence, and not far from Berenson's soon-to-be very famous establishment, I Tatti. Strong's choice settled on an awkward lozenge of land catty-corner to the original Villa Medici, then occupied by his friend Lady Sybil Cutting and her daughter Iris, later the writer Iris Origo. He called it Le Balze, which means in Ialian something like The Precipices or The Edges, or even The Ruffles, because it is literally dug out of the steep hillside slope in a series of man-made buttressing terraces.

To design the house Strong employed a neophyte British architect, Cecil Pinsent. Pinsent, just 25 years old at the time, had recently transformed the old farmhouse at I Tatti for Berenson, and he had also overseen some successful repairs to the genuinely Renaissance Villa Medici for Lady Sybil. For Le Balze's extensive gardens Pinsent joined forces with an equally young British ex-pat, Geoffrey Scott, light on architecture but long on taste (and apparently on looks; five years later he became Lady Sybil's second husband). This clever pair of Edwardian dandies made Le Balze look, at least from a distance, as though it might have been around since the Medici.

The house itself, the villa proper, is long and narrow, large but by no means grand, plain almost to the point of ascetic, coated with biscuit-colored stucco, and topped by a red tile roof. Inside, off a long, vaulted corridor open the three principal rooms, a dining room, a *salone*, or music room, and a library. Five good-sized bedrooms above, with ensuite baths. Behind the dining room there's also a sizeable, two-storied service wing, with the kitchen in the basement, of course. Though generous in scale, the house doesn't have a public room that would pass muster in a millionaire mushroom suburb like Potomac, Maryland, let alone in a place like the Rockefellers' Tarrytown. Its gardens, however, through which I am now making my way, make Le Balze something genuinely extraordinary.

Gardens, not garden. To both east and west the house opens into a series of seven garden "rooms," most enclosed by either masonry or shrubbery or both, far lovelier and more distinguished than any of the rooms indoors. Each is designed in a different formal pattern, with different sorts of plantings. And though they are walled, arches open from one to the next, aligning double, often triple perspectives, of house, gardens, and Florence miles below. In addition, there's also a symmetrically planted ilex grove to the west, and beyond and below the grove two further acres of olive trees, *de rigeur* in any Tuscan country house. Finally, to top it all, literally, a giant exterior double staircase expands to the north.

It's with the stairs, one feels, that, having satisfied the philosophical Strong with the rigorously disciplined house and garden, the impish designers set out to please themselves. Every Baroque inch is covered in seashells and sponges, formed from *spugna*, a kind of petrified limestone. It climbs three flights of low, very broad steps, curving along the way around a deep, (again) sponge-clotted grotto where water plunges into a murky, fishy tank. Everywhere you look on and around the stairs, there are statues. Big ones: Venus, Bacchus, an anonymous philosopher, Triton mounted on an oddly Japanese dolphin. Smaller ones: busts of ancient philosophers, several reclining river gods in bas-relief. The staircase ends, way up on the third story of the villino, at the Loggia, open to the broad Arno plain below.

Father and daughter moved into the house in 1913. I sometimes wonder if Strong named it Le Balze, not because of all those terraces but for the kind of peripheral, edgy life he and Margaret led here. By all accounts it was never even close to a happy place. In any case, Margaret soon left for an English boarding school. She never lived in the house again. Strong stayed for almost 30 years, alone except for a small staff, until his death in 1940. For much of that time he was confined to a wheelchair, completely without the use of his legs. Toward the end of her life Margaret kept an apartment in Florence but never spent a night in Le Balze, though she would come up regularly to have tea served in the gardens.

With no happy memories of the place she gladly gave it to Georgetown in 1979, shortly before her death. And when Maggie and I first lived here, the whole place, inside and out, was scrupulously maintained as a kind of living shrine to a past way of life. Ancient Dino, who had been her gardener, was still in charge. The Marquesa could have been in the next garden: *ci vuole una begonia, per piacere, Dino.* Even earlier, perhaps Henry James taking tea in the library with Berenson, Santayana and Strong. Strong's philosophy books were still on his library's shelves. The Marquesa's lamps, with their delicate, hand-painted shades, still on the consoles. And though most of the staff working then had not worked for the Strongs, they had been trained by the Strongs' staff. We were even given the use of the Marchesa's box down in Florence's Teatro della Pergola.

But as I prowl among them now, I see that though the gardens are still maintained, much of the rest of the fabric is starting to crumble. Signs warning *Vietato*—Forbidden—crop up with increasing frequency the further you move from the main building. Indoors, I saw that Strong's library has given way to dog-eared volumes the students consult and haphazardly discard. The console tables are stained with cup rings. The Marquesa's lamps are nowhere to be found. And all the furniture has been prudently slip-covered in garish, stain-resistant plaids. We could easily be in any better college dorm. Dino is dead. And when I inquired, Marcell says no one remembers anything about the box at the Pergola.

San Gimignano

Back in the Villino Maggie and Cecilia have decided we should drive to much-towered San Gimignano, though it's already mid-afternoon. Cecilia's only here for the week. Then she heads to Boston to start her career as a lawyer. Naturally, we want to crowd as many good things into her week as we can. Our first time here she was 11 years old. The older members of the Villa staff, who remember the little girl with braces and pigtails, maintain this poised and elegant young woman cannot possibly be she. Most of the time I agree.

Despite the crowded Sunday roads, we head off with high hopes.

But first we have to brave the horrors of the plunge down the Via Vecchia Fiesolana, the road onto which the property opens. It's only one lane wide, and a narrow lane at that. And it is virtually vertical from start to finish. What's more, it twists. Which means that as you start down you begin to blow your horn and you don't stop blowing your horn until you get to the bottom so that any until-the-last-moment invisible car coming the other way will in time try to find a driveway or similar layby into which to duck as you hurtle past—calling out with defiance *"Tocca a me."* My Turn! If this does not work—Pfffft. It's never less than terrifying and on a Sunday, with all the tourists out, it is almost suicidal.

Then, once out of Florence, it takes us about an hour to make our way there, but pretty much from the start San Gimignano is not the success for which we had hoped.

First of all, it's too damn hot. We arrived in winter last time, and winter that year was mild and beautiful. But summer in Tuscany this year, like summer in Tuscany every year, is infernal. Of course summer is supposed to end here in August. By rights we should by now be surrounded by hints of early autumn. But this year September continues to feel like August, scorched, mosquito plagued, and record-bashingly dry. Last night, walking the high Fiesole ramparts, we did feel a rare breeze surprise the stillness. Near me a young woman sighed, *"Ah, che bel vento."* "Oh, what a beautiful wind." Her entire frame shivered with pleasure. That wind could have been the virile, puffing god of Botticelli's *Primavera,* so completely did she surrender to its unpredictable, cool caress.

I don't know about her, but I haven't felt a breeze since.

But it's not just the heat. San Gimignano, one of our old favorites, turns out to have become a global favorite also. In 1987 the miniature town with its multiple turrets—you can cross it in something like 20 minutes—was magic, private, untouched by time, a secret pleasure. Now it's mobbed. Even in the Collegiata, the principal church, with its gigantic, primitive murals of the Old and New Testament, crude marvels though by no means masterpieces, you jostle against large, loud crowds. And the tiny jewel box of a side chapel, decorated by Domenico Ghirlandajo to honor the town's patron, Santa Fina, is packed shoulder to shoulder.

I love this chapel. I remember it as a quiet, melancholy retreat, not much larger than a coat closet, just a maid's room really, perfectly suited to the abused and holy maidservant who died of neglect. A Cinderella who never saw a slipper, let alone a prince. On one wall Ghirlandajo shows all San Gimignano grieving her death. Even the mice have come out to mourn, since she used to feed them first with her poor scraps. But to feel Ghirlandajo's spell, you have to be able to sit quietly, and let the sad space take hold. That's not possible this afternoon. Just to get a glimpse of the murals you have to squeeze between shoulders and peer above heads. Everyone is talking, no one is looking. We could be in the lobby of a multiplex.

Nevertheless, we force ourselves to make at least one complete circle of the town, what the Italians call a *giro.* But when we come back to our starting point, near where we parked the car, we quickly agree to drive home, quietly disgruntled since complaining won't make things better.

I pull out to rejoin the main road back to Florence and then, in a distracted moment—who knew it was going to be so hard to remaster stick shift; after all, I learned to drive on a stick shift—I take a wrong turn, a very wrong turn. And before we can discover a place to turn around, we are crossing the Val d'Elsa, the (it turns out) entirely splendid Val d'Elsa, superb in its late summer greenery. It's a nature reserve, valley then peak, peak then valley, all densely forested. We've never been here before—and, delight of delights, nobody else is here now. We have the road entirely to ourselves. Soon we are on an even better road, the 68 heading pretty much straight west, and still miraculously pretty much on our own. And we are wondering how it could be possible we didn't come here in 1987, when suddenly we realize that we have now gone way out of our way, moving toward the mountain top town of Volterra. We can see it on the horizon, an alabaster fortress capping an extinct volcano. Also someplace we've never seen.

And I don't care. No, I'm glad. Even though it is getting late, and we're all three hungry, I can't make myself turn back. Each curve is producing fresh and entirely unexpected rearrangements of green valley, sharply profiled hill and crowning citadel, astonishing figurations that seem to reinvent moment to moment what it means to be Tuscany. From time to time Maggie urges me to find a turn that will get us back to Florence before dark. And I keep promising her to take the next turn, only to keep—somehow—missing those turn offs. And then we are driving up the steep causeway into Volterra, the greenery suddenly gone, the roadway scarcely wider than the car, and the ground dropping off precipitously on either side. We're so high up now we think we can see the coast at Cecina 25 miles to the west. And then we are driving into Volterra, gleaming impossibly high above the valley slowly misting below. Shall we stop here for supper?

Maggie doesn't answer. I look over. She's forcing herself to stay upright, lips tightly compressed, eyes shut. The long hot day has clearly been too much for her. Of course, we should have gone home straight from San Gimignano. —As she asked. No, it was more than asked. I've been stupid and more than usually oafish. I have got to get this into my head. Maggie is not the person she used to be. Because she wants Cecilia to enjoy her week here, she insists on pushing herself as though she is who she once was. She finds it hard, always has, to refuse anything to anyone, especially one of her children. But she is here to convalesce, not play tour guide. And until she begins to get her energy back, I have got to teach myself to become the one who says no on her behalf.

Monday: the First Class
Le Balze's library, originally planned as a formal study for a

single scholar, can comfortably seat ten, tops. There's squatting room only now for the 19 students who've enrolled in the course. (Cleary, Sunday's little pre-orientation had a thinning effect.) Even those 19 aren't likely to feel enthusiasm at finding themselves here. Back home I am known as too demanding, a GPA buster. So, except for a pair I've taught before, I doubt many of the others would be squeezing in here if the Villa's narrow curriculum offered them a workable alternative.

I bolt the heavy wooden shutters against the harsh afternoon sun, unfortunately also killing any chance of a little breeze.

I start by explaining what I didn't get to yesterday. I am hoping to keep and then publish an account of the course in a book I think of calling "With Shakespeare in Italy." Of course, I can't do this without their permission. Which they willingly and spontaneously offer. Much to my surprise, and delight, they are enchanted by the idea of appearing in print. It will be a unique souvenir of their memorable time abroad. With winning naiveté they don't for a moment doubt that such a book will easily find its way to the public. They stipulate only that they should be called by pseudonyms. Despite the oppressive weather there's a noticeable thaw in the room.

I invite them to choose names from the glorious chapter in *The Great Gatsby* that lists the people who went to Gatsby's house "that summer." It has nothing to do with Shakespeare or Italy. I choose it because it's my favorite passage in American fiction. And because *gli studenti* are also a mixed crowd that has come to party in a big (or at least biggish) house. There are seven men and twelve women, but Fitzgerald's catalogue offers far fewer names for women than men, so they choose mostly without regard to gender. Here's what they select. Men: *Benny, Duke, Beluga, Rotgut, Ripley, Clyde* and *Earl Muldoon*. Women: *Duckweed, Claudia, Denneker, Consuela, Klipspringer, Corrigan, Stonewall, Ardita, Jacqueline, Betty, Orchid* and *Miss Haag*.

To keep their identities secret, of course, I can't describe who's who, but I hope an attentive future reader will be able to distinguish them by paying careful attention to what each says.

Now to work: I remind them of the twinned questions I mentioned yesterday. Does it really matter that these plays are set in Italy? And, if it does matter, is there something we can learn about our Italy by studying Shakespeare's?

This time they are indeed paying attention. Maybe yesterday the problem really was the wine, and the tiramisu.

"You want us to talk about Italy, but isn't Shakespeare universal?"

"He's not writing about Elizabethan Englishmen, or Italians, he's writing about being human."

"After all, isn't that why we still identify with his characters after all these hundreds of years?"

"Isn't that how you are able to teach this course, because we can still identify with him and what he writes?'

Before I can even start to respond to this catechism, I get an even stronger protest from Muldoon, whose frown and tone announce he intends to be difficult for the remainder of the term.

"Professor, you admitted yesterday that Shakespeare never saw Italy. So aren't his Italians, like, just English people with Italian names. He can't write about Italians if he's never met them. He can't write about different cultures if he is himself mono-cultural."

Monocultural—he reads. And, clearly, he thinks.

One of my two former students, Miss Haag, tries to come to my aid. "But Shakespeare could have read about Italians. He didn't actually have to go to Italy to know something about Italian culture."

"He did indeed read about Italians," I chime in. "We know that because scholars have recovered the astonishingly wide and deep range of earlier material he used in fashioning his plays. Shakespeare, as you probably know, almost never invented a plot of his own. Every script adapts earlier sources. So one thing we might discover is that Shakespeare is not only a great writer but he's also an equally great, perhaps an unsurpassed, reader."

There's another point to be considered. The plays set in Italy seem, by and large, to require, well, Italy. Their plots reply on more friars and less law than you would find in Tudor and Stuart England. But time has blurred for us the differences between sixteenth-century England and sixteenth-century Italy. They seem to us much more like each other because they are both so different from what we know. And I suspect Shakespeare's original audiences would have been not only struck by the differences between their lives and the lives in the Italian plays, they would have been fascinated by the Italian plays precisely because of that difference, because to London eyes they appeared so *exotic*.

I look around. The score seems now to be: maybe two *studenti* for me (my old acquaintance), one for the guy who knows how to use monocultural (that is: himself), and 16 suspicious of me but unwilling to ally themselves with a guy who on the first day of class would use a word like monocultural.

I press what I hope is my advantage: "And of course we do know that he knew Italians. For a very long time the center of banking in London was Lombard Street, so named because it was originally dominated by the northern Italian goldsmiths, and later the Italian bankers who managed much of Tudor finance. There were Italian doctors at court. There were Italian musicians. And London was becoming in the sixteenth century a great international port."

But it's clear from the look on their faces that this did not help. I try a different tack.

"Look: you've just had a wonderful *pranzo*. No one would turn down *pranzo* here because at home they would order a BLT and a Coke for lunch. So instead of starting with what makes them universal, why not approach the plays the same way? Why not look out for what's different, what disrupts, what's surprising, even shocking in these plays, shocking to the characters, shocking to the original audiences, shocking or at least puzzling to us?"

They look torn. They don't want to leave the comfort of what they know, but they still don't want to side with the show-off.

I've got just about 30 minutes left; I try to make the most of my momentary advantage. We're going to start, I explain, with the very early play, *Two Gentlemen of Verona,* one of his first comedies, dating probably from 1590-91.

[Since the play is not well known, let me briefly summarize it. It's one of what are sometimes called Shakespeare's forest or green-world comedies, in which at some crucial point everyone goes into the woods, where they find ways to unravel the complexities that oppressed and deluded them in the "real" world of the courts and cities from which they have fled or been banished. In this play two friends from Verona, Valentine and Proteus, the two gentlemen of the title, find themselves in Milan and in love with the same woman, the Duke of Milan's daughter Silvia. Proteus betrays Valentine to her father in order to have her for himself, but she scorns him. Everyone flees to the wood where they are captured by a band of outlawed aristocrats. What follows is strangely ugly for this sort of play, with Proteus trying to rape Silvia. But in the end the tyrant duke is forced to make amends to the thwarted lovers, and all ends well.

[In 1971 John Guare, whom we proudly hail as a Georgetown alumnus, and Mel Shapiro turned it into a rock musical with music by Galt MacDermot of *Hair*. It won the Tony for Best Musical and Best Book. But without their embellishments the original is, despite the eminence of its author, somewhat wanting. But since Shakespeare started here, so do we.]

When Valentine and Proteus go from their home in provincial Verona, they expect Milan to be a kind of paradise on earth. But Milan turns out to be authoritarian, oppressive, a nest of deception and betrayals. *Gli studenti* have spent their first Italian weekend not at Le Balze but traveling, mostly to Capri (three guys, twelve girls), the rest to the popular Cinque Terre (six guys). These five tiny towns hug the Ligurian coast a two hour drive from Florence. Established Tuscan families still vacation at stodgy Forte dei Marmi where a family's cabana occupies precisely the same stretch of beach literally for generations. But Cinque Terre is the coastal hotspot for young foreigners. There's not a room to be had for September, at least a room anyone older than an undergraduate would be willing, or able, to sleep in.

"Obviously you didn't discover the same disappointments Valentine and Proteus find in Milan, but what did you encounter that was unexpected?"

"Sheep," says the young woman that I think is Corrigan.

At the hotel on Capri, she explains, they found sheep penned on a lawn near the entrance. They never saw sheep penned at a hotel before. Not in front of a hotel, anyway. And lamb, they insist, was not a specialty of the house.

At the same hotel the college-age son tends bar, and the daughters clean the guestrooms. Nobody back home, they insist, would be willing to do this kind of work in a small family business. Tending bar might give the son some status. Every undergraduate guy dreams of being a bartender. What could be cooler, even if it's his dad's bar? But from their particular horror at the daughters' lot I suspect that at home, under no circumstances, does anyone clean rooms, their own or anyone else's. The daughters on Capri clearly appear lost in a bondage virtually medieval.

Not that *gli studenti* hung around this hotel bar, they want to make clear. Beluga, the handsomest of the men [later my visiting sister-in-law, spotting him as she arrives, will gasp: "Oh please don't tell me they all look like that!"] explains that they quickly figured out they should stay in a hotel they could afford, but drink in one with five stars. And of course, with their accumulated charms, Clyde shyly admits, someone else each evening picked up their tab.

Snell, the other of my former students, joins in. On Capri he was surprised to find that the older men strolling in the evening look much sharper than their wives. This imbalance between men and women, Snell insists, is exactly the reverse of home in New York, where women as they age continue to care mightily about how they look, while their menfolk surrender any claim to style. This is a major epiphany for Snell. I gather his own future appears now to be significantly less dim.

(After class, when I retell this to Heidi, our Administrator, she says yes, it is true, but that's because, especially in the South, Italian women gain status and power as they increase in maternal extensions. "Italy," she insists, "is still a matriarchy." She should know, as stepmother to three grown men. A woman wants to show that she has mothered, and, better still, grandmothered. To look unmaternal is to look like the fate one has proudly evaded, the aging spinster. It would seem then, on both sides of the marriage, for the hen and the cock, there is bliss is the *passagiatta*, the evening promenade.)

Kindly Miss Haag, still working hard to help me out, adds that people were kinder than they would have been at home. When the Capri group showed up without tickets at a local festa on Anacapri, they were warmly welcomed, wined and dined like the locals, all tickets excused. Twelve lovely young American women, and one guy, is it any wonder they were waived in? But I don't point that out. It's still early days.

Not only were the locals kinder, but *gli studenti* themselves grew kinder, and did things, they chime in, they would never have done at home. At midnight, for example, the all-guys encountered a group from another school program wandering from one of the five *terre* to another, unable to find any sort of accommodation. Our six guys spontaneously and unanimously invited them to sleep on their floors.

"You see what I mean about difference," I say. It's not only what one encounters in travel that is unexpected, what's most surprising is what that encounter does to the self." Travel is going to become one of the major terms of the course so I take the chance to expand the frame.

The eminently distinguished Australian historian Greg Dening has brought to the center of contemporaary academic discourse a distinction he makes between the *island* and the *beach*. The island is the other world as it is known by those who inhabit it. The beach is that portion of the world as seen by outsiders, observing it from a distance, the visible edge. (A not insigificant term for those of us living in a place that calls itself The Edges.) The beach makes itself availabe to, indeed welcomes the tourist. And the tourist is content with making the most of what the beach makes available. It is the traveler who, boldly, penetrates beyond the sand, beyond the perimeter, into the hidden, interior, utterly different world, the world of the other. Our temptation this term is to remain merely tourists in Italy. To stay up here comfortably on The Edges. The challenge this semester offers, and the potential reward, is to turn ourselves into travelers.

I can sense now the beginning of interest, if not yet concurrence, among *gli studenti*, when Muldoon once again demurs.

"But none of these things, sheep, places to sleep, is significant. No big differences. No big changes. How can you read Shakespeare's plays around stuff like that?"

He gets nods all around, and then he points out that my time is now up. The others shuffle out. No chatter. No smiles of any kind, except from my contrarian, who grins at me broadly.

Afterwards, I wonder why not just concede, concentrate on Maggie and give them what they want: universal truths embodied in universal persons? Academic tourism. It's not what I believe, it's not what I want, for them or for me, but haven't I got other, more important battles, to fight here?

Lucca

While I have been working Cecilia and Maggie have gone down each day into Florence, despite the random bus strikes. After years of living on a student budget, Cecilia is about to begin earning a real salary, and what better place to start assembling a professional wardrobe than Italy. She has a dance coming up soon after she returns to Boston, the annual black tie event at her new law firm. And she is thrilled to have located on a side street in Florence a shop that produces waltz skirts and contrasting tops in specially commissioned rich vivid silks. She is debating color choices.

But today I am free for the whole day and, happily, the oppressive heat has broken, so we decide to take another drive into the Tuscan countryside. Briefly, we consider Volterra, merely glimpsed on Sunday, but we take too long to decide and finally agree on the shorter drive to Lucca, an easy hour and a half away.

We have been to Lucca before, on an unforgettable April Sunday, and we know it is magical.

There are really two Luccas: the ancient walled commune, built over a Roman town, and enclosed with two and half miles of unsurpassed, still entirely intact walls. Outside the walls there are later, more residential areas of ninetenth-century apartment houses and broad sidwalks with cafes. Lucca was Puccini's birthplace and his home for much of his life. He had a country place near there, the Torre del Lago, now a musuem, and it was on the road from Lucca to that house that he suffered the terrible autombodile accident that destroyed his health. Almost a century later his spirit seems still to linger over the newer town. There's a *fin de siècle* quality wherever you turn, of aperitifs and sentimental assignations in the blue light of late afternoon, Muzetta's Waltz amateurishly played on a bad piano in a third floor room. If you wanted to film *The Merry Widow* you could do a lot worse than film it in Lucca.

I like Puccini's Lucca, but we are there for the walls. Last time we didn't get around to Lucca until a few weeks before we were ready to go home, too late for a second trip. This time we can enjoy a dozen returns.

Of course, the magic in large part last time came from sharing all these wonders with Cecilia and Thaddeus. With children so young, Maggie and I were having two kinds of experience at once:

seeing Italy for the first time through our own, adult, trained and informed eyes, but also seeing it through those very young, teen and a pre-teen, eyes. Reading had showed us how to look, but for the children each new thing was sheer unexpected revelation. Each experience with them wasn't just squared; its square was squared. Now we are diminished, not only because Maggie is weak but because then we were a family, and now we're just a couple—with a too briefly visiting adult daughter whose own real life is about to start up elsewhere.

I don't think it was so hard to find a parking space last time. As I remember, we pulled into town, immediately found an empty slot across from the walls, and started walking. Not this time. We circle. And circle. Until finally I give up and park in what is clearly marked as a space for official municipal vehicles only. Violaters will be fined and towed. It's either take it or turn round and drive back to Fiesole.

Because we've now lost a lot of time and the *intervallo* looms— when all of Italy closes for a couple of hours every afternoon to sleep off *pranzo*—we cut our must-see list down to the church of San Giovanni, luckily close by our illegal parking space, and the great Cathedral of San Martino. We reserve the walls until after lunch. But the very first person we encounter, before we can see anything for ourselves, is a bedraggled, defeated Englishwoman angrily waving us back, lamenting that she has been coming to Lucca since the end of the Second World War to see San Giovanni but it is always being restored. "*In restauro. Sempre in restauro.* I know now I will never see it in my lifetime." It's Dame Judi Dench as Eleanor Lavish in *Room with a View*, virtually papal in her self-assured authority. "You are wasting your time if you hope to get in there. Simply wasting your time." She may not in fact be papal but she does turn out to be something of a prophet.

So we hurry on to the *centro* and San Martino. Lucca was once a major power, a center for the sillk trade, and the cathedral was built to demonstrate the city-state's eminence. I'd like to like the *duomo* but today I find I can't. Overwhelming rather than uplifitng, its blindingly white facade of tier on tier of pretty pastel columns feels bombastic, a sort of petrified wedding cake. Marble should come across as frozen pigment in flawless stone, not spun sugar.

Perhaps if its symmetry had not been destroyed by the insertion of an overscaled campanile, the front mght work, but there's no getting away from the fact that it now looks lop-sided—because it is lop-sided. The left side is several bays shorter than the right. The interior remains a treasure chamber of master works in sculpture, but we are so aware of the looming intervallo that we hardly do it justice.

No problem, however; we came for the walls, not the buildings.

The intervallo closes in, when we learn to our chagrin that without reservations there's not a table to be had in any place we've heard of. When we do finally find some place that can take us, we find that it is true: you can eat badly in Italy

On to the fabled ramparts, their paved tops wide as a Parisian boulevard, planted with lines, sometimes even small groves, of trees. In the 1950s Italo Calvino published a sensational novel called *The Baron in the Trees* about a boy who climbs up into the trees on his estate and never comes down, traveling widely and finding whole societies living easily amidst the branches. At Lucca the trees shade the ramparts, you walk under them, but the elevation gives you a similar sense: a world opened up into a hitherto closed dimension, nominally human but now largely avian. The walls are Lucca's biggest boast, but they are not at all a brag

But our passage turns out to be San Gimignano all over again. Except that it isn't. Sunday, the little hill town town felt not only crowded, but cheapened, exploited. In 1987 you had to search hard in San Gimignano to find an Italian at ease in English. This time around we had to work hard to find an Italian. And the heat was brutal. But today the ramparts remain just as they were, and the weather is clement. The problem today is not with the walls, or even Lucca, it's me.

Of course in these fourteen years Italy has changed. Despite our English friend's disappointment, things here that were shabby a dozen years ago have been restored, in some cases magically restored. Italy was just Italy then; now it's a vibrant partner within Europe. And it has profited mightily from that development. But a dozen years ago much of what was saw was free, and easily accessed. Earlier in the week, while I was teaching, Maggie and Cecilia, down in Florence, decided to stop by the Medici palace to see one of our favorite paintings, Gozzoli's fabulous frescoes of the Magi, spread out on three walls of jewel-like color, a crowded, exotic caravan of princes and peacocks, camels and chargers, all crossing the Tuscan hills to worship an infant Christ. But when they got there they found they would have to wait in line for two hours, just to get the tickets. And then get into another line to go into the chapel. They didn't stay. Cecilia doesn't have four hours to spare.

In 1987 I remember meeting a woman, another of those thirsty-for-high-culture, Italophile Englishwomen. She had come to Florence just for the day, and was openly weeping on the Via Cavour because she had just realized what the *intervallo* meant: everything would be closed for the time she had available. Everything but the Medici Chapel into which I led her, smiling with not a little of the thrill the Magi must have felt went they got at last to the Stable. In those days, you could just stroll into the chapel, for free, at any hour of the day, even when everything else was closed for the afternoon siesta, to gaze as long as you liked in uninterrupted, unalloyed bliss. A bliss that has somehow kept eluding me since we arrived. Italy is clearly richer now, but it is also, I want to claim, poorer.

But it isn't. I know that. It's not poorer, it's different. But even that is not the problem. The problem is I want it all to be fresh, new, unexpected and a discovery. I want the good new to be the old new but somehow new again. But this is the second time around and it can, of course, be none of the things I desire.

Up in a Loggia

For our second class, I lead *gli studenti* up to the Loggia, the highest point on the property. It's an oblong, maybe 20 by 30 feet, open on two sides to a stupendous 180′ panorama of Florence, framing the full passage of the Arno as it approaches, passes through, and finally leaves the city far behind in its climb toward Pisa.

We are dividing the week. The first class of each week will meet in the library to talk about the plays. But for the second class we'll try approaching the plays through performance. Which will culminate, I hope, in that performance of *All's Well*. It turns out that only one of the students, Clyde, has had any acting experience. But the rest seem game to try. Climbing toward the Loggia they chatter away, apparently a lot more enthusiastic about performance than about theory. I'd expected the reverse.

I suggested they come to this class in work-out clothes. Shed self-protection. Loosen your defenses. And they've all showed up appropriately under-dressed. Clyde and Muldoon, my monocultural guy, have even come bare-chested. But that may be just a status-move within the still adjusting group dynamic.

Because rain threatens, I start out fast, putting my notes aside on the ledge.

To begin we need to distinguish between three terms: *script, show* and *play*.

Script is what a playwright writes.

Show is what actors make of the playwright's script.

Play is an audience's response to a specific show.

Defined this way, playwrights don't actually *write* plays. *Plays are what audiences see when actors in shows perform scripts*. That's sound acceptable until I put it more specifically: Shakespeare didn't write plays, he wrote scripts. With his acting companies he then put on plays from those scripts. All those collections titled *The Plays* mislead. They should say *Shakespeare The Scripts*.

This isn't mere word play. We do scripts a disservice when we approach them as novels in dialogue, with prescribed action and preset characters. Scripts—most especially Shakespeare's—provide only dialogue and basic movement, like entrances and exits. Actors then interpret those lines in a virtually unlimited range of ways, and supplement that language with movement and gesture. There is no Lear: there are only the Lears actors perform. There's Derek Jacobi's Lear, utterly different from Ian McKellan's Lear, and both of them completely unlike John Gielgud's. All of them interesting; each of them valid.

In fact, the richer the script, the wider the universe of performance possibilities. In our terms, the wider the universe of possible plays. And this extends to reading as well, which is a sort of performance in the mind. To read a script well we've got to at least imagine a performance. Hence our weekly division: on Mondays we discuss scripts in the library; on Wednesdays, up on the Loggia, we put on a show. In fact, this division replicates the work of professional actors who usually begin the rehearsal process with what is called in the business "table work": actors holding scripts sit around a table, read scenes, and talk about how they can be performed.

In any case, that is the way in which we will use these terms for the remainder of the course (and, indeed, from this point on, for this book).

I just finish this introduction as the rain starts. My notes blow away. Page drifts after page into the gardens far below. Unprompted, *gli studenti* rush down to retrieve them. Minutes go by. Now not only the notes but *gli studenti* have disappeared. The rain gets harder. I shout for them to return. One by one, increasingly damp, they come back, empty handed. I wing it.

We start at the start of *Two Gentlemen*, Valentine and Proteus are saying goodbye to each other in Act One, Scene One, before Valentine leaves for Milan. So that everyone gets a chance to perform, I ask the women to read Proteus, the men Valentine. Actors, I explain, are trained to prepare scripts strategically. At every moment a character is trying to make something specific happen. Everything he or she does, speech, action, gesture, silence, is done to bring about that result. Nothing just happens on stage; nothing lacks purpose. Plot may change a character's goals, but at no point does a dramatic character ever lack goals, or strategies to attain them.

"What is your character trying to do in this sequence?"

Silence.

I'm not worried. I have known this particular silence before, often. It's shyness, and inexperience, and the massive authority of Shakespeare's reputation.

I ask them to start reading in pairs. After we've heard several of them exchange the lines, I invite them to interpret backward from what's being said to the motives prompting these exchanges. What's Valentine thinking when he says "Cease to persuade, my loving Proteus;/ Home-keeping youth have ever homely wits"?

"Well," Snell suggests, "it sounds like he's trying to get away from the other guy."

"And," Rotgut adds, "despite that word *loving*, I think he sounds like he's trying to put the other guy down."

"Or maybe," this is from Muldoon, "*loving* is just a way to soften the blow. I'm blowing this burg, you're staying."

They are off.

Valentine is showing off, they concur. He doesn't just want to get away from Proteus, he wants to make Proteus see that Valentine

is his superior, better at everything. So we try to turn that into action, what the theatre calls *blocking*, moving the action within the
space.

What was awkward to start now becomes funny and fun to do,
as one after another the Valentines cross the Loggia, speaking over
their shoulders to a Proteus, who tries, in vain, to keep his friend
still. Suddenly, this isn't any longer a page of grotesquely tortured,
old-fashioned speech. It's two guys. They know these guys. One is
sweet and a little dumb, and a little jealous. The other is especially
sharp and funny.

And the one who's not as bright, Proteus, what's he trying to
do? The blocking makes it clear.

"He's trying to catch up," Duke suggests.

So we reblock the sequence, using basketball for our model.
Proteus is now guarding Valentine, trying to stop his forward motion, but Valentine has more talent, more edge. And once we put
Proteus in front of Valentine, the tension that is always there between them, which will erupt midway through the script into fierce
sexual rivalry, becomes visible, palpable, even this early on. Claudia, as Proteus, even trips her Valentine, Benny. He's shocked but,
happily, she doesn't stop and then, seeing Benny's bewilderment,
decides to mollify, a little, with a grin. We get texture. Complexity.
Dare I say it: realism.

We're out of time. They're hooked.

Who needs notes?

Shots

Cecilia has gone into Florence to pick up her silks and find just
the right gift for her good friend, Douglas Gordon. Maggie and
I walk up the hill into Piazza Mino, Fiesole's miniature market
center, to restock fruit and vegetables. Tuscan houses have very
small refrigerators. The reason for this we learned last time from
a plumber. The narrow, low doors and twisting stairs of the older
houses cannot accommodate an American-scaled appliance. This
means you have to shop for food every other day. Given the superb
quality of Italian produce, that is no hardship, though it can be,
sometimes, a bore.

The Piazza, the ancient Roman Forum—Fiesole actually pre-dates Florence—fills a rough square a litle larger than half a football field, arcaded by older buildings now used as shops, interspersed with more public structures including Fiesole's cathedral. All of it centered on a heroic sculpture of Victor Emmanuel II and Garibaldi, both on horseback, shaking hands in the gesture that created the Kingdom of Italy. It's here that you disembark from the Number 7 bus, our main link to Florence.

On the way to the *frutta*, we pass the pharmacy. In the window a sign offers flu shots. We remember the standard joke. What's the best prescription an Italian doctor can write you? An airline ticket to Switzerland.

On the spot we decide not to get flu in Italy. Who knows what that could lead to? We are light hearted. But we both recognize, and don't mention the fact, that Maggie has been very sick, very recently. We enter the pharmacy.

An Italian pharmacy is typically more confessional than remedial. No one simply thrusts a prescription at a pharmacist. That would be rude. Nor do you simply request an over the counter medication. Even with prescription in hand, the history of each misery must first be fully recounted. The initial ache, the original blister, that tell-tale wince, those unexpected spasms. And thereafter you annotate meticulously each upward notch in suffering, to the sighs and murmurs, the dismay, the compassion, and the gloom of every other relief-seeker in the shop. *Ah, Signora. Povera Maria Laura. Che peccato, Mauro!* This is not Freud's talking cure, but it comes close. Talking relief, built on a lifetime of rosaries.

There are half a dozen or so people already there. Maggie and I wait patiently. Several of the stories are quite interesting. One is horrific. But with each new entrant we find ourselves thrust a little further from the counter. If we have nothing to tell, we lose all right to ask. Finally, our backs pressed against the door, I pipe up and inquire politely, and in Italian, about the flu shots.

Everyone stops talking. They had thought, tourists, *Americani*, harmless and insignificant. But I have (poor) Italian; my mother was Italian, I spoke Italian before I spoke English. We have understood them. And, instantly, we are transformed: eavesdroppers, interlopers, and probably spies to boot. A wounded and suspicious hush fills the room.

The pharmacist quickly disappears, reassuring the others that we will be dealt with and gone in a moment. I take off my jacket and begin to work on my cuff. The pharmacist returns with two packages and begins to ring them up. We are handed the packages.

They do not give flu shots here. They sell syringes with flu vaccine inside.

We carry the syringes home, convinced we will never use them.

During her therapy, Maggie had to give herself regular shots. She believes she can remember the technique. I suggest she stab herself first and then me. But by the time we are back inside the villino she has convinced me that we can shoot each other up. Five days in Italy and we're about to become junkies.

We remove the syringes from the packaging. Dictionaries in hand, we make sure we have carefully translated the instructions. We are scrupulous and painstaking. Can we be absolutely sure these are flu shots? What is the Italian word for insulin? We even read the small print we never read at home, with all the warnings and the bio-chemical niceties. We exhaust the capacity of our dictionaries. The rest must rely on faith.

We bare our arms, and stare at each other.

"You go first," I say, "you've had practice."

Maggie suggests that a truly manly husband would not behave this way. I think it is extremely, even extravagantly manly to offer my arm first. What if the syringe were to break with the needle in the flesh? Maggie jabs me.

Maggie jabs again.

Maggie jabs a third time, and this time I can feel the vaccine pushing under my skin.

Nursing my bicep, I now examine Maggie's bared arm. I do not think I can do this. I suggest I go back to the pharmacy and buy an extra syringe so that I can practice on an orange, as Thad's wife, our doctor-daughter-in-law Sarah, says she was taught to do.

Fleetingly, I think of calling Chicago to ask Sarah to talk me through this.

Anticipating the honk of derision that will answer my request, if she is not on duty, or exhausted after thirty hours on call, I take up the syringe, and stab. I get it in one.

Maggie agrees that I was much better than she, both fast and painless. The spreading bruise on my arm confirms her judgment.

What else, I wonder, will we be doing to each other before this is over.

A picnic

Cecilia left this morning, Saturday, by a 9:30 flight. We got up at dawn to drive her down to the tiny Florence airport, from which she flew to Milan. From Milan she flies to Boston, and her new, her own real life. She'll be back for Thanksgiving, with Douglas Gordon, but that seems a long way away. So we've returned to Le Balze, Maggie and I, down and blue, not helped by the harrowing drive back up to Fiesole, all hairpin turns and 45 degree inclines.

There's no one around this afternoon except the two of us. *Gli studenti* are away on the second round of weekend excursions—Capri again, for the most part. The big house is empty and alarmed; the gardens are entirely ours. Maggie naps, and then assembles the perfect picnic lunch, which we take out to the ilex grove. We eat, we drink wine, we look down into Florence, the air around us a still and tangerine haze. Our garden. Our Le Balze. Ours alone for the whole weekend.

Even very wealthy people would give a great deal for an experience like this. So why aren't we suffused in bliss?

Of course Cecilia's absence is already an ache. She's so easy to be with, so willing to see and to make a joke, so eager to laugh. When she's around, both Maggie and I are lighter, more amusing and amused. But it's not just Cecilia going. Even stalwart, uncomplaining Maggie now concedes that things have begun differently than we had planned.

Just the fact that we are alone here this afternoon seems strange. In 1987, the very weak dollar forced, perhaps better to say forged, us into a single community. Even the kids from well-off families didn't go away for weekends. No one could pay for the kind of travel everyone now seems able to afford. But this time, as I hear *gli studenti* talk of their travels, I sense that Maggie and I may stay outsiders for the whole of the semester, we in the villino, and the young people sojourning on the other side of the garden wall. Encountering each other four days a week, separated for three. (We and our guests, I should say. Of our 98 nights here, Maggie has figured out that, starting with Cecilia, we've got house guests for 79. This also was not part of the original plan, and I'm already concerned.)

The sun's now a perfect orange disk just over the hills to our right. For the first time today we actually see the Arno, a silver-gray ribbon climbing the hills away from Florence. Earlier it had been lost in the haze. And the venerable city, terra cotta all through the afternoon, has begun to turn a shade of old rose. We have been at this now for hours, benumbed, probing. We decide to pack it in, the picnic and the probing. Carrying the basket, I follow Maggie out of the grove, seeing from her walk the exhaustion she has been carefully concealing.

Inside the villino I lower the heavy, louvered shutters against the now broiling sun. Maggie goes upstairs to lie down. She naps for part of every afternoon, and sleeps in later and later each morning. She insists it's jet lag. Maybe.

I go down to the small study off the ground floor entry, determined to make some sense of the week we've just spent, and, if I can, of the many weeks ahead.

Ironically, I've urged *gli studenti* to welcome the unexpected, to notice and to embrace things that surprise and even, at least initially, disappoint them. But that's not advice I want to take myself. We've come to Italy not for an adventure but as a prescription, and we want it to deliver the relief it promised. We knew precisely what we wanted when we decided to come. That's why we decided to come—to have every single one of our expectations amply fulfilled. But if teachng turns out to be a tug-of-war, and if Italy isn't magic anymore, why are we here? I admit to myself for the first time what's been quietly nagging me for days: that the strain of trying to copy the past, the effort of attempting to cope with the difference, might actually make things worse

And yet why has this particular week left me feeling so melancholy? Yes, San Gimignano was a bust, and Lucca a disappointment. But Volterra was a stunner, and the Val d'Elsa a revelation. Yes, the first classs was a dud, but the second was a thrill. Fairly examined, this week has been a mix, but it has been far from a wash. And yet I feel it has. I feel deprived. Worse, I feel cheated.

Though the window beside my desk, I see two guys, serious

walkers from the look of their spandex hiking shorts, settle down on a rock across from our entry. They've just climbed the steep Via Vecchia. They admire the view down into the valley of the Mugnone. One offers the other a hit of pot. I turn back to me.

In that little break it has unexpectedly come to me that everything now, good and not so good, is colored by panic, by my deep conviction that I will lose Maggie. It's irrational, of course. Her disease has been cured. It's been cured for almost two years. She may be tired, but she is no longer a sick woman. I should be able to rest easy. We found the tumor in time. We had access to the best care, to cutting edge treatments. Drugs now are miraculous. I know all this rationally. But the fear her cancer opened up deep inside me, that terror at losing her forever, it's suddenly re-opened in me and it won't go away. It now colors everything, everything I see, everything I do, everything I think.

And I know why.

Maggie was about to turn 51 when she received her dagnosis of breast cancer. My mother died of breast cancer at 51. I remember that October night, going to bed thinking, Dear God, this can't be going to happen to me twice. Life is cruel, I've always known that, but not this cruel. That's just not possible.

And it wasn't. Breast cancer 1997 is not breast cancer 1963. The name's the same, but everything else is different, utterly different. In my mother's case, the only thing they could do was cut, and then cut again, for ten years, until finally there was nothing left to cut away, and then she died. But Maggie had her lump removed immediately, no more cutting, and then seven months of radiation and chemo, followed by a regime of wonder drugs, and now she is cured, and likely to live a long time.

Those facts should be the only ones that matter to me. But a week here, freed from ordinary life, has unexpectedly opened up the past, the distant past, everything I feared and repressed when I was a very young man. Then I had no way of coping with what turned out to be the collapse of my world. But what I repressed then seems now to have sprung at my throat.

My mother, whom I loved very much, died a few weeks before I began my senior year in college. With her death, the world I knew came to an end as abruptly and finally as though we had just lived through a revolution. I saw that, but I refused to feel it. I can't say I decided in any conscious way to refuse to mourn her loss. I simply blocked, firmly but unconsciously, my grief. I left home, and left her loss behind there. In retrospect, I understand that it was a way to cheat death, to refuse to allow death to defraud me of the life I wanted to lead, the life my friends were leading. Death had taken away my mother, I was not going to allow it to take away anything else. Later, those friends, loving, baffled and not a little hurt, asked me why I hadn't let them know my mother had died. But I didn't want their pity. I didn't want to be sad. My last year in college wasn't the time to be sad. I was, as a young man, and even as a not so young man, interested only in pleasure. I studied English because it was easy for me, and because reading gave me pleasure. I read serious books, but I thought only about their form not their content. In those days I wanted nothing in my life that called for effort, that stirred the depths.

But now it seems—this is uncanny—the time for that long repressed grief has returned. This isn't mere melancholy. This is sorrow. Genuine sorrow. A complex, omnivorous, paralyzing sorrow, and it is coloring everything I see and feel and do.

I look back out the window. The hikers have moved from languorous to amorous. There are kisses now, and a probing finger. I can't go upstairs; I don't want to wake Maggie. I can't stay in the study without becoming a voyeur. I'm stuck I decide discreetly to lower the shutter, but the noise surprises them, and they hustle off. Nasty voyeur, they're probably saying. Another unintended consequence.

So what do I do? Let *gli studenti* do as they please? Watch over Maggie, and worry on my own? Tend our guests? Keep feeding the gloom?

Is that the story of our much needed new? Maggie and John and Shakespeare and *gli studenti* go to Le Balze, only to go round and round in increasingly purgatorial circles. Did I get this completely, horrifically wrong?

WEEK TWO
September 10-16

The Celle
Morning

To distract me from moping about Cecilia, Maggie makes a proposition. She also spent Saturday evening pondering last week's unexpected disappointments, and this bright Sunday morning she has a change of her own to suggest. Let's stop making this a trip down memory lane. The big mistake last week was to start with places we know, San Gimignano, Lucca. We have to stop going back to those places, the ones we loved the last time. They are always going to disappoint us. Let's start looking for places that are entirely new, places we don't know at all. Let's make it about what made Italy so wonderful, discovery. Not recovery.

In other words, the good new!

She's right, as usual. After years of managing complex issues at USDA, Maggie's instinct is always to stop talking and just solve the problem, whatever the problem may be. Mine, I suppose this comes from being an academic, is always just to wallow.

I search out the villino's extensive map collection, left behind by my faculty predecessors here, and come up with Cortona. It's a small town about a two hour drive southeast, close to the border with Umbria, a town we'd never even heard of last time. In fact, last time we scarcely went anywhere east of Florence. Maybe we should take Eastward Ho! as the new motto.

While Maggie puts together a picnic lunch, I head over to the villa to see if we have email from Cecilia announcing a safe arrival in Boston. The villino has no internet capacity. For contact with home we and *gli studenti* depend on a dark, dank computer room down in the old servants' quarters. Nothing there from Cecilia, but there is a message from my cousin Joanne back in Philadelphia. "Please call me. Urgent."

Joanne's supposed to join us here at Le Balze in mid-October, to celebrate her birthday. She's a second-grade teacher in the Philadelphia suburbs. This will be her first trip out of the US, a real new for her. Half the time with us in Tuscany; the other half down in Rome with her cousins the Capolagos. I talked to her just before we left Washington. Everything was set: tickets, passport. What could be urgent?

I try calling Philadelphia. No answer.

Maybe it's not about her trip. Someone in my family is in the hospital? There's been an accident? If anything had happened to my brother, the message would come from my sister-in-law. But who else would make Joanne say urgent? I've been so happy with Maggie's brilliant suggestion for reorientation and now, suddenly, somehow, this makes me feel off balance.

But whatever it is it is not going to be allowed to put me, to put us, off Cortona.

Mid-day

We buzz off out of Florence and down on to the A1 (happily, and economically, we get full use of Le Balze car on the weekends). As we speed along (this is, after all, driving in Italy, a non-stop macho competition) looking for the turn off to the 71, it occurs to me that I should treat this jaunt as a kind of pilgrimage, an idea I don't share with Maggie. ("Why can't we just enjoy ourselves, John?") The town shelters the remains of a thirteenth-century nun, Saint Margherita of Cortona, the third Franciscan, preceded only by the founders, St. Francis himself and St. Clare. The Cortonese venerate her deeply because they attribute to her their escape from the bombardment that devastated most of the rest of Tuscany in World War II. A truly miraculous survival when you see the photographs of wholesale devastation the Nazi withdrawal inflicted pretty much everywhere else in northern Italy. Since St. Margherita could also be a patron saint for Maggie—she came to me as Margaret Agnes Mary O'Keeffe—I can pray at the tomb not only for Maggie's continuing recovery but also to keep me faithful to Maggie's redirection of our stay. I am the kind of old-fashioned Catholic for whom praying to saints is as fundamental as the air I breathe. A practice Maggie tolerates, but only just.

Cortona turns out to be the hilliest of hill-towns. A ziggurat of steep, cobbled alleys, some of them virtually vertical, all colored a kind of baked clay. We circle the walls for a good half hour and finally settle on a place to park a mile or so outside, near a rural cemetery.

Once inside the town I suggest we start off with Saint Margherita in her basilica. I am the only member of the family not repelled by the Italian cult of relics. (Of course, I am also the only member of the family who is also Italian.) As a little girl Cecilia was especially horrified by them. Thaddeus used to promise to go ahead to make sure that the next chapel in a church we were touring was relic-free, only, of course, just as she entered it to say something like—"except for the eyes and liver of Saint Sympherosa." And yet she never stopped trusting him, which tells you something of the rooted power of an older brother. Maggie goes along grudgingly with my suggestion. She says she is praying to find exactly the reverse of what's usually there: exposed under the altar, a sainted mummy in nun's habit and veil.

We climb hard to the saint's shrine at the top of the town. The climb takes us the better part of an hour. There is no direct path, nor anything as simple as orderly switchbacks. You advance almost straight up, single-file on a narrow stony path, only to find yourself every thirty yards or so at a dead end. You then retrace your path, until you spot some hitherto overlooked, oblique opening wedged between houses or garden walls, not leading up in any obvious way, but maybe leading somewhere. You take that. You have no choice, really, except to go back down to your starting point. You hope this aperture may somehow intersect something, anything, an alley, a break in the wall, a paved incline that could start you back on your way up.

The climb is not made easier by the tantalizing scents wafting out from open windows on this warm day, sage, rosemary, onions sweating in olive oil, the start of the preparation for the family Sunday *pranzo*. Why are we heading perversely away from rather than toward our picnic?

And, surprisingly, on this Sunday morning, we are the only people climbing toward the church, though we do encounter lots of folks coming down. Later we realize we are also confronting a key difference between Americans and Italians. In America all of these people would have called out, without being prompted, something like: "Hey, Sir, Ma'am, Buddy, Guys, if you're going up to see Saint Margaret, you can turn right around, because the basilica just closed." The Cortonese don't do that. In fact, they say nothing, they merely stare and pass by. But this is not what it seems, hostility, rudeness, suspicion. Just the reverse: to intervene, to warn us off, would be an unacceptable invasion of our privacy, a terrible discourtesy to strangers, no matter the outcome.

At the crown of the hill, finally, the view is superb, but of course the basilica is tomb-tight. We stare at the various facades, peer down into a convent garden, where a nun hangs out washing. (I always thought it was considered a sin to do servile work on the Sabbath.) We take photographs of the nun, and of each other, staring and peering, and then we start the long descent. Maggie is not unhappy with this outcome. In fact she seems genuinely pleased that I have been baulked of my—to her—morbid desire to see a dead nun. At least we have prudently prepared that good picnic, she reminds me, and won't have to depend on the hospitality of the overly courteous Cortonese.

We return to the car and have Maggie's delicious lunch—in the cemetery, where else?—staring out at a beautifully austere church which the guide books tells us is Santa Maria delle Grazia al Calcinaio. Late fifteenth century by a minor architect, Francesco di Giorgio Martini, but perfect in its lonely, grey and quiet harmonies. It's probably only a fifteen minute walk from the cemetery to the church, but it's also the intervallo. It will be shut and inaccessible for hours more.

Packing up the picnic, restored from our ascent, we realize we have seen nothing but the walls and back alleys of Cortona and decide to risk one more attempt at an interior. Just beyond the town itself, high up on the slopes of nearby Monte Egidio, is a spot I've read about, the *Celle* or Cells. Saint Francis of Assisi came here, some accounts say 1211, some say 1226. In any case everyone agrees he came in flight from his rapidly spreading fame. The cells were then just caves, spaces naturally hollowed out from the rock, large enough for a short man—Saint Francis was scarcely five feet tall—to lie down in if he bent his knees, or to pray in if he stayed on his knees. Gradually, as Franciscans multiplied, the caves became interconnected. A rough-hewn friary emerged. We decide to risk a try. Even the intervallo cannot shut down caves.

Leaving Cortona behind, we drive steadily down off the paved roads onto a series of rough, then rougher single tracks, almost entirely hedged in by rank, late summer vegetation. Were another car to come from the opposite direction, there'd be no room to swerve, let alone turn round. Only a steep drop over the cliff face into the valley hundreds of feet below. Once again we seem to have made a very stupid choice. And sure enough, suddenly, there's a car barrelling toward us, thirty feet below and climbing rapidly. I can't back up round these turns. I edge slowly forward. He appears, speed unabated. And then, just as we are about to collide, the path widens. Miraculously, we pass each other with only inches to spare. A hundred yards further along, the same thing happens again. Speeding car; brief, opportune widening of the path. What kind of place is this, we ask each other? And what does it mean that once again we are the only people heading toward, while everyone else is heading away? Is this going to be the basilica all over again?

Maybe so, but obviously we can't turn round till we get there.

And then we are there. And we are indeed utterly alone.

First a small, unkempt and empty parking area, then a rough-hewn path down through rocks, until unheralded and unmarked they emerge, a high bleached escarpment and then wedged tight against it the cells, rising up tier above tier, stark, terraced, stories high, blank walls, blank windows, stone upon stone, spare, stark. The whole complex vertiginously overhangs what should be a mountain torrent but which, in this prolonged drought, is stone dry. With water rushing along and over the sloping sluice, it might seem lively, engaging even. But on this dry, hot, still afternoon, bony, corrugated, lunar, the only life it seems able to sustain is the life of ecstasy.

Some places suggest holiness like a distilled essence, a fugitive, evocative scent. The *Celle* are not among those places. They say nothing of suburbia's favorite saint, gentle winsome Francis, all garden ornament with bird bath attached. This place belongs to a much tougher, ascetic Francesco that Americans would hardly recognize. And probably wouldn't much like. Nothing gently consoling. Nothing comfortingly transcendent. In fact, the place does not feel sacred at all. Comfortless, the *Celle* are dauntingly, and only, human. You would never find animals here, or angels. Animals, angels, in their different ways, need only what they desire, and desire only what they need. But for some very rare women and even rarer men, a Margaret, a Francis, everything the rest of us desire seems merely superficial, distracting, to be rooted out, if necessary blasted out, leaving behind only a fibrous and tough, resilient something, something beyond personality or preference. Certainly well beyond happiness.

And yet both Maggie and I find we can't get enough of this place. It may not seem sacred to us but it is sublime. In part, it's because we are so alone, as though it had been kept in reserve just for the pair of us. The answer to the question we did not think to ask. But how can there be no caretaker? No guide? Surely there's a resident friar, waiting to panhandle gently for donations? All these windows, all these doors, all these cells. We search. We wander in, and out of, and back into, every available space. We linger for a long time in St. Francis's own cramped cell. In there you can begin to feel why holiness might search out rock as its only source for honey.

But we find we are indeed truly alone. And yet, even after we've walked ourselves to the very edge of the precipice several times, the deep still gorge yawning below, we can't stop seeking. We retrace our steps all over again. Down to the bottom, back up over the top, along each terrace. We are entranced. Nothing could be stranger, more haunting. Cleverly contrived and pretty Le Balze seems very far away.

The afternoon has drawn in. Reluctantly, we realize we have to go home. On our maps we work out a different route back to Fiesole. South almost to Lake Trasimeno and the northern edge of Umbria, then westward onto the 326, looping way down before we head back north after Siena. It will take us a lot longer going home but after this we feel we can't go back the way we came.

Evening
These are slow, meandering, back roads. We drive for hours. It should not take this long but we misread the maps and take wrong turns. We keep driving into the setting sun when we should be heading north. This part of Tuscany, the Val Di Chiana, is weirdly empty, an apparently limitless stretch of ochre, long-since-drained

marshes. Farmhouses are rare, most of them gaunt deserted ruins, isolated, forsaken, crumbling away. Even the light seems sepulchral. We encounter no other car, no person, no animal. It could be the landscape Noah looked out on from the ark, after the flood waters had withdrawn. It's Limbo emptied by Easter, devastated and devastating. We have indeed come this time to a truly new place, a place we not only never knew before but which we never dreamed existed. A place that has the feel of death in it, but not death in the ways we have learned to fear.

Class/Gaps

Last week in the library it was merely hot. Now it's sultry. An oven for the intellect. I remind *gli studenti* that the script proposes, early on, that no one can "be a perfect man, / Not being tried and tutored in the world" (I:3, 20-21). And the ideal location for such tutoring, the script claims, is Italy. Thus, when a father asks a friend where his son can learn to be "a perfect man," the answer promptly comes back "Milan." This was an Elizabethan commonplace. I cite Thomas Nash from just about the same year as our script, probably 1594, calling Italy "the paradise of the earth and the epicure's heaven" (*The Unfortunate Traveler*). A large body of writing insisted Italy was not just perfect, it was "paradise," a place that made human life perfect, literally "heaven." But an equally impressive body of contemporary writing urged the contrary: that Italy was not only not a paradise but gravely problematic. Roger Ascham, Queen Elizabeth's own tutor when she was a young princess, warned families against sending their sons to Italy, insisting they would inevitably be corrupted there. Every sort of vice was practiced in Italy, he bemoaned, every form of debauchery encouraged. And that damnably Papist place was all the more dangerous because it was all done in so decorous, so civilized a way as to be virtually irresistible. But it wasn't simply a matter of sowing wild oats. The worst thing about Italy was that, once corrupted, the young Englishman would never go back to being the virtuous youth who departed England's shores. His lament is the Tudor version of *How You Gonna Keep 'Em Down on the Farm, After They've Seen Paree*—or in this case Milan. The only way to protect young Englishmen of quality was to keep them carefully bound at home.

So when Shakespeare's audiences heard that encomium on Italian travel, they would have begun to watch the action feeling at least uneasy, perhaps even forewarned: is this thing going to turn out Ascham or Nash? A red flag would have begun to flutter in the breeze above the Globe.

So which is it for you, I ask *gli studenti*? Have you come to Italy to debauch or to find a perfect place to make you perfect?

"Perfect place," Rotgut insists, enthusiastically. That's exactly what he's come for. He could be the eager young protagonist of Shakespeare's script.

Uneasy silence fills the room.

"Well, in a way," says Duke. Well-to-do himself, he's here primarily to extend his contacts among the European titled classes. Like several of the other young men, he has even brought his dinner jacket. His father, he told Maggie, advised him never to travel anywhere without black tie. "You never know, Duke, when you'll need it." Europeans, he now explains, are the world's experts at pleasure. And expertise in pleasure is what he's here to learn. (I've already heard him trying to drum up support among his classmates for a Halloween masked ball to which they would ask the Florentine *jeunesse dorée*. And when asked where his group of guy friends plans to spending our long weekend in October, he sweetly suggested to me "Morocco.")

The others demur. They are not on Duke's side or on Rotgut's.

"Study Abroad means," says Benny, "time off from the pre-professional pressures of study at home."

"We work hard at home, but here we just want to have fun," Faustina adds. "If we wanted to work hard abroad, we'd have chosen a program like Oxford or *Sciences Po* in Paris."

"Isn't fun," I ask, "what Duke just meant by pleasure?"

No, she insists, as the others nod their heads in concurrence. Pleasure is heavy. You may get a lot out of it, but you have to put a lot into it. Pleasure can enrich your life, but it's also demanding and risky. Fun just happens. You watch it. Or you buy it. Or you just let it happen. And you can always turn it off.

And what about *Two Gentlemen*? Does it end by supporting its claims for travel? Do the characters find Milan a paradise? Does their travel tutor them in perfection?

No, says Judy, right away. Just the reverse. She was surprised by what happened. Proteus and Valentine became outlaws, criminals. They experience banishment, betrayal. One of them tries to commit rape. Italy turns out not to be a paradise at all. The best of all possible worlds turns out pretty much to be the worst. It's pure Ascham.

So what does Shakespeare seem to be saying to his fellow Londoners? Is the problem with travel itself, or with Italy, or simply with the two young men at the center of the plot? Or all of the above?

Silence.

It's the wrong question, of course, or rather it's the wrong moment for this particular question. It's a mistake in teaching that I make much too often, especially for someone with my years of experience in classrooms. They can talk about their own experiences, and they can talk about what happens in the script, but they cannot then easily and smoothly leap from clear text to problematic context. My question forced the pace, throwing them off balance, a sort of rushing the receiver.

I stop and reverse. I apologize for my stumbling-block of a question. It made them think they had to guess my intention: which of those three options, the characters, travel, Italy, did I think was the right answer. Hence their silence. *Gli studenti* do not like to be wrong. Actually, I did not expect them to choose. I thought they would answer all three. But I didn't make that clear.

I approach again, from an entirely different direction.

In 1966 the Philadelphia architect Robert Venturi published what became for me (and for a great many others) a mind-changing book, *Complexity and Contradiction in Architecture*. With compendious, overwhelmingly persuasive illustrations from iconic buildings ancient and new, he showed not only that the greatest architects routinely broke all the rules but also that the enduring power of their buildings roots in those anomalies. I had been raised on the contrary aesthetic, organic form: the greatness of works of art emerges from the way in which everything finally fits together in a coherent whole. Venturi's book made me see that I had been deluding myself, ignoring unassimilable features staring boldly back from the texts I thought I knew. The great works contest, they refuse to conform, even to their own ostensible intentions.

This helps us return to Shakespeare. The scripts are incomparably polysemous. They contain the ground for many different, even contradictory meanings. Indeed, that's part of the way in which they function as scripts, as we saw last week. Actors can be perform them, directors can shape them, in an almost endless variety of ways, because they are complexly layered to generate an unequalled range of different but valid readings. Specific performances are individual readings of the polysemous scripts, but no performance is ever definitive, can ever accommodate or express the whole range of a script's possibilities.

When we perform we have to choose and stick to our choices, making them clear and crisp, but when we read we do exactly the reverse: we attempt to locate and register the full range of possibilities. And we do that best, following Venturi's title, by looking for and making much of complexity and contradiction, the places — gaps, fissures, impasse — where the text seems to open up rather than to cohere.

And so we return to ponder Italy and travel and our two dubious young men.

But as Lear predicted to Cordelia: nothing will come of nothing. It's too much, too late, too badly delivered. Here in this oven of a classroom we face a gap, but it's not a gap from which meaning emerges.

Class ends; they file out. I lost them. Again.

Urgent

I finally get through to my cousin Joanne. Her message is about her relatives in Rome, the Capolagos, Dora and her husband Waldo, the people she is going to stay with after she leaves us. Their younger son, Ivo, has died. They are not in fact related to me. But in Italian families, cousins of cousins are still connections. Joanne had called to see I could represent the American relatives at the funeral. Hence the urgent. But of course by now I've missed the funeral. I promise nevertheless to try to get down to Rome to pay a condolence call after classes end this week. Joanne doesn't know how the poor guy died. He was very young, I think, 22 or 23.

Dora and Waldo were very kind to us the first time we came to Italy. Thaddeus still wears a ring we had made from an Etruscan coin they gave him. And Cecilia treasures a jade elephant that was their present to her. They even wanted Thad to go live with them in the summers. But we never met Ivo, the boy who's died. Of course he can't really be called a boy anymore. I remember that he graduated from MIT just this May. From all accounts, a smart, vigorous, athletic guy. He certainly wasn't ill. We would have heard that.

I decide to call Rome. Nobody answers.

Even though I never met Ivo, this news throws me. I guess it is because I suddenly realize how far away we are from Cecilia and Thad.

Midweek: An Alumna Calls

Going back from the villa to the villino at the gate this afternoon I am stopped by a woman, late-thirties, deeply tanned, in plum latex. With cleavage. And Fit. Extraordinarily fit. An alumna, she explains, not only of Georgetown but of the Le Balze program. She has written to the Director for permission to visit. I let her in and we start to cross the gardens toward the house. She grabs my arm, hard.

"I have to tell you: I spent the happiest year of my life here. Nothing's changed. Where is Dino?"

Dino, the old gardener, she recalls him carrying in fresh figs for breakfast every morning, "in his beautiful, gnarled hands, the most beautiful hands I've ever seen." I tell her he died last year, aged 98.

Dino was indeed a very kind man. He once described to me in exquisite detail how he had served tea to Henry James when James came to Le Balze to call on Strong. His girth. His bald head. How he held his cup. What he admired in the garden and the view. It was only when I got back home and reread James's life that I realized James was not in Italy after 1913, the year Le Balze was completed.

Dino, the exemplary servant, giving each of us exactly what he believed we required.

The Alumna sadly accepts the inevitability of Dino's death but is disappointed to learn that Clara the cook is also no longer here. And then her disappointment becomes a little more like irritation as one by one she lists the faculty who taught her, only to hear that each of them too is gone. This is not, she hints, what she deserves.

We continue across the gardens toward the house.

"On Halloween we put fig leaves and masks on all the statues in the gardens, and played hide and seek in the dark. There's no better place for Halloween."

I think of asking her to become the honorary chair for Duke's masked ball, but catch myself. The Villa administration is not happy about the masked ball.

We've got as far now as the Triton fountain. "Why is it dry?"

Somewhere in the piping, I explain, there seems to be some kind of unlocatable, unfixable leak. We'd have to tear out a large section of the villa's retaining wall to find the problem.

She fell in love by that fountain, she tells me, with an Italian boy. "Here's where we'd sit, and he would quote Dante to me. I thought it made him special. I didn't know then that's what they all did. Do."

She told her parents she was dropping out of school to marry her Dante-spouter. They threatened to disown her. She's already managed to make it quite clear to me that there was—is—a lot to own. Regretfully, she dropped the boyfriend. Went on to get an advanced degree in Art History. And when that didn't produce a career, she went to law school. "An even worse idea."

I am having a good time. She is in just about equal measure impossibly pretentious and cleverly self-deprecating. "Before Georgetown my family sent me to Choate. That's a boarding school in New England. They thought it would turn me into a lady."

"And not just a druggie?"

"Oh that too, of course."

Inside the house, surveying the changes in décor, her dismay begins to verge on anger.

"It looks like a truck stop."

I suggest at least a better sort of truck stop, but now she won't be amused.

"We had a life here you couldn't find anywhere else."

She remembers the Principessa Corsini who would show the students through the superb galleries in her palace on the Arno, still without electricity in the 1980s. She rattles off the titles of other local aristocrats, and the nicknames of their sons, Nicky, Ricky, Tino. The Dante spouters. "They came here. We visited their houses."

We visited their houses. It rings a sad little bell. Last night we had our long-awaited reunion dinner with Stefano. He only visits Florence now, on the weekends. During the week he holds the chair in Hittite at the University of Trieste, in the far northeast of the country. A very good new for him, but a loss for us.

Stefano mentioned that the woman who lives next door to him is an alumna of Le Balze. She came back as soon as she graduated, and married an Italian. Others of our alumni and alumnae are dotted around Tuscany. For them Le Balze set a standard. It cored out in them a need America and Americans could never afterwards manage to fill.

Of course, Maggie and I know something of that.

But my Alumna is not dwelling in the past. She knows Italy well. She has just driven over from Cortona (Tuscany is a small world) where her parents keep a house. Though her Italian is not very good, it is very easy. Clearly, she's spent a lot of time in Italy since her year here. And she knows now she can't get from Italy what she has missed in her American life. But until this afternoon she believed she could still find waiting up here, carefully kept at Le Balze, preserved for successive generations of young people, an impermeable domain of privilege, to be re-visited and crooned over. It should have remained the same, she insists, even if she had to grow up and leave it behind

I do my best to apologize and explain why all these changes had to be made, but she makes it clear that all she wants now, and badly, is to get away from me. I'm nothing but bad news. She thought I was Peter, opening up the pearly gates. I've turned out to be a Cerberus, at the mouth of Hades, barking bad news with every one of my three heads. She wants me away before I make things even more hellish. I excuse myself, claiming the pressure of work. She quickly agrees to let herself out.

"Before I go," she says, shaking my hand, "I would like to spend a few minutes in the chapel. Alone."

I hesitate.

"The grotto." How can I not know this, I can see her wondering. "Under the walls, near the olive groves."

She means the stone shed down at the edge of the gardens.

"You can see it, of course. But it's not a chapel anymore."

"Why not? It was so beautiful. It was perfect."

If I were raising a gun to my shoulder, she could not look more petrified. I equivocate. After all, I am Jesuit-trained, and a Jesuit employee for over thirty years.

"There's no one to say Mass. We don't have priests."

"We used to have Mass there every evening. Before *cena*."

She's going to find it whatever I say.

"We use it to store vegetables now."

Back in the villino, Joanne is on the phone. She's heard something from Rome but she won't say what. Now she wants me to drop the whole thing. Don't call the Capolagos, she insists. And don't, don't! go to Rome.

What does she think happened?

"What can I tell you, John? I don't know."

What does she suspect?

"It's something pretty terrible, I think. But that's only what I think. No one said that. No one says anything. Except drop it. I don't know anything. What can I tell you?"

Edging Gender

Up in the loggia today we move to *The Taming of the Shrew*.

[Though the plot of *Shrew* is well known, its Prologue or Induction is sometimes cut in performance and may be unfamiliar. In form and function it is a kind of curtain raiser, a staple of most theatrical performances before the twentieth century, a short, usually comical, even farcical play that got the audience in a good mood before the main, and quite separate action, began. In this Prologue, an English Lord back from hunting encounters in the nearby inn a sleeping drunken beggar, Christopher Sly. The Lord orders his servants to bring Sly to the manor, put him in the Lord's bed dressed in the Lord's finery. He also orders his page, Bartholomew, to dress up as a lady and pretend to be Sly's wife. Fortuitously, a group of players arrives and the Lord instructs them to perform for Sly when he awakens. When Sly does awaken, he's told he's had amnesia for years and is actually a gentleman. At first skeptical, he becomes excited by the possibility of his wife, the disguised page, joining him in bed. He's put off for the moment, and instead, lolling, watches the strolling players perform the story of Petruchio and Katharina (also Katherine and Kate). Once the Italian plot begins the Sly frame disappears.]

I begin by suggesting that perhaps we should not even try to perform scenes from this one. *Shrew* has to be for us these days a very ugly, almost unbearable script, with its pernicious delight in violence against women. To be watched comfortably it has to be tamed, to be kidded into something like Cole Porter's musical version, *Kiss Me Kate*. But Porter's theater-savvy librettists Sam and Bella Spewack understood that even as a musical Shakespeare's story had to be back-burnered, upstaged as it were, while downstage the main action followed the traditional plot of the backstage musical.

And then I ask *gli studenti* if—given the gender issues central to this off-putting script—if it's important to remember that boys played women on Shakespeare's stage. Are we really grappling with a script that shows men being violent to women if on stage the violence was male-male, albeit man against boy?

That's insignificant, they unanimously insist, merely a convention of the time, irrelevant to us. The audiences understood the boys were women on stage and that's how we should think of Bianca and Katharina also.

To counter, that is: to make it complex, I improvise a crude summary of Stephen Orgel's subtle argument in *Impersonations*, a landmark study of the boy actors in particular, and Elizabethan ideas of gender more generally.

Orgel shows how the boys' cross-dressing was not a meaningless or merely accepted convention. It was a peculiarly British practice. Everywhere else in Europe on stage women played women. Foreign visitors to the London theaters were shocked by the practice. And all sorts of home-grown anti-theatrical groups, notably the Puritans, denounced it as irredeemably corrupt. In addition the scripts themselves repeatedly call attention to their frequently risqué representations of gender slippage. In the Prologue to *Shrew*, for example, the Lord seems perversely titillated to think that his boy Bartholomew, cross-dressed, is going to flirt in bed with the drunken Christopher Sly. We are left with the strong impression that this is not a behavior the boy will find unfamiliar or repellent.

Of course, it helps to understand that Elizabethan biology did not think of gender as we do. Their medical science insisted it was the amount of heat generated in the act of conception that separated a male from a female embryo. Males were conceived, literally, because of hotter sex. And even after birth little boys were dressed as girls and lived with women until they were "breeched" at four or five. (A practice that continued well into the nineteenth century.) Even pubescent boys, like the apprentice actors, were still imagined as somewhere between fully male and fully female. Only with the maturing of the genitalia and the appearance of secondary sex characteristics like face hair did a boy become fully male. Playing women, then, the boy-actors certainly cross-dressed but they did not, at least not quite as they would in our time, also cross gender.

At this *gli studenti* seem somewhere between appalled and titillated. I suspect they are beginning to fear what I, Lord-like, may next suggest they do up here on the Loggia. But I am not interested in titillation. Nor do I want them merely to naturalize or appropriate the scripts to our shared cultural norms. Shakespeare's *Shrew* is not just *Kiss Me Kate* sans songs. As I said on the first day, I want them to encounter this script, and all the scripts in the course, not as the familiar beach but as the strange interior of the island: unexpected, even off-putting, contradicting our expectations, exposing us to the strange, the other, putting us on edge. And I particularly want them to see how Shakespeare is most unlike us as he consistently treats identity not as fixed but as lambent, fugitive and almost weirdly malleable.

To move in that direction I ask them if they were staging the play would they do it with or without the Christopher Sly Prologue.

Beluga thinks the Prologue is funny and since the play is supposed to be a comedy it seems better to retain those first scenes.

Miss Haag disagrees. The writing is much weaker there, more stereotypical and broad, almost as though it's not by Shakespeare but added on by somebody else. Whatever we think of the Petruchio plot, it's better off without the Lord and Christopher Sly.

But isn't it important that the Prologue make this explicit about an English audience watching a play set in Italy, I ask? It is, after all, set specifically in Padua.

And that's why you need to keep the Prologue, Italophile Rotgut insists. Because it's not about Italy. It's about England. These

are the Lord's English servants putting on a play that is only ostensibly set in Italy but is really about life as they know it in their
village.

Where there's probably at least one shrew, adds Duke.

Rotgut: "We shouldn't even be reading it in this course." He
does love Italy.

But then, I suggest, should we not conclude this is how Shakespeare thought his English audience thought about Italy, as a place
of bitter, shrewish women and brutal, narcissistic men, a place of
ugly and constant violence, verbal violence and physical violence.
The taming here, the rape in *Two Gentlemen?* Should we imagine
Londoners watching this play like WASPs watching *The Godfather*:
"Well, of course, that's how *they* [read Wops, Dagos] all behave."
Sonny and Connie Corleone as Petruchio and Kate? A script, then,
of almost infinite ethnographic condescension?

Clever Beluga suggests they all watch *The Godfather* on tape before we meet again and on this meeting-half-way note we part.

As the others leave the Loggia, Muldoon asks if he can speak
to me privately. I've sensed this coming. Since that first class, he's
been turning himself, literally and figuratively, further and further
away. On the Loggia he spent the whole class sitting on the balus-
trade almost with his back to me.

Once we are comfortably settled in the *salone*, Muldoon explains
that he has studied Shakespeare before. Now he's afraid my course
is "taking Shakespeare" from him. That is his phrase. He wants instead to keep Shakespeare in what he calls his "comfort zone." It's
clear he's quite bright, a committed student, and a clever reader. It's
also clear he hates where he, rightly, sees the course going.

Take *Shrew*, for example. Shakespeare, he argues, can't possibly
stand behind, or want his audience to get behind, Katharina's famous final speech.

> *I am ashamed that women are so simple*
> *To offer war where they should kneel for peace,*
> *Or seek for rule, supremacy, and sway,*
> *Where they are bound to serve, love, and obey.*

He offers instead a reading Ripley Snell suggested earlier in the day. Katharina's taming is an example of the Stockholm Syndrome, the name given to the recurring phenomenon of the abducted who come to depend upon and ultimately to defend their abductors. Katharina as Patty Hearst. Petruchio kidnaps her, starves and terrorizes her until she senses that her very survival depends on introjecting every single thing he insists she believe. Her taming is the price she pays for surviving. It's a very clever way to read the script. It would make for a very powerful modern-dress staging, a production that would leave Katharina enormously appealing, and the play very dark indeed.

Of course, Katharina can indeed be played as Patty Hearst. Or she can be plausibly played for laughs as a farce vixen forced to reform (the Porter/Spewack version.) Or as a traumatized woman in a patriarchal family, who senses in Petruchio someone who actually values her and singles her out. Sort of Katherine Hepburn in *The Philadelphia Story* (a very obvious rewriting of *Shrew*), tamed by Cary Grant. Or as Hillary Clinton, going along with the ways of a man's world because she knows that's the only way she'll ever get what she wants and needs. I try to make it clear that this range, in fact much wider than anything I sketch here, becomes possible just because these are scripts, designed for, and completed by, performance. That's why we spend every other class exploring performance options on the Loggia.

Clever, agile Muldoon quickly makes my point his own. If what I say is so, why can't he, then, read the script to suit himself? Isn't that just what I have been saying actors do, interpret roles to make them their own? What's the difference between a performer playing, and a reader arguing, his preferred interpretation? Why shouldn't what works on the stage also work in the study?

I could at this point refer back to the distinction between the beach and the island, between performing a single coherent interpretation and deep-reading the text as polysemous. Successful teaching always depends on this sort of redundancy. To lodge an idea effectively you have to find ways to repeat it over time. Students are inundated with new information, new ideas, new paradigms, all day long, all week long, during the term. They go from class to class, from Econ to Bio to Comparative Political Systems, and each class is a kind of geyser. No one, no matter how earnest, can take it all in. The judicious teacher figures out what he wants to secure as a take-away from the course, and that's what he finds ways to repeat, usually in three stages, first securing the student's theoretical understanding of the idea, moving on to recognition of its appearance in specific locations, and then—the goal—to a student's ability to use the idea on his or her own independently. The trick is to repeat without boring. No mean trick.

But instead of the island metaphor—Muldoon is resolutely anti-theoretical—I reply with a story told to me by Inge-Stina Ewbank of Bedford College, London, when she was translating Ibsen's Norwegian for the Royal Shakespeare Company. True, it's a story about Ibsen, not Shakespeare, but it is about the Royal *Shakespeare* Company. It's also a story I consider a touchstone.

The first text she translated for the RSC was *John Gabriel Borkman*. Each morning during the initial table work a car would whisk her from the college to the theater across the Thames. There the director, Peter Hall, and the cast read through the script scene by scene while she sat by to tell them what the original Norwegian had been, in case there was a question of precise interpretation. The leads were Sir Ralph Richardson, Dame Wendy Hiller and Dame Peggy Ashcroft, than whom there were in those days no more glittering stars in the theatrical firmament.

The first scene was read. Professor Ewbank marveled: well, this is why they are who they are. On the first reading they got to the heart of the script. What I uncovered after months of work. Delighted, she was turning to the next scene when the director asked if everyone was satisfied.

Sir Ralph said something like, "Well, I could also do it this way." And Dame Wendy said. "Well, if you do that, then I could do this." And Dame Peggy said. "Well, of course, if you two did it that way, then I could try this."

And so they read the scene again. And this time Inge-Stina said to herself, "I thought I knew this play. But they've just found something new there."

And again, the director's quiet "Is everyone satisfied?"

And this time it was Dame Wendy who suggested something different.

And so it went through the entire afternoon, reading after different reading, all of that same scene. Interpretation after dazzling interpretation, unpetalling the script like a giant, creamy peony.

The choice of a specific interpretation to stage only came much later, after every possible way of thinking about and representing the script had been exhaustively held up to the light, tested, evaluated.

And this doesn't apply only to the greatest stars I remind Muldoon. Each week I'm having *gli studenti* read chapters from the terrific collections of essays in Cambridge's *Players of Shakespeare* volumes. There you get actor after actor, some very famous indeed, and some whose names ring bells only for theatre buffs, all telling stories like Professor Ewbank's. The good rehearsal process unlocks the full potential within the script. Exactly what a good reading should do.

Great texts should stretch us. But that can happen only if don't pounce on a reading to which we then hold fast. We need to try to suspend judgment for as long as possible, so that we can explore all the possibilities that crowd around the edges.

Muldoon has listened politely and now excuses himself. *Gli studenti* are waiting for him to go up to the Irish pub off Piazza Mino. "Thank you very much for your time, Professor." I know he's convinced that I'm wrong. And I'm pretty sure I've lost him. What I don't know and what I'm left wondering is: will he be only the first?

A Call from Rome

A woman calls from Rome. She's called Fran; she doesn't offer a last name. Fran is a friend of Dora Capolago. Dora wants to see me next week. It's urgent. (Urgent, again.) She's getting back tomorrow from Brazil.

Brazil?

Fran explains it wasn't a funeral, it was a memorial service that Joanne hoped I could attend. Actually Ivo was buried quietly just after his death and a few days after that Dora and Waldo and their older son, Carlo—the family calls him Chip, which the Italians spell Cip—all left for South America. They had planned the trip months before, for the four of them. They decided to treat it now as a godsend, and just get away.

But Dora has changed her mind. She is flying home tomorrow.

The friend warns me not to call the Capolagos' apartment. Dora thinks her phone is bugged. That's why the friend is calling me. Dora will find a way to contact me. And I should not call Joanne. That's very important. I should tell no one anything. Dora will explain it all when she sees me next week.

Maggie, when she hears all this, tells me to be kind when Dora calls but she also urges me to keep my distance. We're in Fiesole, Dora is in Rome. We are not Italians. We're relatives of relatives, not really family. We only met the older Capolagos once; we never met Ivo. Whatever is going on, she urges, don't get involved. "You're here to teach and to write. I'm here to get well. Don't let us get sidetracked."

Other Edges
Ouch.

Maggie's office called this morning. Some arrangements have fallen through. They need her to stand in at meetings next week in Rome, London and Dublin. Of course she said yes. They've been so understanding, allowing her this time away, she could hardly refuse.

But—though I can't say it to her—she's not really up to a week of flying between the capitals of Europe. Any gains she's made with these past two weeks of quiet are sure now to be squandered. That's the unselfish side of my gloom. The selfish part is that I'm already missing her. Since her illness even the shortest separation, for whatever ordinary cause, brims me over with almost unmanageable anxiety. When I was a little boy I used to believe there were alligators hiding under my bed. No amount of patient, or impatient, explanation from my parents could persuade me that (a) alligators were unlikely to be living in the second floor of a Philadelphia row house or that (b) alligators could not mysteriously reappear in my room after my parents had thoroughly checked all hiding places. I feel the same way now about Maggie going. I can't talk myself out of fueling my worst fears.

Right now she is in the garden, painting. Over the last few days she's worked out a routine for herself. Very typical of Maggie; she does best within sturdy structures. What she may have hated most about her time in chemo was the way it undermined her need to organize. Now, in the mornings while I prepare class or write in the villino, she uses the gardens to draw and work at her watercolor. For which she has a strong talent. Watercolor, that is, not drawing. That's the morning. After *pranzo*, she takes her needlepoint out there, and later on she reads. And thinks. She keeps her hands busy so her mind can rest, and find focus. She hasn't said it but I know she doesn't want me out there with her. Maybe later, but not now.

So here I am in the study, feeling very sorry for myself, even though I know that's just childish. She'd certainly stay here if she could. She's doing her job just as I am trying to do mine.

Throughout that harrowing autumn and winter of her cancer treatments I would play, when I was alone, my CD of Gluck's *Orfeo*, repeating over and over again that most haunting of all arias, *Che farò senza Euridice?* We don't have a CD player in the villino. I don't need one to hear it now.

Her surgeon was so happy to be able to assure me that Maggie's operation had found clear margins; no signs of cancer in the surrounding tissue. But there other sorts of margin, margins where the watchers share and can't share suffering. Those margins aren't so very clear, then or now. It's another sort of being at the edges.

A Cena

Maggie flew off this morning. To Rome. This evening the Villa took pity on my sudden bachelordom and invited me to take *cena*, the evening meal, with *gli studenti*. The table is surprisingly full. Usually there's no one here on the weekends. But the first set of papers and tests arrives next week. It looks like only Duke and his dashing group are gone.

The meal is pleasant, but it's a cold Saturday supper—choice of pizza or quiche—and very brief. The pub beckons my companions. But just as I am about to head back to the empty villino, Eva, one of the four students not taking my course, asks to speak with me.

We stroll the same paths I walked a few days earlier with the Alumna. Like most of the others, Eva is here only for a semester, but after these two weeks she thinks she wants to stay the year. She's been given to the end of the September to make a final decision. Her family thinks she should come home as scheduled. They fear this is an infatuation, quickly fostered and quickly deflated.

We come to the parapet that runs along the south front of the garden. Lights are just beginning to twinkle in Florence below. The sky is indigo in the east, fuchsia in the west. A breeze has come up. The non-pub-goers have taken their coffee and wine out to the terrace. One of them strums a guitar. They have already begun to quicken to the sweetness of *villegiatura*, the centuries-old life of the villa, wine, music, conversation, the garden, turning simple, ordinary, necessities into pleasures, and making those pleasures linger. Duke had a point.

Why, I ask Eva, does she want to stay here?

Something is happening to her here, she says. A new part of herself is opening up. Back on campus she's a leader, with a full social and curricular life. She is never alone, never has a moment to think. But here it's not unusual to find someone reading alone in one of the gardens, or just walking and looking about. You never see that on campus. Before *cena* Rotgut told them he's going down to Florence later to a memorial service for the late actor Vittorio Gassman. Several of the students decided to go with him. They're the ones now out on the terrace. When Eva and I finish, she'll join them, and they will take a bus down to Florence, to stand in a crowded piazza, to watch on film an actor speak Dante in Italian. It's astounding.

I try out on Eva the word *introspective*.

That's too much. She says, instead, *reflective*.

That's what she wants more of. She wants to read here, to think here, to look about her and to grow

I say: why not, what could you lose?

But I wish we'd had this talk before the Alumna arrived. I might not have reassured her about Le Balze's continued powers, but at least I might have disappointed her less.

WEEK THREE
September 17-26

Sunday *un dramma italiano*

The American Consul in Florence has sent up a warning to lay low. Take the name plate off the entry. No one should wear a shirt with a school affiliation, not just Georgetown, any American school. There are credible threats of violence against American citizens in Italy. An Italian-American, Derek Rocco Barnabei, convicted of murder in Virginia, has just been executed there. Like the rest of Europe, Italy cannot imagine how a civilized country justifies the death penalty. The death penalty here is what abortion is in the States. Except that here the entire country is united against it. It's just about the only thing that does unite Italy, except for soccer, suspicion of law enforcement, and contempt for politicians of every kind.

The Sunday newspaper does not just cover, it headlines the story *"Barnabei, un dramma italiano."* The dramatist of that *dramma* could have been Puccini. Here's the lead (my translation): "In the arms of death in Greensville [Virginia], Rocco encountered his mother and brother who nevertheless did not have permission even to touch him. The youth had requested to donate his organs, but the laws of Virginia and the poison from the injection prevent this. His last wish: 'a pizza.' All appeals for clemency have failed after the appeal from the Pope went unheard."

What more can drama do? The cruel arms of death preempt the mother's loving embrace, and the brother's, denied their natural right to touch. Inhumane, hyper-juridical Virginia versus a moral, compassionate appeal from the Pope. Which of course is not simply refused but goes unheard. And not even that pizza.

But this is not Puccini; this is something even more essentially Italian. In the venerable language of a pious Catholic practice, the Stations of the Cross: at the fourth station Jesus on his way to Calvary encounters his mother. The newspaper's Italian captures that precisely: *ha incontrato la madre.* I'm willing to bet that's a direct quotation from some Italian manual of devotion. The innocent victim, torn from the arms of his fainting mother, before a cruel, un-justified, unjustifiable death. This is *a*, if not *the*, fundamental Italian story: on the one hand, the Family, on the other hand, the State. On the Family's side love, and life. The mother's arms. On the other, the State's, side, only *Nel braccio della morte*, the arms of death.

For Italians, Family is fundamental; the State, deadly. The Family's touch enlivens; the State's embrace kills. Of course many Americans also revile the State as enemy. From the Right, where less government is always better, or from the Left, where institutions always fail our real needs. But Americans make this a conflict between State and Self, the corporate countering the individual. That's not Italy. In fact, nothing could be less like Italy. In Italy the State threatens not an individual but the Family, because in Italy you only become an individual when *touched, nel braccio,* in the arms of, embraced *by* the parent, the brother, the sister, the child.

Not, significantly, by the spouse.

I was raised by my Italian grandparents always to guard the line marked by blood. My uncles' wives were my aunts, but they were not family. They didn't share our blood, and they could never be trusted completely with the real family secrets. In fact, with any sort of information. Over and over when I was young I would be told, after one of my uncles had visited us: Remember, don't tell your aunt. That aunt being his wife. Italians feel they *need* nothing and no one outside the family. And any claim on the family from outside can only be fraudulent, a form of theft.

Shakespeare didn't get this. His Italians have no mothers, ex-cept Juliet, stuck with the cruel and narcissistic Lady Capulet. May-be this absence was simply another result of boys playing women. Even a very talented boy is unlikely to make a convincing mother playing opposite another boy his own age who's supposed to be his daughter. Certainly, when there are mothers and daughters, as in *Winter's Tale* or *Pericles*, their time on stage together tends to be very brief indeed. And of course there weren't that many boys to go round, particularly in the romantic comedies where you need-ed them for the girls and their maids. But I don't think this is re-ally about the resources of his particular theater. His Englishmen have mothers—all those mad and maddening queens. And so do his classical figures like Coriolanus. And some of those boys must have been just terrific cross-dressed. Who played Lady Macbeth? But when we turn to his Italian families they almost always consist only of dads and daughters, or dads and lads.

Which gets Italian life dead wrong. Our academic director Marcello tells me he lives across the street from his mother-in-law who comes for after-dinner coffee every evening. Her thirty-something bachelor son, who, of course, still lives with her, also comes most nights. When I murmur something about how difficult this must be, Marcello cuts me off, insisting without a hint of reservation or irony: "It is so good to be able to live within the family." Each weekend he adds, he and his wife and their little daughter go out to the country near Siena to spend Saturday night and Sunday morning with his parents. He wouldn't think of missing it. His emotional and physical health depend on it.

And Stefano says much the same thing, in his characteristic way, when he explains why he travels back and forth by train every weekend, *every* weekend, between Trieste and Florence—a distance of 245 miles—to have Sunday lunch with his mother here. "You know, John, the Italian mother, she is terrible." As a goddess is terrible, tremendous with the touch and power of life, giving life, denying life.

And this newspaper item has absorbed me, I realize, because at first unconsciously, and now consciously, I am constantly awaiting that call from another *madre* who has lost her son. From Dora.

First Encounters

We have arrived at the first really significant play in our syllabus: *Romeo and Juliet*. (Obviously, no plot summaries needed for this one.) Greater plays by far are still to come, notably *Merchant of Venice* and *Othello*. But now we have moved light years ahead of *Two Gentlemen* and *Shrew*. Later in the week, up in the Loggia, I want *gli studenti* to perform the scene where the lovers first meet. Today, to prepare for their performance, we spend the entire class reading that extraordinary first exchange as closely as possible.

Romeo: If I profane with my unworthiest hand
This holy shrine, the gentle sin is this:
My lips, two blushing pilgrims, ready stand

To smooth that rough touch with a tender kiss.
Juliet: Good pilgrim, you do wrong your hand too much,
Which mannerly devotion shows in this;
For saints have hands that pilgrims' hands do touch,
And palm to palm is holy palmers' kiss.
Romeo: Have saints lips, and holy palmers too?
Juliet: Ay, pilgrim, lips that they must use in prayer.
Romeo: O then, dear saint, let lips do what hands do:
They pray: grant thou, lest faith turn to despair.
Juliet: Saints do not move, though grant for prayers' sake.
Romeo: Then move not, while my prayer's effect I take.
                    [*He kisses her.*]
Thus from my lips, by thine, my sin is purg'd.
Juliet: Then have my lips the sin that they have took?
Romeo: Sin from my lips? O trespass sweetly urg'd.
Give me my sin again. [*He kisses her.*]
Juliet: You kiss by the book. (I:5, 92-109)

Gli studenti respond: it's a sonnet (they've read the notes in their editions), which means, they agree, that Shakespeare wants us to find the exchange stilted, contrived, artificial. I concur to the sonnet part of the claim. Fourteen lines, carefully rhymed. But by the time we finish this afternoon I want them to hear—and relish—the erotic energy and fiercely compressed wit that pulses through that sonnet.

They seem skeptical; they know what the notes said. It's not spontaneous. It's conventional, and that means it has to be boring.

Let's start with Juliet as a role to be performed. No less a figure than Kierkegaard considered it one of the greatest challenges the young actress can face. Actually, of course, it's rarely played by a very young actress, since it requires such formidable technique. Within only a couple of days within the story line Juliet has to develop from a very young, very naive girl just out of the nursery, still reliant on her Nurse, to become a figure of extraordinary independence, of passionate feeling and profound thought. Romeo starts off an impetuous boy, all hormones. And after a few days he dies, still an impetuous boy, all hormones. From beginning to end Romeo's a guy's guy, completely dependent on his buddies, his priest, and his girlfriend. But Juliet becomes the woman who soon understands: "*My dismal scene I needs must act alone.*" The actor playing Juliet (the term actress has been banned as sexist; after all, we don't say doctoress, or professoress) must find and then play a convincing arc that will stretch smoothly and speedily from ingé-nue to heroine. In approaching a script as a guide to performance, no scene registers entirely on its own. You need to put it in context. What does it follow from? What is it leading toward?

So where in the script's action does Juliet's arc start? Should the actor initiate the through-line here, at the moment of her first en-counter with Romeo? Does the actor have any other good option? After all, the next time we see Juliet, in the iconic balcony scene, she's already smitten with Romeo. Doesn't that mean, then, that the actor has to start the arc here? Before she can even phrase her anxiety or give her fears a name, does she not have to show that the undertow is pulling her away and speedily, in a direction no one, least of all Juliet, can determine?

And if that is the case, then the interchange can hardly be read or played as mere convention.

Gli studenti read through the lines again, several different pairs of Romeos and Juliets, but there's no difference in what they find there. It's still in each pair's treatment conventional, contrived, ar-tificial.

We return to the first quatrain, which Romeo starts. Remember, I say, the pair has never met before. Disguised as a pilgrim, he is masked. (A masked ball, that should help at least Duke to sympa-thize.) He had come unwillingly to be with his friends and he is loudly smitten with another lady, Rosaline. Juliet of course has no idea what he looks like, or who he is.

> *Romeo:* If I profane with my unworthiest hand
> This holy shrine, the gentle sin is this:
> My lips, two blushing pilgrims, ready stand
> To smooth that rough touch with a tender kiss.

Me humble pilgrim, *you* saint in shrine.

Beluga doesn't want to give up the on the artifice. He's willing to reconsider Juliet but he insists Romeo is just recycling what had become for the Elizabethans a standard formula, the four-hundred-year old stew of religion and lust we now call courtly love. The lady always towers above the lover, the *donna* as Madonna. The suitor's *rough* hands are of course *unworthy* to touch her, but then, equally of course, it's always appropriate to kiss the statue, the relic, the shrine. That come-on is so standard, he observes dismissively, it was tired by the time of Dante. (One of the Villa's courses is in Dante, so he is talking about what he actually does know.) To play it right, Beluga continues, you'd have to do it by rote. Romeo's not even trying. He's just marking time until the music ends.

Maybe so, Ardita concedes but, she says, Juliet then bowls him over. Returning his tired gambit, she in one large move checks his king.

> *Juliet:* Good pilgrim, you do wrong your hand too much,
> Which mannerly devotion shows in this,
> For saints have hands that pilgrims' hands do touch,
> And palm to palm is holy palmer's kiss.

Juliet is being clever, witty, piling pun on pun, playing on *palmer* as another word for his "pilgrim," because pilgrims often carried away blessed palms from the Holy Land shrines. Better yet, she easily takes up and teasingly rearranges Romeo's own rhymes. His greeting-card *hand/ this/ stand/ kiss* effortlessly becomes her *much/ this/ touch/ kiss*. And she confounds all his codified expectations. Romeo thinks it's the guy's role to sue, beg, coax, cajole, all the while pretending—just pretending—he's blueballed with frustrated desire. But Juliet hasn't listened to her Nurse's incessant bawdy talk for nothing. She is cleverly, eagerly able to give as good as, better even than, she gets.

At least the women among *gli studenti* are beginning to like it. Even to respect it. And their new enthusiasm catches on.

Ripley Snell pushes forward. Romeo at this point forgets, entirely and abruptly, the old girlfriend, Rosaline. If this exquisite young thing wants to play, and can play so handily, then who wants a madonna?

Romeo, as Snell sees it, now raises his bid. "*Have not saints lips, and holy palmers too?*" Forget about hands. It's lip time for the pilgrim. And you can forget about *unworthiest* and *rough*.

Since the scene has now begun to earn pretty much everyone's interest and respect, I try to complicate matters. For a romantic play to work, tragedy or comedy, there has to come a moment when each lover realizes this person is different, consequential. We've agreed that this exchange shows Juliet more than just piqued. Is it possible that Romeo also finds his parallel epiphany as early as this first meeting?

No, the guys all insist.

Muldoon: "This is a hook up."

Clyde: "It's about cool lines."

Duke: "It's about getting moves on."

Willy: "Romeo knows he's got only this dance to score in. He's got to move fast."

They are united.

But Faustina points out how at this moment Juliet takes a prudent step back. "*Aye, pilgrim, lips that they must use in prayer.*" Why this sudden switch, she asks, if Juliet's not suddenly aware of something more complicated in the moment, not just inside herself but coming also from him What else explains her sudden retreat?

"No," handsome, flirtatious Benny smirks, "she likes his flattery, and wants more of it. She's teasing him."

Betty, surprisingly, supports him: "Juliet just wants to have fun."

Orchid: "Juliet has no second thoughts, no reservations."

Claudia: "There's no foreshadowing, and certainly no guilt."

Boomerang. Now the young women have joined sides with the young men, Faustina and perhaps Ardita alone trying to probe below the surface. I had hoped they would make the scene real, make it their own, and they have, but that also means they see it now as a hook-up.

Luckily, Faustina is fighting back.

Romeo: Oh then, dear saint, let lips do what hands do.
They pray; grant thou, lest faith turn to despair.

I try to help her. Listen to the rhythm. In Shakespeare, himself an experienced actor, the performer always finds the best guide to the affect of the moment in the rhythm of the line. There are two breaks per line, we call the breaks caesuras, cutting into the ongo-ing rhythm. And in the second of those lines the sense breaks off after the first two words. This is not the easy, confident calm of the initial speeches. Something different is emerging here, something marked by that word *despair*.

Despair is one of the two sins in the Christian scheme there's no going back from, one of the two sins that cannot be forgiven. The other is presumption, the expectation that you can do anything you want without suffering negative consequences. Presumption and despair are the only two terms in Romeo's lexicon. It was all presumption in the first part of the exchange, and now it's all the reverse. He does not deal in in-betweens. Nor will he permit them to her.

Is this then a mutual moment where Juliet realizes she is en-countering in him something like the same force she is encounter-ing in herself? Does she realize here that she has met a force that she cannot, that she is unwilling to, circumvent? So that, swept up, she tells him to do what he wants. She will neither help nor hin-der. "*Saints do not move, though grant for prayers' sake.*" At which the impetuous Romeo immediately pushes home his advantage. "*Then move not, while my prayer's effect I take.*" The first kiss.

But he oversteps, and she panics. He brags after the kiss: "*Thus from my lips, by thine my sin is purged.*" The religious language re-turns literally with a vengeance. Her body, Christ-like, purges his body of sin. But Juliet takes that language, and that theology, gravely. "*Then have my lips the sin that they have took.*"

Miss Haag: "Sin may be only a word for Romeo to play with but for Juliet it is a reality.

"He's a guy," Claudia insists. "A guy does what he wants, then he tears off to his buddy, the friendly priest, makes a quick, easy confession, and then he's back in business, and moving on. But women," she concludes, "for women sin matters."

We go back to the text, to the final lines of the sonnet sequence. Romeo is now over the moon, swept up in the intoxicating mix of Juliet's sweetness and his own cleverness, which excite him equal-ly. "*Sin from my lips? O trespass sweetly urged!/ Give me my sin again.*" And then the second kiss, which he takes without any thought for her consent, or pleasure. My sin, what a joke. What a conquest. And the best of it to pretend that what he's done she's *urged*.

To which, cutting him off, Juliet concludes, wonderfully enigmatic: "*You kiss by the book.*"

What does she mean?

They are unanimous. She means, "You are an awesome kisser. That was even better than I expected."

I demur. In the clipped rhythm breaking the hitherto regular iambs I hear the possibility of something else. There is no pleasure, no expansion, no delight in the falling pulse of her line, particularly in that swallowed diphthong *book*.

They are deeply suspicious of the dark place to which I'd like to take this reading. They want to know more about the *book*. Rotgut thinks it could be the book he's just read about in Dante's *Inferno*, the book the famous lovers Francesco and Paola read the fatal afternoon that dooms them to death and hell, the rhyme of Lancelot. Dante's lovers read about Lancelot's kiss, they look at each other, and that afternoon they read no more.

It's a clever and tempting suggestion.

Beluga, who these days seems eager to contradict anything he hears from Rotgut, suggests it's probably just one of the many amorous manuals that circulated in the Renaissance, all heirs to Ovid. Whatever the Shakespeare course is or is not doing for them, the Dante course is clearly paying off.

But is it really from Juliet a compliment? Could this be her last attempt to pull free from the attraction that has all but submerged her, one final attempt to dismiss with a word what her heart can't relinquish?

"Nope," jolly Faustina insists. There is no way she is going to let me reinsert this scene into a tragedy. "Juliet ends this way because she sees the Nurse bearing down on them and wants to look as though she's putting down this brash intruder."

I could press on, though there is really not much time left. I could align Juliet with the other major tragic protagonists in Shakespeare: Macbeth, Othello, Lear, Hamlet and Antony. They are all undone by delusion: by persistently holding on to an error despite mounting evidence to the contrary. For Macbeth, Hamlet and Othello that delusion is prompted by someone or thing outside the self. For Lear and Antony, like Juliet, the delusion emerges from the self. In her case from her belief that Romeo is reliable, that she can trust him and trust in his love. She is literally *fascinated* by this masked, honey-tongued and bold man. Fascination comes from an ancient Roman word for the power of the phallus, for sheer male sexual energy and promise, the *fascinum*. And out of that fascination Juliet projects on him the man she wants and needs Romeo to be. And that is her tragedy. Romeo turns out to be exactly right about Juliet, she is everything he thinks her to be. She is exalted. But Juliet, aroused, thrilled, about Romeo is just about equally as wrong.

But I say none of this. All I want for them to do at this point in the term is to grapple with the script's richness. And they have. For the first time we all exit a Monday meeting pleased.

Back in the villino, my pleasure slackens when I find a message that Dora called and will try again later in the week.

A Garden Walk

Maggie calls from Rome. She's there for a session of the grandly named Codex Alimentarius, the international body that sets standards for world trade in food. The meeting is going well, but her office now wants her to go on another trip next week, this one to Brussels. That means we'll be together only on weekends till the end of the month. And after that our house guests start arriving. Our time, the time for just the two of us together, has suddenly evaporated. And this bachelor solitude in the villino has already begun to feel like a confinement. Except for two or three hours when I am in class I am entirely alone. I haven't exchanged a word with another adult in almost four days.

So I'm delighted when Marcello invites me to the villa for *pranzo*, to meet Allen Grieco who oversees Le Balze's gardens. I plan to behave very well, and look very pitiable, and very hungry, so that they'll invite me back at least once more. But I'm also wary of wearing out my welcome too soon, in case these trips take Maggie away for the remainder of the term.

Allen is quiet, and funny, and, though an academic by profession, clearly also a very capable garden manager. Actually, his real job involves the gardens at the much larger establishment over at Harvard's, formerly Bernard Berenson's, Villa I Tatti in nearby Settignano. He manages our considerably smaller operation only part time. After lunch he offers to lead *gli studenti* on a tour of Le Balze's gardens, and he invites me to tag along. As we walk, I am delighted to hear his informed, professional view confirm things I have been feeling for a while now about Le Balze's oddity.

Allen explains that the Villa itself rests on top of a giant, man-made cistern. Nothing could possibly grow naturally on this originally barren hillside. So the first thing the architect Cecil Pinsent did was plan an enormous water tank and feeding system from which, even today, the gardens are watered. To the somewhat incredulous students, Allen answers that yes, the cistern is still there. He points with his toe to some of the paving stones. Removing them would disclose water deep as the hillside is high.

Beluga, who has been lamenting the impossibility of strenuous exercise at the Villa, suggests that the cistern might be rethought as a pool. Allen, two thousand years of Italy winking, agrees that "yes, anything is possible."

We begin to move counter-clockwise, starting at the grand main entrance with its double staircase, moving west into the ilex grove, then along the south terrace, and back eastward into the enclosed garden with the camellia tree. We will finish in the first garden, called the orange garden, though the orange trees are these days for some reason all in the next, the camellia garden.

It's a bright, hot afternoon. The garden looks slightly past its best. Indeed, we see the three gardeners, pruning, clipping, and carting away the late summer excess to give the autumn plants their chance. It's all blue and yellow now, with undertones of purple. The choice of colors, Allen says, was his. He thought something cool-looking this year because of the unusual heat. "There will be more red in the next few weeks," he promises. He changes the colors each year, "to amuse myself." It doesn't matter historically. Neither Pinsent nor Strong cared for flowers. For both designer and philosopher, gardening was all about form not bloom.

Although Le Balze borrows from Renaissance models, its garden is essentially Anglo-American, Edwardian actually. Quintessentially English in its feel for cozy little rooms. A genuine Italian garden would be much more committed to prospect and vista, with more and longer promenades. Here, except for the narrow terrace that looks down to Florence, the views are always blocked, and the space strictly contained.

The site probably made this constriction inevitable. Strong bought a property shaped, Allen says, like a sausage, long and narrow. And of course hilly. *Le Balze*, the bulges, the edges. His choice to call the place after those precipices seems telling. Though he built it while mourning his wife, he didn't call it Villa Elizabetta, like the Villas Diana and Iris down the hill in San Domenico. Nor Villa Forte, punning on his own name. And certainly not the Villa Rockefeller, in homage to the money that made it possible. Nor even Villa Margarita, to please the lonely little girl who lived there with him. He named it instead after the *balze* because, clearly, they are what intrigued him. The difficulty of the spot, the inhospitableness of it all.

I ask Allen why anyone would choose to build a house here, descending at something close to a ninety degree angle, requiring massive excavations all done—in 1912—by hand. They built it here, he answers merrily, "because labor was cheap."

Maybe it's just my increasingly disgruntled mood, but I can't help but recall now a bitterly satiric poem Rudyard Kipling published in 1911, the year Le Balze was begun. It's called "The Glory of the Garden." "*Gardens are not made/ By singing*," Kipling wrote, but "*by better men than we*," who "*go out and start their working lives/ At grubbing weeds from gravel-paths with broken dinner knives.*" On this hot afternoon I think of those men with their broken knives grubbing. One of them could easily have been my grandfather, who migrated to Philadelphia from Italy in 1913. I imagine him, and dozens like him, working for a pittance, to fulfill the perverse fantasy of Strong and Pinsent, who if they weren't singing were surely, as Kipling says, "*siting in the shade.*"

Does this imaginary memory make me angry?

No. My grandfather got away, and built a decent life, the foundation for my own exceptional life. But it does help me understand why I don't quite feel at ease here. I am sufficiently Yankee now to believe better any Paradise Earned than a Paradise merely Married Into.

As though hearing my thoughts, Allen is now describing the artifice and deception of the place. "You think the north walk traces a straight line from the gate at the east to the statue of the philosopher at the far west end, but look back and try from here to see the gate. You can't. It's off by almost ninety degrees." The whole place is based on optical play. It's all skewed. We have stopped in the secret garden. By a nice coincidence, Frances Hodgson Burnet published her much-loved *The Secret Garden*, in 1911 the year Le Balze was begun. In her immortal fable the secret garden restores life to the children who recover it. Our secret garden seems just the reverse. Stone's strange turning away from life still stamps the place. And it gives me the creeps.

Allen concurs. "Oh yes, there is nothing playful in this garden."

No wonder the Marchesa chose not to live here. And no wonder she left it away from the family, to a university she'd never heard of before someone suggested the gift, a place with which she and her family had no connection. How better to rid herself of what Dickens once called "the crowding ghosts of many miserable years"?

But this is not, happily, how the students see it. Duke and Beluga have been conferring apart from the group. They now ask Allen how much it costs to keep such a garden going. Without exceptional expenses, he says, a little under $100,000 a year. They are surprised. They had thought it would cost much more. I Tatti, he tells them, larger and more elaborate, costs about eight times that annually. That's nearer their guesstimate.

It is clear theirs wasn't an idle inquiry. A garden something like this each of them confidently expects to own sometime in the future. It's the end of the twentieth century, the era of the dot.com millionaires, who all have made it by thirty. But this time, for them, it would in fact be Paradise Earned.

As I leave for the villino the guys are debating how much Le Balze is now worth, and how much they would be willing to pay for it on the open market. They've been told it could probably sell for between 2.5 and 3 million. Dollars. That's the cost of a mid-sized townhouse in Georgetown. So it's a bargain, they conclude, if you are looking for a third, or maybe a fourth house. Too small for anything else.

No room to put in a tennis court.

No pool.

Kissing

Performance day. Up in the Loggia.

We return to work on the scene where Romeo and Juliet meet, this time trying to perform it, turning script into play. After the last class I divided *gli studenti* into pairs. Because there are more women than men, several Romeos have two Juliets. (I don't think *gli studenti* are ready yet for same sex public pairings.) I asked them to memorize the brief encounter, and to practice it with their assigned partners. It's only 18 lines divided between the pair. Not a demanding task. I also asked each pair to figure out a way to block the action, keeping in mind that the characters are dancing.

Almost immediately after class I started getting phone calls, or being pulled aside while walking in the gardens.

"Do we have to do the kisses?"

"How else can you do the scene?"

I am at a loss. These days, I thought, college students take kissing in stride. On campus undergraduates even insist on doing the nude scenes in scripts like *Six Degrees of Separation*. But *gli studenti* are not actors. They are students in an English class. Not only that, they live in a small group, less than two dozen, in very close quarters. So it turns out that even a pretend kiss, let alone a kiss in front of everyone else in the villa, is nervous-making for the girls, and close to sick-making for the boys. They are obsessed with the dreaded moment. It drives out every other thought. As we assemble, the Loggia feels the way classrooms do on the morning of a final exam.

Boldly volunteering to start, the unflappable Duke pairs off with Claudia. His Romeo is a lounge lizard, all oily charm. Duke's Romeo has seen this, done this so often, he's on autopilot, very shallow and entirely convincing. But Claudia has taken the saint in a shrine image literally. And her choices are rich and fascinating. She leans against a covered sawhorse. Remote. Guarded. Granting him just the flick of a swift glance. A strikingly lovely young woman, she is also at this moment a wonderful Juliet. You see at once how and why Romeo would choose as his gambit those courtly/sacred images.

Much applause when they finish, and relief. The kisses went by without a blush or hesitation. Muldoon and June agree to follow.

Despite his reservations about me, Muldoon is the class's alpha wolf. He can't bear for anyone else to grab the lead.

He and June build the scene as an exhibition of Ballroom Dance. (It probably comes as a surprise to people not in touch with college students, but these days ballroom dance is a major activity on most campuses. There are even leagues for intercollegiate competition.) But Muldoon suffers from an almost pathological inability to memorize. At the second line he freezes, and trips June. She recovers, but the speeches don't. The pair has taken on something far too elaborate for their level of skill. It's hard enough just to get the words out without adding the samba. But Muldoon is proud. He keeps on pushing, literally, until finally at "*Give me my sin again*" he really thumps June, and over she goes, hard, on her back.

As her friends set June back on her feet, I get the guys to help me retrieve some ladders the gardeners stored here on the Loggia. We arrange them on their sides to pen in the remaining couples, so they can only talk. Bewitched, fine. Bothered and bewildered, of course. But I draw the line at bruised.

Muldoon and June retire to the sidelines, but his panic is now contagious. None of the guys who follow gets through even the first speech without going up on lines. The *Oh Shits* pile up. All the young women have their words down faultlessly. They say their bits and wait. They are even sweet about it. One after another they turn to assure me *he knew it perfectly when we rehearsed it*. But the guys hobble through like amnesiacs. We start. We stop. We start and stop again. In most cases it's hard to locate any kind of interpretation, so lame is the delivery.

Clearly, it's all about the kissing. A good third of guys actually refuse to kiss when the moment comes, and airbrush against a cheek, or, in a few instances, simply stand stock still and pause. In the end no one but Duke kissed.

Who would have thought it?

Afterwards: Snell finds me sipping a lonely Scotch on the Loggia watching the sun go down. Generously, he decides to stay and chat even thought the rules prevent me from sharing the Scotch. We talk about the kissing crisis. He's one of the two who have been my students before, so he feels quite comfortable explaining to me how completely I have misread Shakespeare. He is also happy to share his mastery of the plot.

All Romeo wants is to hook up, he explains, but Juliet, she keeps upping the ante. And he can't lose face in front of her. He doesn't want to complicate things, but he doesn't want to look like a wuss either. So each time she makes a demand, he's got to follow through. The reason why Romeo gets so upset by the middle of the play is that he can't figure out how to get out of this. He doesn't want this commitment but he can't lose face either. So he goes along with her demands, and finally it kills him, kills the both of them.

Explains a lot.

222

Le Balze is beginning to live up to its name. Without any company, I feel more on edge and at the edge with each passing day. And I am becoming not entirely unaware of the consequences that come when a lonely Scotch at sunset becomes a lonely Scotch at every sunset, and then lonely Scotches at every sunset, so I am making an effort to get out onto the 222 each chance I get.

I am convinced Providence has shown me the 222.

Up through last week, after negotiating the horror of the Via Vecchia plunge, Maggie and I tended to drive out of the city on the four-lane highway between Siena and Florence that all English speakers here call the Si-Fi (Firenze being the real name for Florence). But on a whim, on Sunday, on a solitary drive, just outside Siena, I suddenly peeled off the Si-Fi at San Damazo. I just couldn't manage the anxiety of the next sixty minutes jockeying against eighteen wheelers at 140 kilometers an hour. And then, unexpectedly, there wasn't another car in sight. Let alone a truck. And I got that rush you feel when you replace a faded, frustrating video with the Criterion Collection. I had been led to the 222.

It's a two-lane country road running almost parallel to the Si-Fi but between 5 and 20 kilometers east of the big highway, bisecting western Chianti. On the Si-Fi you ride above and peer down into Chianti. On the 222 Chianti becomes yours.

So much of this week, whenever I've found myself with the odd two hours on my hands, I turn my back on the Scotch and go out on the 222. If I have an empty morning or a free afternoon, I'm all the way down the 222 and back. If the time is short, I divide it in half, getting as far as I can toward Siena as I can, turning back toward

Florence when I must. I rarely stop. I go nowhere in particular. No, that's not true. The Jesuit poet Hopkins talks about "going in Galilee." That's how I feel now. I am going *in* Chianti.

I have begun to need Chianti the way I imagine addicts need a fix. It soothes me, it comforts me. You are spending the autumn in Tuscany, the envy of everyone you know! Yes. And yet, as Adam knew, even Paradise grows stale without Eve. But now I've found Chianti, not the wine, thank goodness, the place. It consoles me. That's its charm. Chianti tries to *make up to* you. For what? For everything. Everything I've ever lost. Everything I've ever feared losing. For what Hopkins meant when he asked the question that became the title of one of his greatest poems: "For What Serves Mortal Beauty?" Chianti consoles you for the fact that all beauty, to be beautiful, must also be mortal. Chianti insists instead: *'I'm here. I've always been here. Rely on me. I won't ever let you down.'* And you believe it.

Why? I don't know yet. Nothing is in motion here, nothing moves here. Each part is still, and it seems composed of many measured parts, fields, hillsides, little hillside towns, perfectly still. Chianti has been still for centuries and will (God willing) be still for centuries to come. The 222 offers Rousseau's ideal, a moderated movement without jolts or lapses. Its easy inequalities promise to smooth every sort of broken surface. I'm like a new lover. I am completely and only attracted, and I don't care about why. Indeed, part of the attraction comes from abandoning myself on the 222 not caring about why.

Dora calls and a star comes calling

Morning: Last night Noah's own weather, apocalyptic winds, sheets of rain. This morning, what I hope is the first cool breeze of autumn. For the first time since our arrival the smoggy scrim between Fiesole and Florence has entirely disappeared. The great city of art now gleams below us like an infinitely intricate mosaic, what the Florentines call *pietredure*, ten thousand roofs each a coral bit, and every skylight a crystal. I station myself in the garden, ostensibly to read, but really because I can't get enough of this view.

Mid-day: Getting back to the villino for lunch, I hear the phone ringing. The heavy locks delay me. The ringing cuts off before I manage to get inside. But luckily, just as I pass the study, it starts to ring again.

Dora. She's calling from the apartment of someone she calls the Monsignor. I start trying to offer our condolences on Ivo's death but she cuts me off. She only has a few minutes. She will meet me in Fiesole on Monday afternoon. I explain that I teach on Monday afternoons, but I can meet here at the Villa afterwards. No, she's told Waldo she is going to visit his cousins who have a villa near San Domenico, just below Fiesole. The real purpose is to talk to me but she can't risk being seen with me.

She will try to come on Tuesday. Do I know the small Franciscan church at the top of Fiesole? Yes, it's an out of the way place, of no historical or aesthetic importance. Even the most intrepid tourists tend to give it a miss. She'll meet me there in the tiny cloister next to the church.

If Maggie were here now what would I say? I know what she'd say. Don't!

If Maggie were to be here on Tuesday, would I still walk up to the little church? She'd never let me out the door.

I begin to explain to Dora that the demands on my time here have become unexpectedly heavy. I wouldn't want her to come all the way up to Fiesole and find that I have stood her up.

She cuts me off. She's heard nothing I've just said. "I can't talk about it. Not over the phone. I will explain everything to you next week."

Then, just as she is hanging up, she adds. "Don't tell Joanne. Don't talk about this to anyone. You could put yourself in danger."

I could put myself in danger? How could whatever it is that's happened to her family down in Rome harm me? This autumn is about Maggie, not about keeping things secret from her, not about risking harm, to either of us. And now Maggie is not even around to share my bewilderment and offer sane, sage counsel.

And there's this other matter that I am just beginning to sense. Left to myself these past days I've begun to see clearly and for the first time what Maggie's illness has done for me. Of course, nothing like what it did to her. But this near panic after just a few days' separation has uncovered anxieties I've refused to recognize, fears I have been tamping hard down. I begin to see I've spent the three years since Maggie's diagnosis doing just what I did when my mother died. Once again I've refused to feel. But now, with so much the time alone, my defenses are coming undone.

Two weeks ago I thought this was going to be Maggie's time, the survivor's story, with me along as tour guide, concierge, comic relief. I don't think that anymore. Maggie's not the only needy person living in the villino. She may not even be the needier of the pair.

So what if I don't go to see Dora? What if I call her back right now and cancel? What if I start protecting myself and don't show?

Won't that repeat what I've been telling myself to undo?

But danger, what kind of danger?

Evening: And then at sunset, in the zigzag counterpoint that is rapidly becoming the shape of my life here, an entirely unexpected surprise. Mel—I can't call him Mr. Gibson now—pays a call. Yes, that Mel!

He's in Florence scouting locations for a movie he's think of producing about the fifteenth-century Pazzi conspiracy. The Pazzi was the most serious of the many attempts to get rid of the Medici. On April 1478 the conspirators trapped the brothers Giuliano and Lorenzo (later Magnificent) in the cathedral. Lorenzo managed to escape into the sacristy. Not as lucky Giuliano was stabbed nineteen times and bled to death on the marble floor of the sanctuary. Obviously a story idea with lots of appeal to the star of *Mad Max*. Because our Marcello is one of the world's experts on the Medici court, he's been consulted on the project. He happened to mention Le Balze to Mel, and Mel asked to come by and inspect. It seems he's buying or has bought a big place in Connecticut and is looking for ideas for his gardens.

Unfortunately, Marcello seems not to have told the great man that *gli studenti* also live here. Mel made it safely through the first two gardens and then froze as he came onto the south terrace to find all of us clumped around the center, gaping.

Generously, he submitted to a group photo, and then his entourage of Personal Art Historian and Screenwriter whisked him up to the Loggia. Heidi and I were invited to follow, with the retired Villa cook, Clara, respectfully trailing with a glass of Coke on a silver salver.

Once free of the crowd, he relaxed and showed what a genuinely nice and funny and smart guy he is. We talked about John Milton, yes, we did, I swear it, and Milton's journey to Italy. He found it funny that just because Milton once visited here in the seventeenth century the Florentines, worshippers of any sort of artistic achievement, have named a street after him, Via Giovanni Milton. I suggested he drive up the mountains behind us to the heavily wooded monastery at Vallombrosa. There he'll find an inscription in Italian identifying exactly the spot which inspired the *Inglese* poet to devise those lines in *Paradise Lost* that describe the newly fallen angels "who lay intrans't/ Thick as Autumnal Leaves that strow the Brooks/ In Vallombrosa." And up on the loggia we are of course almost exactly where Milton imagined Galileo viewing the moon through the then new telescope: "At Ev'ning from the top of Fesole."

In return he tells us about visiting the Old Sacristy at San Lorenzo, the site of the Medici tombs. Oh to be a star! It's been closed for restoration. I've tried and tried but can't get in. He, of course, has been given a private tour. He was shown photographs of the exhumed skulls of both Giuliano and Lorenzo, to whom Mel refers, one magnifico to another, as Lorenzo the Mag. He says there are huge chunks missing for Giuliano's skull. The Pazzi must have gone after him with awls.

He also confirms that the skull proves that, even without the nose, Lorenzo must have been one of the ugliest men God ever fashioned.

From Milton we go on to talk about Shakespeare. He may soon stage *Hamlet* in California. He talks about how remembering the lines, even in that outrageously long part, is never a burden. The rhythm, he says, Shakespeare's rhythm, always carries you through.

The sun sets. Galileo's moon comes out. Below us Florence has never been more lovely or lovable. Graciously kissing the cook's hand, our star departs. And all the other stars in compliment come out.

Volpaia

Ever since I first met her Maggie has made everything in my life not only good but better. And she's just done it again. She appeared at the villino, unheralded, very late last night. Close to midnight. A complete surprise. I didn't expect her until late today. But she made herself take a terrible slow local train to Florence so we'd have the whole of today together. (House guests start tomorrow.) Even with the slow train she should have arrived by dinner time. But someone jumped under the train, stranding them for hours in the middle of the Romagna. An interval enlivened by a Chinese man who tried to improve her Italian. No easy feat since his perfectly grammatical Italian lacked the letter R. Maggie says after about an hour of this she also was ready to throw herself under the train.

But none of this matters now because this morning, as early as possible, I whisked her off to enjoy my new discovery. And because Maggie was with me, the 222 decided to surpass itself and give us the one thing it had lacked before, a town. Volpaia. (The old Italian promise: ask for much, get even more.) We discovered it for the reason that impels many of travel's best finds. We needed a pit stop. We were in the middle of nowhere. I don't mind using the shelter of an available tree. But all the trees before and behind us were birches. I'm 6'4. A skinny birch won't do it. In any case Maggie is not comfortable with the protection of even very protective trees. And then we saw the sign. Volpaia.

I can write about it here only because I have promised myself, and promised Maggie, that I won't give a hint about how you can find it. I'd like to think that the next time we come back to Tuscany, it will be there still, exactly as we saw it last. But of course its privacy won't last. Still, I'm not going to let you know where to turn. Don't bother to look it up. It's not even indexed in the Blue Guide to Tuscany. And, happily, it's so small it's not on many maps. I have to keep this secret. You can't betray what you love so well.

Volpaia is ancient and tiny, high and walled, built throughout in the same dark brown stone. It's got a central four-story keep, the remains of a medieval garrison. Around the tower a range of two-story dwelling houses interconnect through a tricky labyrinth of courtyards and alleys. Enclosing tower and houses there's another, irregular range of buildings, more houses interspersed with the occasional church and barn. There are three churches. All Catholic, of course. How many people can live here? Surely far fewer than fifty. You can see everything in the town in ten minutes. On the ground floor of the keep they sell the local wine and olive oil, and very handsome, heavy-duty kitchen aprons. Facing the cantina across the entry square is a small shop with coffee, pastries and sandwiches made to order. And the toilet. That's just about it. And it is perfect.

Again, I can't say why's it's perfect. Because it is miniaturized, I guess, and everything miniaturized charms us. Because it's harmonious. Frank Gehry at his best couldn't manage proportion better. Because it has tucked itself away and does not care to be known. And because, I think this is what gets me most, I don't understand how people manage to live here. The shop and the cantina couldn't possibly support an individual let alone a family. There's no other kind of work going on. The entire place is immaculate, not just beautifully but lovingly kept, every bit of it. It is clearly prosperous. And yet it seems to lack an economy. And that alone in today's world makes it magic.

I don't care what damage Dora's visit brings with her. I don't care what next week threatens. I don't even, at this moment, care about houseguests and Maggie's trip to Brussels, or even about my having houseguests on my own while Maggie is in Brussels. Today we've shared Volpaia.

Who could ask for anything more?

WEEK FOUR
September 24—30

A Dark Drive

Maggie and I want something fresh for our first house guest, Kyra, who arrived last night from London. Kyra has just retired from an exorbitantly demanding life as an international banker to concentrate on her formidable gift for painting. She is also a formidable hostess. With Cecilia, we were guests for the millennial New Year's Eve at her chalet in the French Alps, all *Écrevisses* and Taittinger *Blanc de Blancs*. This is in our small way an attempt to return that extravagant hospitality. She is also the most experienced traveler we know. One year her work took her to a hundred and ten different countries within twelve months. She has been virtually everywhere, and she has certainly seen virtually everything worth seeing. Today must be exceptional.

So, pouring over maps and guidebooks while we sip morning coffee on our terrace, we determine on Stia. Kyra says she knows nothing about Stia. Nor do we. All we know is what we read in the guidebooks. It's the northernmost *significant* town in the National Forest of the Casentino, high in the Apennines. This would be our second national forest this trip. The Val d'Elsa was unforgettable on the first Sunday. Why not take a chance on the Casentino?

We head almost due east from Fiesole, on the 667, following the course of the Arno upstream. After about an hour the road starts climbing. We turn off the highway at Sandetole, where the Sieve enters the Arno, and begin to ascend precipitously. Now we enter the forest, the unvarious Casentino, a sober, demanding part of Tuscany that tourists rarely visit. Easy to see why. Constant hairpin turns spiral you up then quickly down steeply banked, densely forested roads. For a while you pass the occasional small house, a small flock of sheep nearby, and just beyond, no doubt, wolves. But soon all signs of ordinary habitation disappear. You climb higher and higher into the beginning of the Italian Alps.

These mountains call to mind parts of Washington State or of the Blue Ridge, though even in late September without any hint of the color we associate with autumn. Everything here is steadily evergreen. And you never get anything as sentimental as a view. Instead, at the tips of some peaks, if you leave the roads for dirt tracks, you can make your hard way toward ruined oratories or remote monasteries, like La Verna, where St. Francis received the stigmata. Up here you can well believe the transcendent might make itself visible. And the form it would take would be wounds.

From time to time we pass stern, wiry men, in chamois and corduroy, who have forgotten how to smile if they ever knew, out with their guns on Sunday to bag wild boar, a Tuscan autumn delicacy. At lunch last week I asked Marcello about boar. Growing up on a farm near Siena, did he ever encounter them? Yes, in the summer. He would finish helping his father and uncles in the fields, and then go to a pond on the property to swim away the grime. Frequently, coming up from a dive, he'd find the entire shore lapped by boar drinking. Dangerous? The males, he says, would leave you alone if you splashed a lot on your way to the bank. But the sows, if they were guarding their young, would attack as soon as look at you. Sometimes he was still treading water till well past sunset, in the increasingly chilly pond, waiting for the last of the moms to trundle home from supper.

Half an hour or so into this vertiginous climb Kyra begins to feel unwell. When we pull off the road, we can hear the regular report of rifle fire cracking in the middle distance. It was of course the grandfathers of these hunters who composed those fierce and unforgiving bands of Partisans that made life hell for the retreating Nazis. This is a place, I hear myself thinking, where I don't want to be. A place where I find myself praying the car won't break down. For the first time in Italy I feel fear. No, for the second time. I recognize in hindsight fear is also what I felt when Dora hung up.

We have no sense in the States of this grim, tough *montagnard* Italy. This is a genuine beach v. island moment. Italy is for us the cities of art and the medieval towns, the farming countryside, even the seaside. And of course the eateries. All welcoming abundance. Set in those places, conventional Tuscan memoirs in English never encounter anything worse from their Italians than petty chicanery. And that's always the temporary exception. The ruined farmhouse does get heat, finally, and running water. The unfriendly neighbor provides the cheese and the eggs just when they're needed. And some shy passerby has left on the doorstep that fragrant bunch of wild fennel and broom.

To find the dark, resilient landscape into which we've driven this afternoon, *tough* Italy, you need to look in other books, back to the Italian novels and stories of Henry James and E.M. Forster, where the innocent heroine is ruined or more often dies, or in our own time to the many excellent mysteries set in Italy. To Donna Leon, Timothy Williams, Timothy Holme, and perhaps even more so to the wonderful, strangely undervalued Magdalen Nabb. You don't find in these books the random violence or casual cruelty of the American dark side. Our crime fiction depends on a clear divide between the good and the criminal, a boundary carefully tended by incorruptible policemen or their surrogates. No matter how vicious or cruel the perps may be, we can rest assured they represent exceptions not the rule. Order is basic, and reliable.

In Italy, outside the tourist zones, and the narratives written to entice tourists to visit, even the mere notion of such a boundary seems naïve. In the real Italy self-interest always masters principle; indeed, principle is hardly more than façade. There might be rare heroic goodness, but never ordinary disinterest or simple altruism. Italy is not a civil society as we understand society, a community, a commonwealth, but a world of monad-like individuals embedded in families, not vicious, just unrelentingly suspicious and self-protecting. It's the world of the Barnabei: in which the only relationships are mother to son, brother to brother, never friend to friend, let alone stranger to stranger. Here you count on blood, and only on blood.

I am not surprised when Kyra is ill again on the drive back down. We found a wonderful *trattoria* for *pranzo* and she was able to buy several lengths of richly red woven wool direct from the factory. But the dark approach never entirely lightened.

And when, much later in our stay, I think back on this Sunday drive, I see how carefully it has been offered to me as an overture.

Preposterous

"Don't you find *Romeo and Juliet* preposterous?"

I borrow *preposterous* from the distinguished scholar, Patricia

Parker, who takes the term back to its literal meaning, derived from the Latin for 'before' *pre* and 'after' *post*. Something is literally preposterous not because we find it absurd or ridiculous but because it disrupts the order we expect things to follow. The preposterous puts its *afters* before its *befores*, upsetting cause and effect, and thereby subverting plausibility, challenging our customary ideas of order. Professor Parker has argued that, in this sense, all Shakespeare's plays are—deliberately—preposterous.

Think about it, I ask *gli studenti*. A guy meets a girl at a dance and within 18 or so lines of highly formalized verse repartee, knowing literally nothing about one another, they fall deeply, madly, lastingly in love. Surely that is preposterous by any set of standards? And then just look at what follows. Later that night they meet again, briefly, in her garden. The dance took place Sunday night, now it's very early Monday; the days are set into the play. And after five minutes' more conversation they decide to get married. His priest who certainly should know better, and entirely contrary to Canon Law, agrees to marry them Monday afternoon.

At the point at which they marry they have spent perhaps a total of ten minutes together, a couple of minutes dancing, a few more minutes on the famous balcony. (One of the really curious features of *Romeo and Juliet* is how little time Romeo and Juliet are actually on stage at the same time together and alive. Over the course of the entire play the lovers share the stage for about fifteen minutes tops, and never, alive, after the midpoint.) They consummate the marriage Monday night. Tuesday morning early, Romeo flees into exile; Juliet learns she is being married to Paris the next day. Tuesday night she takes the drug that simulates her death. Wednesday night she's buried. Romeo comes back later that night, is duped, dies and, waking, so does she. It's not yet Thursday dawn. The entire play covers fewer than four full days.

Surely we are meant to notice that this is—well, *preposterous!*

Muldoon is immediately hostile. "Just because at the end of the twentieth century we find a 400 year old play strange doesn't mean Shakespeare's audience did," he insists. Or that Shakespeare wanted them to think it preposterous. "You are talking," he accuses, "about the difference time makes, not about something inherent to the play itself. You are doing exactly what you've been telling us we can't do, imposing your values on an older text."

How often the best student is the angry student. How rarely does the angry student know how to let his anger help him learn.

Of course we are talking about the difference time makes, I concede. But is that all we are talking about? I ask Muldoon to read Romeo's speech comparing his love with the families' feud, a speech that comes almost at the start of the script, while the text is still framing for us how to watch it.

> Here's much to do with hate, but more with love.
> Why, then, O brawling love, O loving hate,
> O anything of nothing first create,
> O heavy lightness, serious vanity,
> Misshapen chaos of well-seeming forms,
> Feather of lead, bright smoke, cold fire, sick health,
> Still-waking sleep, that is not what it is!
> This love feel I, that feel no love in this! (I:1, 175-181)

Muldoon reads the speech but at once, acutely, responds: Romeo's describing here the *chaos* of the feud, and his trivial love for Rosalind. Those are the things that only *seem well*. He's not describing his love for Juliet. He's not making sense of the script with this speech. He's describing, accurately, what the script is about to refute and refuse.

I could reply that nothing in the text suggests a significant difference between Romeo's swift falling in love with Juliet and his equally swift falling out of love with Rosalind, for whom of course he was literally love-sick up until the moment he spotted Juliet. In the words of another lyricist: when I'm not near the girl I love I love the girl I'm near. But I don't want to antagonize Muldoon, so I quickly concede his point and ask him about Friar Laurence's speech on the herbs (Act II, scene 3), the herbs that will do a lot of the later damage.

This is a notoriously difficult speech to deliver because the chiming couplet rhymes inevitably make it sound like nonsense:

> The earth that's nature's mother is her tomb;
> What is her burying grave, that is her womb; (II, 3, 9-10)

Surely, in a reasonable world tomb and womb occupy opposite poles of life. Here they are the same. Life becomes death, death life. The distinctions on which ordered thought and ordered life depend appear to collapse under close scrutiny.

> For naught so vile that on the earth doth live
> But to the earth some special good doth give;
> Nor aught so good but, strained from that fair use.
> Revolts from true birth, stumbling on abuse.
> Virtue itself turns vice, being misapplied,
> And vice sometime's by action dignified. (17-22)

Before I can even ask about these lines, Muldoon forestalls me. He is really on his mettle today. This is a speech about *fair use*, he says, and *misapplication*. Laurence is not denying the difference between the vile and the virtuous. He only says that the virtuous can be used vilely, and the vile can be turned to value. That's obvious. Anything can be misused. He glows in anticipated triumph.

Exactly so, I concur. That is indeed precisely Laurence's point. I want Muldoon to win this. I am so delighted at his energy, his eagerness, and his insight. But think of what it means, I ask, to live in a world in which all the signs are so unstable, in which opposites can so easily blend into and become each other. How can anyone in such a world be sure of what is virtuous and what is vicious? How can someone then separate romance from tragedy, family from futility? How can anyone, that is, avoid contributing to the tragedy of Romeo and Juliet. Where and how can these people learn what they need to know to live?

Silence. Is he taking me seriously, or merely resisting?

I review the plot that follows from the gathering of the herbs. Laurence is convinced that marrying the lovers will reconcile the families. Wrong. He is also convinced that Juliet's drug-faked death, using these herbs, will save her life, and Romeo's. Wrong again, doubly wrong. Repeatedly, for the best possible motives, and with all the skill and knowledge available to his world, the Friar winds up causing the harm he is trying to avert. Isn't that why the lines have that ding-dong sing-song quality. It's like greeting-card verse, full of bromides that don't stand up to the stern texture of experience.

I wait for Muldoon's reply. He merely turns his back to me. But I know he can use that keen mind to synthesize his view and Parker's. I just have to find a way to stop alienating him.

No one else has said a word all class. No one else speaks now. They all seem to sense that this is it, the big duel between us that will determine the rest of the term.

List everything, I ask *gli studenti*, you find preposterous in the story. If Muldoon is going to participate, he's going to do it to show the others he's smarter than they, not because of anything I can stimulate.

They all write for a bit, and then we collate a master list. When we finish, *Romeo and Juliet* no longer looks or sounds anything remotely like a romance about innocent and admirable young lovers undone by blind prejudice. That's *West Side Story*, Shakespeare's tragedy sentimentalized and distorted. What we find instead in a script in which Shakespeare seems to test and find wanting all the models of loving available to his culture. And which finds nothing else to be guided by, in the domestic (the parents), the civil (the Prince), or the religious (the friars) sphere. No play could be more totally negative. No design for living is left standing at the end. And as a result almost no young person is left standing either.

No one in the class is happy with this reading. Now it's not just Muldoon. What's the point then, why should we care, their truculent silence implies, if it's all, and only, preposterous.

This is teaching? This is why we've come to read Shakespeare in Italy? Why, why am I doing this? Why, class after class, do I let this happen, make this happen? I've been doing this for decades; I know how to teach. What's really going on here? Do I insist on disappointing them in class because outside the class that's what keeps happening to me?

I find myself now the most preposterous thing in the room.

Pericoloso

Maggie and Kyra are down in town looking at art supply stores. No surprise: Florence is famous for the quality of its colors and brushes. Kyra is eager to sample the wares. (Later, we will receive from her two magical contrasting oils, made from the colors she buys today, one called Assisi, the other Florence.) I wait by the phone for Dora, hoping she calls before Maggie gets back. The phone rings. It's Heidi, our administrator. She's swamped organizing a major conference on study abroad in Italy. Can I show the gardens to a visitor? I know I should wait by the phone. But the hell with Dora. For now.

Which is how I find myself trying to remember what Allen told us, while touring the gardens with the charming, Chicago-based, garden specialist, Jane Harvey. She's just finished work on the restoration of the famous gardens at Villa Noailles in the South of France, an iconic early Modernist house dating from the 1920s. Now she is planning a book on our architect, Pinsent. She says he is an unfairly overlooked genius.

Well, it's her field, not mine. She certainly dismisses out of hand my suggestion that there is something about Le Balze that is fundamentally perverse.

We begin to stroll. She looks something between shocked and appalled at how shabby everything seems. We do what we can, I explain, but Le Balze came to us from the Marchesa without an endowment. In 1995 we spent a quarter of a million dollars restoring the gardens. More recently we laid out almost a million dollars on infrastructure: new septic tanks, roof, kitchen, shoring up the terrace and rewiring the telephones. But despite these efforts fifteen years of hard student use have taken their toll.

She concedes our efforts to maintain the residence, but remains pretty much adamant that most of what we've done in the gardens has been wrong. We ought, she insists, to make restoring the Triton fountain the highest priority. And we need to have water back in the garden. Moving water is a hallmark of the Italian garden. All our basins and fountains are dry. And we certainly should stop storing vegetables in the former chapel. That sacrilege shocks her almost as much as it did the Alumna. "The children," she insists, "the children need a place in which to be quiet." I decide not to tell her that the *children* have not expressed such a desire.

She is literally stricken at the condition of our euonymus. If expertly treated, she assures me, it would carpet like soft gray-green velvet the walls of the villa's external stairs. Now it's brown, brittle and mostly dead. And then just as she recovers her equanimity and is ready to move on, Heidi, passing by, blithely explains that they will soon be tearing down a wall of jasmine in order to restore the stucco beneath. Jane looks as though she may faint.

Taking me aside, she urgently whispers that I must, *must*, tell *them* that the jasmine can easily be detached from the wall during the repairs. Nothing would justify tearing it down. In winter it will send out sprays, *sprays* of white flowers, with a *Heavenly* Scent. Of course, she allows, it does need trimming. Everything here, she says, needs trimming. But please, she begs me, *please*, you must not allow them to tear it down.

I don't bother to explain that I have pretty much over the course of a month lost control of both my teaching and my personal life, so it's hopeless to expect me to make any kind of difference with jasmine. Instead I tell her something about Strong that I have just discovered. It puts him in a good light, so it's not a story I am glad to share. But I feel I ought to offer her something nice in exchange for the very happy hour she is sharing with me.

In the late 1930s, when he was in his seventies, the long widowed Strong fell hard for an Anglo-Prussian countess, Elizabeth Van Arnim (1866-1941). She had written a once very famous and still remarkably strange garden book, *Elizabeth and her German Garden* (1898). But she is now probably better known for a novel that got adapted into film, *Enchanted April*. She was born British as Mary Annette Beauchamp. And after Count Von Arnim's death in 1910, she returned to her roots to marry that Earl Russell who was Bertrand Russell's elder brother. We used to have Strong's copy of her collected works, beautifully bound, in the library here, but they have disappeared since my last stay.

Even though septuagenarian and confined to a wheelchair, Strong pursued Lady Russell across Europe, when it wasn't easy for even an able-bodied man to pursue anyone anywhere, given the imminence of World War II. He paid court to her in all the major capitals, and several of the minor spas. But she would hear nothing of it, though it's permissible to think that she wrote something of it into the autumnal lovemaking that kindles the pages of her novel. He begged her to spend Christmas with him in Le Balze. Having spent a winter here, I don't blame her for writing back that she preferred the warmer comforts of her villa at Grasse, surrounded, as she told him, by her children, her lovers, and her dogs. Which, we can hope, she could tell apart. In any case, Strong seems to have been better off in his solitude since she wrote in her garden book that despite the comforts, indeed the splendors of her position, she wished above all things that she were a man. And if she had been made a man, the first thing she would have done, she said, would have been to go buy a spade.

Jane takes this story as entirely consonant with her image of the maker of Le Balze. And I enjoy having my former pleasure in this place restored by her generous and expert eyes. Still, before she leaves, I can't resist taking her outside to show her the original entrance. You get to it by the grandly named Via Degli Angeli, which is in fact a narrow, stony, donkey track snaking between our walls to the south and the looming bastion of the Villa San Giralamo to the north. At its widest it's perhaps three feet. Maybe it was actually made originally for angels. Flesh and blood would have had to dismount from carriage or car and walk some fifty yards along this lunar trail before coming all of a sudden to the ornate doorway, then Number 5. Of course, once the doors parted, you found yourself transported into the high loggia, with all Florence exposed below.

Jane is puzzled. With her lovely manners, she cannot understand how or why you'd want your guests, in the extreme climate of Tuscany, to undertake this strange approach. Why conceal the entrance so carefully with so many easier, more inviting ways available?

I've got her.

"Oh now," she says, "oh yes, now I see what you meant by perverse."

Leaving, she warns me that the walls supporting San Giralamo above and behind us are collapsing, and that if we don't do something soon, very soon, hundreds of tons of rock will cave in over us. This is an even more pressing crisis than the jasmine, a situation, she says, *pericoloso, molto pericoloso,* dangerous in the extreme.

Going Like Lynn

A morning of departures and arrival. Kyra is heading home to London and Maggie is about to fly off to Brussels. And my cousin Joanne, house guest number two, enters just as they go.

After Brussels Maggie will fly to London to join Kyra for a day or two of sightseeing and then they will use the Chunnel to drive across France to Kyra's place just opposite Mont Blanc. They'll wander there around the *alpage*, the high meadows where the cattle spend the warmer months. They will hunt for those incomparable Alpine wildflowers that Kyra will paint and Maggie draw. Then they will drive down here through northeastern Italy, Savoy and then Piedmont. I would be close to despair at Maggie's going except that she announced this morning that she's decided this is it, the last work-connected trip. She will refuse if anything else is offered. After this, if there's travel, we travel together.

She sees it now also. If for the rest of our stay we're together only on weekends, with guests, we've both lost all hope of finding let alone being able to hold on to what we came for.

When they have gone, Joanne, bravely fighting off jet lag, takes the bus down to Florence where she will spend the day. I stay up in the villino to work. I'll meet her in town for dinner at Benvenuto, near Santa Croce, one of our great favorites from the first stay. Fond as I am of my cousin, I dread this dinner. How do we keep off the topic of Dora? I am an unskillful liar. *No, I haven't heard anything either.* All the while I am preparing to meet Dora up the hill.

Of course as soon as we settle into the restaurant, Joanne asks if I have heard anything more from Dora. Stalling I explain that Benvenuto was our favorite place for lunch when we came with the children, but that Cecilia never managed to finish a meal here without bursting into tears. Though she was only eleven, we made no concessions to her age. By the time we'd finish a long morning of church-viewing and museum-trawling, the poor mite would be spent. Even before the pasta appeared, she would have dissolved.

But the Benvenuto people took it in course.

Of course, says a woman at the next table. Everyone becomes family here, just by sitting at a table. Though we have never seen one another before this, our fellow diner suddenly becomes our friend. She is called Lynn Portnoy, and she is heaven sent. All mention of Dora preempted.

Lynn writes guidebooks for women traveling alone, called *Going Like Lynn*. She started writing her books because other women envied the ease with which she traveled to New York and then Europe to supply her boutique back home in Detroit. I ask isn't Detroit too crime ridden to sell expensive clothes. She laughs me off. But it turns out that her boutique is now in a suburb. "I moved my boutique out of Detroit after the shoplifters stopped showing up. When the shoplifters stop showing, you know things are dead. There's no crime in Detroit, there is nothing in Detroit."

She is fearless. Women can travel anywhere safely, she insists, if they are smart about it. She tells us the names of the hotels she uses. Hotels where the concierge always know of places where women can dine pleasantly alone. Like Benvenuto. She tells us about shops where women are treated respectfully, car agencies with drivers you can trust. (I'm not going to give names. Buy her books.)

My cousin listens avidly. Almost as soon as she got off the bus today, she was picked up by a man, "from the world of film," who told her he could make her career, if she'd meet him at 3:00 P.M. Then, at lunch, the waiter, considerably her junior, but with dazzling teeth (she says), asked if she'd meet him at 2:30, to conclude the *intervallo*. And after lunch, when she tried to get into a small museum, the director refused to sell her a ticket. Instead he personally showed her through all its three floors. He was called away before he could suggest the inevitable rendezvous. Lynn is full of congratulations, and Joanne begins to see her afternoon in a different and ego-boosting light.

As though to recognize a peer, Lynn gleefully shares her knowledge of where to look tomorrow for leather, that grail of Tuscan shoppers. There is no greater gift in Florence than a solid tip about bargains in leather. The three of us couldn't be chummier. Tomorrow Lynn goes on to Paris. We agree that if there is one museum you have to see in Paris, every time you go there, it's the Musée Nissim de Camondo. Joanne doesn't know it. Lynn begins to describe its beauties and then its sad end, when the Jewish Camondos, who had bequeathed their exquisite collection to the French state in memory of a son who died in World War I, were betrayed to the Nazis and sent to their doom in the camps.

Lynn begins, God bless her, to cry as she talks about their last days. Their house isn't for her merely a site of acquisition. It is beautiful for her because the Comondos are real to her. I've rarely met anybody so alive to the world, because, I think, so grounded within the world. She represents everything contained in that promise of the deep and revelatory goodness of travel.

If I can only somehow annex the sane good cheer of people like Lynn and Jane Harvey, maybe I can get through tomorrow with Dora, and then maybe I can even begin to find my own way abroad and home.

Dora

Fourteen years ago Dora was a still pretty and clearly prosperous lady in her early forties, generous in sharing the good things life had given her, and commanding. She gave easily but she was also used to being in charge and obeyed.

The woman I meet today in the Franciscan cloister is unrecognizable as Dora. She is haggard and unkempt, cloaked in the deepest mourning, black dress, hose, shoes. No jewelry. Her hair pulled rightly back, her hands unmanicured. She is the ruin of her former self.

What follows here is not quite what Dora had to say. But it is what I could make out of what Dora had to say.

On the morning of the Friday before we arrived in Italy, another in an apparently endless series of hot, airless days, Cip Capolago, Dora and Waldo's elder son, left the family apartment in Rome first. A passionate amateur pilot he planned on an entire day in the skies. Perhaps getting as far as Milan before having to turn back. Now in his late twenties, with a two-year old American MBA, Cip was the family's future. At the end of World War II his grandfather, a mason, had started a small construction business, mostly rebuilding bombed-out houses, capitalized by the savings of the American cousins. One of whom, Dora, on a visit liked Waldo and Rome so much she stayed and they married.

Buoyed by Italy's post-war boom, the so-called Italian Miracle, the Capolago concern mushroomed. Gradually the sites that at an earlier stage they had built for others they began to own themselves. Eventually the more ambitious Waldo replaced his father as head of the operation. He continued to grow the construction unit, but soon involved the family in hotel chains, office parks, and then finance. Competitors claimed that Waldo, though a model of rectitude, was also somehow unsurpassed at sustaining business in the fierce, corrupt arena of Roman commerce. But in the past few years it has been Cip who has spotted ways to grow what they al-

ready had into something even larger, indeed global. Harder working even than his father, he indulged himself only with these rare
days off in the sky.

Waldo left the apartment next that morning, only a bit later
than the older son who had moved from child to partner. Waldo
was going to visit his mother-in-law, who was also his aunt. Dora
and Waldo are first cousins, the children of sisters. He not only
loves his mother-in-law as though she were his own mother but
perhaps even more importantly respects her as the epitome of that
dignified, reticent courtesy he treats as the staff of life. Dora has
energy, drive, edge. He adores her, and proudly attributes to her
their almost fantastic success. But with his mother-in-law Waldo
can be entirely at ease. Unlike Dora she makes no demands. Most
days he tries to stop off at her apartment on the way to or back from
work. But at least one day a week he tries to spend the entire morning with her, having first called in at their favorite *pasticceria*, for an
ample supply of the different pastries each prefers. She has coffee
waiting. The Italian family.

Ivo was the last to go. By the time he was up and dressed, the
maid had arrived and was serving coffee to his mother on the
shaded terrace. He was going to spend the day at the beach, he
explained. As one of his graduation presents he had been given a
Porsche. It had been waiting for him in Rome while he had been
traveling in the States, saying goodbye to his American classmates.
Back home now only a few days, he was eager to see what the car
could do. Especially since he would have to leave it shortly when
the family left on their long-planned trip to South America. He
would drive to the seaside, swim for a bit, and then be back in time
for *cena*. He promised.

Dora didn't describe Ivo to me. And, curiously, I have never
seen a picture of him. Cip is almost the movie-star young Italian,
olive skin, black hair with a slight wave, blue eyes, lean and broad-
shouldered, perhaps more good looking than strictly handsome,
but with spectacular American-tended teeth. Ivo may have looked
like that but brothers often pull from opposite sides of the gene
store-house. I don't know.

When he didn't come back in time for supper, Dora grew worried. Cip returned a little later, to change before going out again,

and laughed at his mother's anxieties. His brother had probably hooked up with up a girl at the beach. They weren't likely to see him before the next morning. *Late* the next morning.

Dora insisted that Ivo always either kept his word or called to explain when he couldn't. He knew she worried. He never caused her needless anxiety.

Saturday morning she saw that Ivo still hadn't come home. Still nonchalant, Cip's new suggestion was that Ivo had taken the girl to the family's villa in the Alban hills. Dora had called there, she said, last night and this morning, but there was no answer. Of course, there was no answer, Cip laughed.

By Sunday morning, she was beside herself with worry. Waldo, who had been urging they spend more time at the villa to escape the inferno of late summer Rome, now got her to agree to go. She packed a cold supper, and they set off in mid-afternoon. Cip said he would join them by evening.

When they arrived at the villa, they found the Porsche, as Cip had predicted, parked in the courtyard. Waldo said he would go ahead, to give Ivo warning in case the girl was still there. Dora started getting their things out of the car. She heard Waldo comically banging on the front door and then pushing it open. Then he began to scream her name. She thought he was having a heart attack.

Rushing up into the foyer she found Ivo, naked, hanging from a noose attached to the high central lantern. Waldo was trying fiercely to push the body up, to take pressure off the neck. But Dora could see from the color and the rigor that Ivo was dead, and had been dead for some time. Gently, she disentangled Waldo and got him sobbing into a chair. Then she called Cip, who called the police.

At this point in her narrative Dora had to stop. She excused herself and walked back into the oldest section of the friary, where a saint had lived, gesturing for me not to follow. In about a quarter of an hour she was able to return and continue.

The police came quickly. She and Waldo were led to their bedroom while the investigation started. Cip stayed with the police. Husband and wife were left entirely alone for hours except for a brief visit from Cip to ask if he could bring them their supper. Both refused. Dora told him to offer the food to the police. Waldo could not stop crying. Dora found herself surprisingly dry-eyed, and numb. She believes now she was in shock.

Just before midnight Cip came back and asked his father to come with him to talk to the policeman in charge. Waldo managed to pull himself together and left Dora alone in the bedroom. After a while Cip came for Dora and led her into the main room of the villa. She could see into the foyer. Ivo was gone. The chief policeman, a detective in a suit, was waiting for her.

This is what she remembers of what he said. "Signora, we are all so sorry for this terrible loss you have sustained. And the terrible way in which you had to discover it. We do not wish in any way to add to your pain. We have advised your son, and your husband, that we think it best if there is no investigation, that you take immediate possession of your son's body, and that you bury it as soon as possible. The heat of the day. He has been there—a while. Your husband and your son agree. We have called for a priest, and he has already anointed the body. He is waiting in the dining room, if you would wish to see him and to pray with him."

Dora felt she could not believe he had said these words to her.

"No investigation! My son has been murdered. How can you not investigate?"

The detective said nothing. After a moment he bowed to her and left the room. Cip knelt by his mother's chair and took her hands in his.

"They have examined the body, Mamma. There are no signs of a struggle. He was not murdered. He took his own life."

Dora couldn't believe her ears. All the numbness was gone. She pushed Cip away and began to go after the detective, demanding he get out of her house, that he admit he was lying, that he and all his crew were incompetent. Her son had everything to live for; he had no reason to kill himself. They were delusional, insane, corrupt.

The detective gestured toward Waldo and Cip.

Cip managed to get her back into a chair. The police believed that Ivo did not intend to kill himself but he did put the noose around his neck. The room, the body, there was no possible explanation of what they found except that Ivo had taken off his clothes, stood on the chair, and put the noose around his own neck, and then probably accidentally, certainly not intentionally, he had kicked the chair away. The chair was the only thing disturbed in the entire house. Did she understand?

Dora refused to hear any more. She was going to call the American embassy. The boys had dual citizenship. If the Italian authorities were incompetent, she would insist on an American investigation. Keep everything as it is, she kept insisting; let someone see it who really understands his business.

"I told them it was impossible. He wouldn't have to do this to himself. There were always girls in his life, He was handsome, popular. He wasn't lonely, frustrated, solitary."

But the police wouldn't listen. Ivo had been away for most of the past four years, in another country. Even in the summer, he had stayed to work in New York. They had learned all about that from the father and the brother. The family had seen very little of him. Just brief holidays at the end of the summer, and then a few days at Christmas. He left them a boy, and as he became a man, the detective explained, he must have changed. Picked up different habits. Acquired other tastes. It happens. The police insisted there could be no other explanation, until even Cip and Waldo agreed. "It must be true."

Dore realized then, without her son and husband, she had nothing left to fight back with.

She then allowed herself to meet the priest. He led her to view the body which had been laid out and decently covered. The family prayed together, and then a hearse came for the body. They next evening, Monday, Ivo was buried in the family crypt.

And a few days later the three of them left for Brazil.

But on the long flight (it takes about as long to get from Rome to Rio as from Los Angeles to Sidney), as Cip bit by bit revealed more of what the police had said to him and what he had said to them, mother and son began to compare what they remembered seeing themselves. Dovetailing one with the other, they could spot gaps. Cip remembered how odd it had seemed to him that Ivo could have kicked the chair out of the foyer and into the next room. There seemed no way that even someone much more muscular than Ivo could have kicked it that far. Shouldn't it have just toppled over? He had actually asked about that. One of the policeman said that yes it was odd but not impossible. He had seen things like it before. Just the right angle, one terrible final involuntary kick.

Dora remembered that some of the things in her bedroom, on her dressing table and her night stand, weren't as she always placed them. Not disordered, just different, in ways the police could not have known. And in their bathroom there was no toilet paper. But about that sort of thing she was meticulous. Waldo insisted that all three of their houses, every room in each of them, be ready to use at any time. They also had a place in the country, in the Abruzzi. Going up to one or the other of those places on a whim was something he liked to do. He expected to be able at any moment to decide to spend the night or even longer and to find everything prepared. Nothing could convince him that the recent increase in robberies in the countryside meant you couldn't leave silver and electronic equipment in houses people knew to be empty for long stretches of time.

Waldo wouldn't listen to any of this exchange. They, however, could talk about nothing else.

Everything that night had been so rushed. None of the neighboring villas was contacted. No one looked into who else might have been passing by. Had they dusted even that chair for fingerprints? Dora and Cip were both sure they hadn't seen any dusting powder anywhere in the house. After the police left there had been nothing for the family to clean up, straighten, re-order. It was a house that looked as though nothing at all had happened within its walls.

And there hadn't even been an autopsy. Who knew what they might have found if a pathologist had had the chance to examine the body, now embalmed and entombed.

Dora flew home. Waldo refused even to consider going with her. Cip thought it best to stay on with his father. Waldo had by then stopped communicating with his wife.

In Rome she immediately went to see the detective who had been at the villa. He patiently explained there was no case to re-open. There had never been a case. They don't even have a file in Ivo's name. Now she is trying to hire detectives.

It's evening by the time she finishes. The Franciscans have passed us on their way into the church, and on their way out. She has to rush to get her train back to Rome. She wants to be ready for Waldo and Cip. She and Waldo have not exchanged a word since she left Brazil.

But why me, I ask. Why has it been so important to see me, to tell all this to me?

"Because I know you write. I am going to discover the truth of what happened to my son, and you are going to write it, and publish it so that the truth will be known by everyone. I want you to know everything that happens. You will find out whatever we learn when we learn it. And then I want you to put it into a book.

"Rumors get out, people love scandal. His classmates, his friends in the States. Sooner or later they will hear this false, ugly, vicious lie about him, about how he died. I owe my son that his story gets told. And you are the only person I know who can tell it. That is why you were brought here."

By here she does not meet the Franciscan church, she means Italy. Her story, she believes, is the story I am here to tell.

She won't let me see her to a taxi, let alone the train. She thinks she may be watched. We won't meet like this again, she insists. And then she remembers Joanne. "When does she arrive?"

"Yesterday."

I am to say nothing about this to her, nothing. I point out that Joanne will be going down to Rome next week, to stay with the Capolagos. She is going to have to be told something, isn't she? Dora says she will think about that on the train and let me know what she decides. She is entirely in charge. It never occurs to her, even in passing, that I might not want to write her story, that I might have other commitments, other plans. Any instrument she can find to right her son is hers to command.

As I make my back to the villino, along the now dark stone ramparts that lead from the church to the Via Vecchia, cosmopolitan, vivacious Jane Harvey and Lynn Portnoy seem very far away. Despite the distance I am much closer now to Stia and the hunters.

"You will find out whatever we learn when we learn it. And then I want you to put it into a book."

Loggia and Lecture
After the debacle of last week's failed kisses, I decide today to ask *gli studenti* about others' staging of the play rather than inviting them to attempt their own.

How does the performance of *Romeo and Juliet* in the blockbuster film *Shakespeare in Love* differ from Shakespeare's script? The film ends with the first performance of *Romeo and Juliet*, and indeed the plot of the film offers Tom Stoppard's reading of the gestation of Shakespeare's script. It's not the Stoppard of *Rosencrantz and Guildenstern Are Dead,* the Stoppard who is Beckett's epigone and Shaw's theatrical heir. The film is clearly Stoppard slumming, but still Stoppard is Stoppard.

"That's easy," says the reliably quiet and always smart Willy Voltaire. "*Shakespeare in Love* has a happy ending."

Indeed it does! The powerless Prince of Verona of the play gives way to the omnipotent Queen Elizabeth, in all the glory of Dame Judi Dench's Oscar-winning performance. In Shakespeare's script the Prince concludes the action by bidding the Veronese, and by extension the audience: "*Go hence to have more talk of these sad things*" (V:3, 306). It's not over. Start thinking. "These sad things." This is complex—it needs *more talk, and much more serious talk.* On screen the queen suddenly pops out from the Globe's upper reaches and resolves all the issues, handily and happily. Will, the film's Romeo, will go on to become SHAKESPEARE. Viola, the Juliet, goes off to the New World where we see Gwyneth Paltrow confidently striding ashore, a la Kate Winslet at the end of *Titanic.* Another Oscar-winner that turns tragedy into a reassuringly happy ending, even if, in the case of the Titanic, that is accomplished through the wedding with a thousand drowned, apparently drip-dry, ghosts. *Go hence and think no more.*

Our lives, lives in the US, the great cultural critic Slavoj Žižek insists, are plagued by, and addicted to, fantasy. We consume fantasy with every magazine we buy, during every moment of television we watch, in every mall we trod. Even the warnings on airplanes about how to manage emergencies are fantasies; all those happy, confident and nicely dressed people (nobody on airplanes today looks anything like the figures in those videos) walking calmly and in line to the pre-arranged exits. As If. The US, apparently, cannot take very much reality. And so of course, from the tragedy of Romeo and Juliet, we manufacture *Shakespeare in Love.* We don't want tragedy, or *Romeo and Juliet,* or the Shakespeare who wrote *Romeo and Juliet* because, these days, we can't take *Romeo and Juliet.* We can't take Shakespeare. He's too tough for us, too—in the word of the preceding class—preposterous.

But—here's my plea—if we use Shakespeare's theatre as he

seems to intend, the preposterous can foil fantasy. The preposterous gets us thinking. As we think we can begin to see at least the edges of the fantasy that enwraps and continually de-natures our lives. Though the preposterous may thereby undercut our confidence in the things we take for granted, it can also stretch us, invite us to reach out for parts of experience we would not otherwise even know were there to grasp. The preposterous is what gets us to go home and think differently: *to have more talk of these sad things.*

This is too much for genial, generous Benny. These are movies, he explains to me. We don't take them seriously. We watch them for entertainment. For fun. That's why we are here in Italy. For time off. We know they are not real. Just as our time here is not our real life. We know what is real. "We know," he concludes, "what to take seriously."

"This is just a course."

I should leave it there but I can't stop thinking of Ivo Capolago, of what he might have said in a classroom like this, of what he might have learned in a classroom like this. Is there something he could have taken away from "just a course?" And what would Dora say, if she were here, listening. Would she believe these young people, only a year or two younger than her son, know what to take seriously?

Let's go back then to reality, I suggest, to where we started four weeks back: our Italy versus Shakespeare's Italy. We've now read the first three of his Italian plays. We're coming to the end of our first month, one third of the way through the semester. What can we claim—or at least hypothesize—at this point about Shakespeare's Italy?

Beluga has clearly thought about this. Shakespeare's Italy, he says, is all about authority. "We are here to do what we like. Over here there's no authority over us—no campus police, no deans. Even you—."

Ruefully I acknowledge the obvious. Even I, here, entirely lack authority.

But, he goes on, in Shakespeare's Italy authorities are everywhere, and they are not only omnipresent, they seem pretty close to omnipotent.

Muldoon counters that in *Two Gentlemen* Proteus easily dupes the Duke of Mantua. And the others escape without incident from the Duke's court.

Beluga quickly returns: But the Duke then shows up in the woods almost at once, and is completely in charge.

Betty adds: and although Baptista, Katharina the Shrew's father, can't manage to suppress his daughter, he can hand her over to a Petruchio who can do pretty much anything he wants to her.

I try to make this a bit bigger. Doesn't this suggest that Italian Katharina is the exact opposite of the heroines of the non-Italian comedies, like Rosalind in *As You Like It* and Viola in *Twelfth Night?* The non-Italian heroines tame recalcitrant or reluctant men. But in Italy a brute easily and lawfully imprisons Katharina, and then tames her violently. It's a completely different sort of story.

Is it just comedy? What happens, I ask, with tragedy.

Miss Haag takes that up with alacrity. Juliet can only go from her parents' house to their tomb.

Muldoon: Romeo manages to get away

Beluga: But he doesn't really get anywhere, except the tomb.

I try to frame it more broadly. In Verona all the authorities, the Church, the State, are notoriously ineffectual. The Prince is always trying to get the feud to stop. The Friar is trying to make peace between the families. But they fail because the families' authority is absolute. You are a Montague or a Capulet and you can't ever do anything about that. When you try, you die. By the end of the play all of the bright young people are dead after trying to find something that might seem to produce real change.

Muldoon will have none of this. Yes, he agrees, but in the other tragedies (here's where his previous course work comes in handy), *Hamlet, Lear,* terrible things happen. Because these are tragedies. We're not talking about Italy, we're talking about genre.

I step back. Either they see it or we drop it.

And then, after a very long moment, Rotgut. What he sees in the play is what he sees in Italy now. "Italy's crowded."

Muldoon is derisive. These are plays about travel. Unhappy in Verona, why not try Mantua? Poor in Verona, go "wive it wealthily in Padua." The whole point about Italy then is that it wasn't Italy, it was a lot of other, smaller places, and you could move pretty easily between and among them. Shakespeare knew that.

And then Benny, always the realist: I don't know about anybody else but I feel pretty crowded here. There's really no privacy. I met some Italians. They have no privacy from their families.

I seize gratefully on this. If you know plays like *A Midsummer Night's Dream* or *As You Like It*, there are these marvelous forests, green worlds, into which you can disappear and experiment with alternative selves. You can have different erotic partners. You can even have different erotic identities. And in the tragedies there's movement, or at least the possibility of movement: Wittenberg and England for Hamlet, the whole of Scotland for Macbeth, France for Cordelia. But Shakespeare permits Italy no green, no empty, no free zones. In his Italy, Rotgut is right, you are always watched, always observed, in crowded piazzas, in tightly walled homes. You can get about a bit, maybe, but mostly only to cells, to confess. Otherwise you are certain to bump into just the people you least want to encounter, generally with pretty nasty results. It's this density, backed by an established usually familial authority which, when it strikes, strikes powerfully, that makes everything in Shakespeare's Italy consequential, for real. There's no room for play here, for pretend. You feign death, like Juliet, and you die. Unlike Shakespeare's other settings, or the Italy of *gli studenti*, Shakespeare's Italy lets you get away with nothing.

And it's all so brutal, so cruel.

I have got to stop. I am beginning to lecture and that is always a bad sign. And I know, even though *gli studenti* don't, that I am no longer talking about Shakespeare or the plays. I know I am talking about Ivo and I can't let that happen

Books are closing. Backpacks are rearranged. My time, they signal, is up. We have come to the end. They quietly file from the Loggia. They know something was up in there and they also know they don't know what it was

After dinner, word arrives that Muldoon has dropped my course. He has arranged instead to take a tutorial with Marcello on ideas of sin in the Middle Ages. He had so much to offer. I should have kept him. But for the life of me I can't figure out how.

Basta così

This morning autumn seems finally to have smashed a way through summer's long, hot clinch. It's raining hard. The Villino is clammy, gray. Before Joanne joins me for breakfast, I need to think this through. What does Dora really want from me. Write what? Is there anything to her insistence that I could also be in some sort of danger? Even if I am not in danger, can I teach *gli studenti* the course I came to teach without infecting it with this terrible, urgent tragedy? And, most pressing, can I risk Maggie's recovery, my recovery, by taking on --taking on what?

No! Enough.

As the Italians say, *basta, basta così*. Enough. Enough for now.

But also, as Jane Harvey warned, *molto pericoloso*.

OCTOBER

WEEK FIVE
October 1-7

"Educating in Paradise"

I have to put Dora and the Capolagos on hold because I am registered to attend a conference down in Florence, "Educating in Paradise." This is the conference Heidi has been working on for the better part of a year. It's sponsored by AACUPI, the Association of American College and University Programs in Italy. There are a whopping seventy-six of these programs now, up twelve percent since 1992, and the number is still growing. Heidi is a key member of the steering group. I considered not showing up, but I've decided after all to go. In part, it's out of loyalty to Heidi, but I am also open to anything that can limit how isolated I feel up in the villino with no other adults. Except for Marcello, I almost never see, and certainly never speak to, the Italian faculty. They appear to teach their classes and then immediately leave. Most of them have other jobs, I think. The apartness of the villino sets up a kind of purdah. Little wonder I'm becoming morose.

But I also hope to learn from experts at teaching abroad something that can help me to turn around what I have begun so poorly. Maybe the old hands can offer a helping hand.

The Conference opened this morning at the Palazzo Vecchio, Florence's city hall, once the palace of the Medici Grand Dukes, in a room called the Sala dei Cinquecento. The Hall of the 1500s. It's a hangar of a space, easily fifteen, maybe even twenty times larger than the White House East Room, entirely frescoed by Varsari and associates with allegories of the rise of Tuscany and the glories of the Medici. From the start, it's clear that both organizers and speakers take the conference title with tongue in cheek. Portia Prebys, the chair, starts off by noting that Thomas Jefferson, despite his villa with the Italian name built in an Italianate style, had wanted to prevent young Americans from traveling in Europe. Too likely to corrupt them. (Shades of Roger Ascham.) He also wanted to keep most Europeans out of America. Too polluting. America was the real paradise, he thought, because it was close to Nature. Europe could only be safely seen by the mature and already formed. Jefferson certainly felt there was nothing beneficial in studying abroad.

Along the same lines Walter Kaiser, the eminent director of Harvard's Villa I Tatti, reminds us that the original Paradise was hardly a place friendly to education. When Adam and Eve tried to know more, they found themselves getting expelled. At best, he wittily concludes, education in Paradise is always uphill work.

The Italian speakers, being Italian, are even more sardonic. We live here, they say in their different ways, so we know it's not paradise. Despite the treasures, Florence suffers all the problems of a city of its size and age. Traffic. Poverty. Homelessness. Overcrowding. Just before the Conference started, the Director of the Uffizi told me they have to limit visitors to six hundred and forty at a time. There is no way around this cap, because the gallery cannot expand beyond its current footprint. During the warmer months the wait to get in can last up to four hours, all spent outside whatever the weather, with no toilets available.

All this growth has accompanied a profound cultural transformation, a change which Bob Callahan of our embassy in Rome distinguishes with the terms our class now knows well: travel and tourism. For me it's the speech of the day, because it puts sharply into context why I feel so befuddled.

Up until the early 1960s, the end of the era of the transatlantic liners, choosing to go abroad invariably meant travel. Travel was pretty much restricted to the well-to-do (with time and money) and the professorate (just time). Even the fastest boats took at least a week to cross the ocean, just to get to England. Longer to reach the continent. But travel didn't only require time. Even more it was a question of attitude. Travelers turned their backs on America for a Europe they imagined as not only better, but superior, for some even vastly superior to what they left behind at home. Perhaps few would be as extreme as William Waldorf Astor who thought that only people who couldn't afford to live elsewhere would live in America. But most travelers felt that culturally the US was far inferior to almost any country in at least Western Europe.

The great age of these travelers coincided with the great age of the big steamers, which from the 1890s on had made the risky part, the ocean voyage, not only safe but luxurious (discounting odd mishaps like the Titanic). Perhaps its last great advocate—exactly parallel to the end of the great liners—was Jacqueline Kennedy for whom, even as American First Lady, everything French was trumps. Even recently, Kyra could feel entirely at ease introducing us to some Parisians as "my American friends, but they are very sophisticated Americans." There spake Travel's authentic voice. Nevertheless, while a few travelers like Kyra remain, largely as expatriates, almost all the Americans in Europe these days are tourists, including *gli studenti*.

Later participants concur: Study Abroad would be better termed Academic Tourism. Unlike travelers, tourists come to Europe for relatively brief stays, a few weeks at the most. Students of course stay longer, but more often than not these days only for a semester, rarely a full year. Of the group at Le Balze right now, just five of the twenty-five will return after December. But, in a curious way that would have baffled Jefferson, if anything could have baffled Jefferson, their tourism turns out to be a way, not to acclaim Europe, but to reclaim America.

In the world that built Le Balze travelers like the Strongs tried to live like Italians, not like all Italians, of course, but certainly like Italians of the "better sort." They came to be immersed in, even subsumed by, the older, richer and more nuanced culture. Tourists come now not to be subsumed but to consume. While here they continue to live as Americans, emphatically. No matter how good those things they consume, they find some way to complain. It proves or keeps them genuinely American. A US woman I met through Stefano complained that the Uffizi Gallery didn't put English captions under the pictures. "But this is Italy," I said. "After all, the Met in New York and the National Gallery in Washington don't subtitle their pictures in Italian." Yes, Stefano's guest countered, but who goes to the Uffizi to stare at the pictures? I didn't then have today's answer: six hundred English speakers out of every six hundred and forty visitors per hour. In fact, the number of Americans visiting Florence each year is actually larger than the permanent population of its Italian citizens. Almost all of them baffled by what they're looking at. As the same woman concluded: "Why is all the art so religious? Did those people ever do anything but go to church?"

Of course, like all dichotomies this one blurs at the edges. Our disappointed Alumna, Lynn Portnoy, Dora Capolago, not one of them fits easily into either category. But this brief history of the traveler-tourist distinction does help clarify something that has confused and troubled me since we arrived a month ago. In 1987, the students were, almost all of them, genuinely ardent travelers. Except for one or two slugs, the majority couldn't seem to see enough of Italy. The older the sight the better. If we let drop that we were driving to Urbino or Orvieto on the weekend, we'd have to fend off volunteers for empty places in the car. To Gubbio we actually drove with our children sitting on student laps. And once they got there they scrutinized every mural, pored over every façade. Now their successors seem to live in an American bubble of the bar and the beach. They see what they are shown, but demonstrate slack interest in anything beyond. On the weekends they use their Eurail passes to go visit fellow students studying abroad in places like Antwerp and Prague. And their favorite hang-out in Piazza Mino is the Irish Bar.

A few Fridays back I spotted a group of them, going off on a jaunt. They were leaving for Perugia, they said, for the Giotto Festival. How encouraging, I thought. On Monday they were back at Le Balze complaining about how sick they got at the Festival. Giotto made them ill? No. It wasn't a Giotto Festival, it was a chocolate festival. The unsaid didn't need to be spoken: of course we wouldn't have gone all the way to Perugia for Giotto.

True there are exceptions. The most notable of them is Rotgut. He cares passionately about Italy, a passion that seems to mark him off from the others. Some weekends he seems to be the only one still in Italy. But the others, if pressed, will cite, as their reason for being here, something like President Clinton's claim that all American students should study abroad for at least a semester, not to soak up European culture but to function better in the global marketplace.

And in fact exactly that point is made at the Conference by the Italian participants. But in reverse. They want us to open our programs to Italian students. Italians, they say, can't afford to study abroad. But to compete in the new world order they have to learn American ways. If we don't voluntarily open our programs to their students, Italy, they warn, will consider insisting on it as the price of our continued operation here. In future Study Abroad, it begins to look as though Americans will be not the students but the subject. Which means that even Thomas Jefferson could be wrong, sometimes. And that if he had lived on to see the age of tourism, he would have realized he needn't have worried about the American young.

Unexpectedly, after this tonic dialogue, returning to Le Balze, I see it in a new way. Or rather I see it in the old way afresh. It is in fact astonishingly beautiful. I've become so used to it, I don't really see that anymore. Educating in Paradise, indeed.

And then it starts to rain. Fiercely.

Siena

Yesterday's fierce rain continues. Nevertheless, I decide to drive Joanne down to Siena. We can't let the weather waste her few days here cooped up in the villino. Luckily, the concentration needed to hold my own in a monsoon on the Si-Fi suspends conversation. It's not a day for the 222. And in any case Joanne, terrified by her first experience of the Italian highway, has shut her eyes tight. Her clenched lips murmur. I can't hear what she is saying but I know without hearing the words: "Mother Dear, oh pray for me, whilst far from heaven and thee, I wander in a fragile bark o'er life's tempestuous sea." Tempestuous sea is no exaggeration for this rain-soaked speedway.

But it means I can think hard about Dora without making Joanne suspicious.

My instinct is to get out of the Capolagos' way. Be polite to Dora, of course, if she calls, sympathetic, but nothing more. And certainly I should not agree to meet her again. Maggie is right: nothing good can come of this connection. Besides, it has nothing to do with me. Dora is Joanne's cousin not mine. And yet all that is really beside the point. I know it's a specious argument. The truth is: I don't want to become involved. Whatever happened to Ivo, it's sad, and it's ugly, but what in the world can I actually do for his poor grieving mother? I want to write a book about Shakespeare and Italy—and at the same time I need to help Maggie recover. The Capologos don't fit anywhere into that. To write about Ivo, I'd have to stop everything I'm doing now, scrap everything I've done for the past month, and start over again from scratch.

But with the regular swish of the windshield wipers something keeps niggling at me, insisting that ducking Dora is wrong, and not just wrong but evasive, cowardly, stupid.

I keep hearing Dora's voice: "you write… you are going to write it, and publish it so that the truth will be known by everyone… you are the only person I know who can tell it. That's why you were brought here." In the shadows of that old and shabby cloister, she spoke with absolute assurance, conviction, with authority. It wasn't a plea. It wasn't the sentimental *dramma* of the Bernabei. It was a command, the words of a sibyl or a prophetess, especially the latter, sacred, ancient, oracular. "That's why you were brought here."

Of course I know what she means by that. She thinks my being here is part of what she would call God's plan. Evil took her boy but God will give him back. The truth will come out. Ivo will be vindicated.

But I don't believe in a god who plans. Planning is clearly and merely a human function.

Still, I can't ignore or evade the uncanny coincidence, that we came to Italy the day he died. Planned or not, from the start his story has been mixed into, mixed up with, ours.

And then there's the other problem this steady, gloomy downpour is forcing me to face, try though I might to evade it: whatever God may or may not have planned, what I planned isn't happening. From the start nothing has developed as I had expected. There's been almost no time alone with Maggie. And from now on we have houseguests virtually non-stop. My teaching keeps running into roadblocks. It has already alienated one very talented student and seems to have left the rest at best indifferent. I've lost any sense of the design for the book I had planned. So was Stefano wrong: no good new for us? Or is this the new he meant? Not a good new, for God's sake, the guy died, but certainly entirely and unexpectedly new.

In one of his *Journals* the Trappist monk Thomas Merton noted: "Inexorably life moves on towards crisis and mystery." Merton, poet and mystic, wrote what became the major book of my boyhood, his autobiography *The Seven Storey Mountain* (1948). Curiously, in a house that had no books we had that book. It must have been a gift. (Even more curious is the fact that I grew up in a house that had no books to become an English professor. Despite, or because, we had no books? In any case, thank you, Andrew Carnegie, for the Free Library of Philadelphia, the Paschalville Branch.) *Seven Storey Mountain* was one of the two or three books that made me me. And I have returned faithfully and fruitfully to Merton's many works during all the years since.

I've been thinking about Merton's sentence a lot recently because I often use it when I teach drama. Drama finds life to be profoundly irrational. The crises of its plots inevitably leave the characters, and the audience, looking for answers but finding only mystery. How could they squander the Cherry Orchard? Is Brutus a patriot or a dupe, a hero or a villain? Why can't that great and wise man Oedipus evade his terrible fate? He tries so hard. And of course it is fundamental to all of Shakespeare, not just to these Italian plays. I haven't quoted Merton's line in class yet. But it's still early days.

And yet the real reason Merton's sentence stays lodged in my mind and resurfaces regularly at times like this is that it so powerfully describes my life. The great crisis of our shared life is Maggie's cancer. But the great crisis of my individual life is the evening in November of 1979 when I died, twice. On the Monday after Thanksgiving I was alone with the two children, then seven and four; Maggie had flown to Kansas City on Agriculture business. My throat had been sore for days, and by mid-afternoon I had lost my voice and was finding it hard to swallow. My doctor thought it was Strep and took a culture. He advised waiting to see what the culture showed.

That evening, I put the children to bed and then decided to go to bed myself. But the minute my head touched the pillow I seemed to hear words inside my head, my own voice, saying: you are very sick, do something about it. I'd felt much worse in my life but somehow that voice was clarion. I got the children a baby sitter and drove myself to the Georgetown Emergency Room.

After a couple of hours of X-rays the attending took me aside to say, "Mr. Glavin, we think we know what's wrong with you. We are going to admit you overnight and... " But before he could finish, I grabbed a pad of paper and a pen and scribbled: "I am choking." It was like a cork being stuffed into a bottle. No matter what I tried to do I could not pull air down my throat.

Calmly, the doctor answered: "I know you are." Took up a knife. And cut my throat.

And then I died. My heart stopped. I had to be paddled back into existence.

After they had stabilized the tracheotomy, they decided to move me from the ER into the main body of the hospital, but when they lifted me onto the gurney my heart stopped again. And once more the paddles, and once more I was brought back into time.

I was unconscious for twenty-four hours and spent the following two weeks in Intensive Care strapped to and kept alive by machines. When my department chair asked a friend on the hospital staff what he thought of my condition, this was this reply: Well, he might not survive and that could be best because if he survives there will be a lot of brain damage and certainly, best outcome: no brain damage but he will never speak again."

None of which happened.

It was something called epiglottitis, the epiglottis swells blocking the flow of air to the windpipe. In the eighteenth century it was called The Quinsy and George Washington died of it. (Tourist alert: we had taken the children to see Mount Vernon that Thanksgiving morning.)

When I think of that crisis, I also imagine what would have happened if I had not listened in time. Thaddeus coming into my room in the morning to find his father dead and himself alone in the house with his even younger sister. Or if I had delayed and lost conscious while driving, destroying not only myself but, horrible thought, others on the road. But neither of those things happened. Instead, I had the peak experience of my life. I learned, in those fourteen days strapped to a hospital bed, that all life is gratuitous. There is no more reason that I should draw my next breath than that my next breath should not be my last. Every single moment of every single day, whatever its content, is sheer gift.

Crisis. Mystery. Inexorably. Moves on. *On* the key word. Merton did not write simply moves. That would mean something very different from move on, which always implies to advance, to progress.

Siena signs start appearing. I need to concentrate on the road.

When she returns, I decide, I will tell Maggie everything, and

Joanne nothing. And if Maggie doesn't adamantly refuse, I will do anything I can that Dora asks.

Inexorably life moves on towards crisis and mystery; however, at this moment the crisis and the mystery center on trying to discover a place to park that won't get us drenched on our way to lunch.

And the mystery is unsolved, since we do get thoroughly soaked running from a parking space near the stadium to the piazza, a mile or so away. But then we find seats at the excellent Ai Mangia at the top of the incomparable Piazza Del Campo. Tended by the most solicitous of waiters, we start to cheer up. These inclement skies don't flatter Siena's varied shades of rose and pink. When the sun is shining, especially the cold clear winter sun, there is probably no more beautiful man-made space on earth. If petals were bricks, Siena would be a bower. The first time we saw it was a Sunday of *Carnevale*, the prelude to Lent, and the square was filled with adorable bunnies, and chicks, and pussycats in beautifully hand-sewn costumes, tossing confetti at each other. But even on this dull and chilly day Siena works her venerable charm. Much of Florence looks harsh and can feel brutal, all those massive, dark, rusticated walls, the massed work of greed and ambition. In contrast, Siena seems a sort of confection, all of a piece, humane, reaching out to please, the consolation prize it was given for falling from the pinnacle of power just as the Middle Ages came to an end.

And Siena, largely auto-free, is also a walkers' dream. After lunch there's a break in the rain and we head toward the Duomo, but it is crowded and we know at once it's not for us today. Instead we wander through the alleys and small squares, doing a little light shopping, a tie for me, boar's sausage for Joanne ("Really, John, boar?") intoxicated by each new revelation. It's already displaced Florence in Joanne's affections.

Toward the end of the afternoon, dry now and apparently encouraged by her earlier success among the varied males of Florence, she flirts outrageously with some Sienese policemen guarding the Sunday soccer match.

"I'm just being friendly, John. I'm a people person."

I manage to drag her away before they do.

Driving home, it continues to clear. I take the hint, and introduce her to the glories of the 222.

Much Ado Part One

Toward the end of *Twelfth Night* Feste the Fool sings: *the rain it raineth every day*. Clearly, Feste spent an early autumn in Tuscany. Nevertheless, I happily splash my way from villino to villa. We are about to begin *Much Ado About Nothing*, one of my favorties, and Merton's mantra has suplied me with a plan.

The script is famous for its sparring lovers, Beatrice and Benedick. They're the pattern pair for centuries of witty, well-off and well-matched partners who fight as foreplay. Jane Austen's Darcy and Elizabeth begin with Benedick and Beatrice, as do *The Philadelphia Story's* Dexter Haven (Cary Grant) and Tracy Lord (Katherine Hepburn); indeed Katherine Hepburn spent most of the 1940s playing versions of Beatrice to various Benedicks, most often Spenser Tracy. Sugared they become Rock Hudson and Doris Day. Sentimentalized they are Nora Ephron's Harry and Sally.

The PLOT: think Romeo and Juliet in a comedy and dropped down from Verona to Sicily. This time they are called Hero and Claudio (she's Hero), and they occupy the subplot. Early on, they become engaged to marry. This time they enjoy everybody's blessing, including that of the Prince, Don Pedro of Aragon. As they prepare for the festivities, the engaged couple and their allies try to entrap an older pair, Benedick, Claudio's best friend, and Beatrice, Hero's cousin, into admitting they love each other, something utterly obvious to everyone but Benedick and Beatrice themselves. This conspiracy plays against the machinations of Don Pedro's bastard brother, Don John, who persuades Claudio that virtuous Hero is actually a whore. Claudio breaks off the match at the altar. Hero faints. Benedick then restages Romeo and Juliet's final act by having everyone believe Hero is dead while Don John's villainy is exposed. The truth now told — it's all been much ado etc. — both pairs wed. It was wonderfully filmed in 1993 by Kenneth Branagh, also playing Benedick to Emma Thompson's ravishing Beatrice.

I won't belabor the parallel to *Pride and Prejudice.*

I start off the class keeping my powder dry, the only thing in the room that is not damp, and only ask what they think of this new script. It turns out they have strong feelings. Strong negative feelings. But not all of them, at least not at the start. At first, their response breaks down by gender.

The guys admire the magisterial prince, Don Pedro.

Willy Voltaire singles out Don Pedro's early speech explaining to his junior officers how ladies are won. Pedro claims the juniors should trust their senior officers not only to know what should be done to win ladies, but also to do the work on their behalf. "Thou lovest," he tells young Claudio as the play begins, "and I will fit thee with the remedy" (I:1, 306-307). Pedro is enviably self-confident. (I think back to the kissing fiasco on the Loggia.)

As Duke puts it: he's got the moves. At the dance that follows (is Duke pining for his masked ball?) Pedro expertly whisks aside Hero, with the dashing "Lady, will you walk a bout with your friend?" (II:1, 80).

Beluga admiringly points to his last line as they disappear from view, cautioning Hero: "Speak low, if you speak love" (93).

Clearly, the guys find Pedro something of a paradigm.

But then Betty: she has a strong grievance against *Much Ado*. The play is "insincere," everyone in the play is "insincere."

Immediately, disparaging echoes, male and female, pop off in a row like corks. Not even one of the young men who so admired Pedro will defend the larger script. Its playful ambiguities, its delight in flirtation, they equate these with evasion, bad faith, surrender of integrity. In this story the characters, all the characters, they insist, dishonor their *real selves*. They fall in love because they are duped. They marry because of subterfuge. Plays, they all concur in this, should ask our respect for characters who seek out and honor their *true* selves. And they should make us turn away from characters who merely conform, or who are made to conform, falsifying what they really feel and are.

For them this script exposes a world that is merely artificial, superficial and irredeemably false. And they reject it.

I am tempted to scuttle my plan and to introduce instead an idea from the great British psychoanalyst, Adam Phillips, the author of *On Flirtation (1994)*. In that infinitely suggestive work Phillips offers a crucial distinction between taking sincerity as your core value or instead giving that emphasis over to play. What should you want more in a partner, he playfully asks. Someone who insists on you being your true self at all times or someone who invites you to explore the untold variety of selves you think you have it in you to be.

What will give you and your partner greater pleasure? Sincerity: the true and single self, or Flirtation, all the selves you togeher can summon? I know my choice but I don't think it will be theirs and so I, reluctantly, put off Phillips (I hope) for another day.

Instead, I ask them to imagine dramatic action as a *parabola,* an idea I first found in the great French playwright Racine, but have since found operating in everything that feels genuinely dramatic. (It would seem that Racine himself found it in Euripedes and the other Athenian dramatists.) *Gli studenti* will remember the parabola from high school geometry, right? A line starts off in one direction but finds itself inexorably (here it comes) curving until it ends going in very much a different way. It's the curve that insists *you can't get there from here.* And every dramatic script endorses that line. In drama, no one gets exatly what they set out after, no matter how good or bad the goal. Merton—Racine—they come down pretty much in the same place.

We can refine this even further and talk about five stages that constitute virtually every dramatic plot.

Typically, a character makes a *Choice,* which he or she puts into action (*Commitment*). Soon, however, the character discovers that the outcome of that action—*Consequence*—is not at all what was expected, often exactly the reverse of what was expected, and generally disastrous. Of course, then the character usually tries to reverse course, only to find the way back blocked (*Counter-Cast*). And so, inevitably, the character is forced to endure an unexpected *Conclusion* strikingly at odds with the original choice.

Here's *Romeo and Juliet* reread as a parabola:

1. After meeting her at the dance, Romeo decides *(choice)* he has to see more of this girl. Which leads to

2. The balcony scene, where he promises to find a way for them to wed *(commitment).*

3. But as soon as they are wed, they discover that Juliet is going to be married to Paris, the next day. That will make her bigamous at best, a clearly unexpected *consequence* of having married Romeo.

4. Romeo struggles valiantly and inventively to find a way back to her, but all his attempts to evade and escape their dilemma are foiled *(counter-cast).*

5. And thus, inexorably, we arrive at the unexpected *conclusion*: they do get together, but only in their tomb.

Having started out to wed Juliet, Romeo's choices, thus, step by step, cause her death. He sets out to choose his life with her only *(inexorably, crisis, mystery)* to end up sharing her tomb. A perfect *parabola.*

There is of course a lot more going on in the play but that's its spine.

Ripley Snell is way ahead of me. As I have been outlining *Romeo,* he's been thinking about *Much Ado.* There's no way, he says, you can do this for Beatrice and Benedick. "You said Racine. So the parabola works for tragedy—maybe. But it doesn't work in a comedy. And that's the whole point of why we don't like the play. They don't make choices, they are duped."

Clever Ripley. He's perfectly correct if we think the script centers on Benedick and Beatrice. But though they are the wittiest characters, they are the best friends not the protagonists. The plot is in fact driven by Claudio not Benedick. Just as *Merchant of Venice* is driven by Basssanio, though the characters we remember most are Portia and Shylock. And *Measure for Measure* is driven by the very dull Duke while we obsess with his deputy, the gelid Angelo.

What happens, I ask Ripley, if we think of the play as driven by Claudio's choice? Gamely, he starts off:

Choice: Claudio, returning for the wars, chooses to marry Hero. And then.

Commitment: He asks his leader Don Pedro to propose on his behalf; Pedro succeeds, and Claudio is promised Hero's hand.

There's a pause. Willy Voltaire chimes in.

Consequence: But then Claudio is duped into believing Hero is not virtuous but "a stale," a loose woman. He's thus gained, he thinks, the very opposite of what he thought he was getting.

And then? This time it's Miss Haag.

Counter-Cast: when he tries to get away, an unexpected revelation of the plot to destroy Hero forces Claudio to mollify her father by agreeing to marry her cousin.

Ripley comes back to finish:

Conclusion: he marries the cousin, a woman he has never seen before—talk about unwelcome conclusion—only to find once they are wed that he has in fact be given his original intended.

Much Ado thus confronts Claudio with a doubly unexpected

conclusion: (a) forced marriage to a woman not his intended, and (b) the happy discovery that his wife is his all-along intended. A fittingly doubled curve to conclude a play that throughout has relied constantly on doubled situations. But more important for our purposes, the play's *parabola* has brought about a kind of maturity in callow Claudio that would never have taken root were it not for the plot's doubling back against his plan.

Drama always turns on the inevitability, and therefore the potential, revealed when the unexpected unconceals. You make a plan. The plan fails. You find you can't back up or out. Then you may find yourself overwhelmed in a situation from which there is no release. Tragedy: Romeo. But you also might uncover, in this painful situation, something entirely new and revelatory about yourself and/or the world. Comedy: Claudio.

Though they are silent, I sense something has happened. I dare not call it a breakthrough, but, this time, the silence suggests something, some part of some thing, has hit home.

For them.

For me.

In fact, how could I have missed it? Life comes to us, and through us, but life, real life, almost never comes from us.

Sometimes you have to teach something in order to know it.

Drying Out

This morning, deluded, I was sure the deluge had finally concluded. The three solid days of rain had been a significant hardship because, as with most Italians, our apartment lacks a clothes drier. Washing machine, yes. Drier, no. So early this morning I quickly tossed an overdue load of underclothes and pajamas into the washer. Delusion. The rain immediately returned. And now every available chair, table and railing in the place is festooned with damp boxers, t-shirts and socks. Hard on Joanne.

This afternoon, however, truly cool breezes have begun to blow and Florence has started to glow. By cocktail time I can hang everything out on the line. As I pin and drape them I can begin to pick out every tower and parapet in the city below, and beyond them, for the first time in over four weeks, I even make out the sandy bulk of Cole Porter's itty-bitty Pitti Palace on the far side of the Arno, the

Boboli gardens rising in terraces behind. I've lived here a month and didn't realize I could see that far.

Underclothes and pjs banished, the apartment returns to something like decency. Without realizing what I've done, I find I've had to close the windows, wide open since we arrived. Luckily, they are all broad enough and high enough that closing them does not cost the view. Even the far off southern hills have managed to emerge now. I discover hamlets and churches outside the city unseen through September. Close up, walking its twisted, dark and narrow, and smelly, streets, Florence is a city of the early Renaissance always on the brink of internecine feud. Guelf v. Ghibelline. Medici v. Pazzi. Everybody v. Savonarola. But seen from this vantage, in this light, it looks like an illumination in a Book of Hours, all salmon, and cream, and pistachio. Or perhaps like one of those magical towns in a fifteenth-century painting, glimpsed through casements, in front of which the Virgin, startled, listens to the amazing news of an Annunciation.

I decide not to be jealous now of Maggie and the Alps. After all, I am educating in paradise. But just as I'm boasting to Joanne about my virtuous forbearance, Maggie calls to tell me how jolly it was joining grape pickers in Champagne as she and Kyra crossed northern France. Kyra even got a marriage proposal. (Later, I find Kyra gets exactly the same marriage proposal every autumn.) To take advantage of the beautiful weather, they are going to extend their stay in the Alps. I wouldn't believe the wild flowers, she insists.

Really, when does more than enough become just too much?

Rotgut

In class, up on the Loggia, the light and the air are magical. We should all just sit by the railings and meditate on the view. However, we are supposed to be staging *Much Ado* Act IV, scene 2, working with the clowns Dogberry and Verges. And so we all reluctantly set to work. It is very difficult for amateurs to make sense of this kind of low comedy with its largely antiquated word play. *Gli studenti* say they found it tedious. Maybe playing it will let them in on the true splendor of the earthy jokes. But all their efforts are in vain. They can't get beyond Rotgut.

Though he has been cast as Borachio, one of Don John's hench-

men, he ostentatiously refuses to participate. He sits on the railing of the farthest arch, facing away from the rest of us, toward
Florence, and he won't speak. He is trying deliberately to frighten
us, I fear. Perched so close to the edge of the rail, he could at any
moment just slip over to fall the several stories between us and the
gardens. The rest of the class tries to perform but it's clear nobody
can concentrate. They're mesmerized by this mute upstaging. What
has happened? When the term began, no one was more enthusiastic, more eager to absorb new experience. For the first few weeks if
I could count on anyone it was Rotgut.

After class he stays behind and asks to speak with me.

Here we go again. While I was obsessed with Muldoon, was his
double in development?

I am over-reading this play, he explains. The only play of Shakespeare that can sustain very close reading is *Hamlet*. That is because,
he informs me, *Hamlet* was not written for performance. It could
not have been. It is too complex. All the other Shakespeare plays
were written to be staged, which means they can only be treated as
entertainments. *Hamlet* is too complex to be an entertainment, ergo
it cannot have been written for the stage.

I ask if that applies also to *King Lear, Antony and Cleopatra* or the
two parts of *Henry IV*. He says he has not read them. Which does
not bother him.

Patiently, I think, I outline the evidence that all the plays were
written for the stage. He will have none of it. It is impossible, he
says, to make such a claim for *Hamlet*. It lasts four hours in uncut
performance. Obviously, there would have been no audience for
such an ordeal. I try to condense *Hamlet's* tangled textual history.
We have two quite different Quarto versions, plus that in the Folio.
Exactly which represents the acting text for Shakespeare's company is a vexed matter on which experts differ. And then we believe
that acting was faster on the Tudor stage. He will recall *Romeo and
Juliet* talks about two hours traffic upon the stage. But all this is
beside the point for him. Shakespeare's audience was too dumb,
he announces, to take in a play we read so complexly. They were
uneducated merchants and their apprentices, right? How many of
them could even read?

Well, Shakespeare was also, in effect, the court playwright, I offer in return. The Comedies especially, like *Much Ado,* seem aimed at aristocratic audiences, audiences that could relish the wit and find their mirror in the action on the stage. And then I name some other writers he might recognize, writers who, we know, combined complexity and popularity: Jonathan Swift and Jane Austen certainly, preeminently Dickens, writers accessible to the general readers of their own time, but also richly responsive to the most discriminating scrutiny. But again he has swept on before I can offer even the beginning of this argument.

This is not the keen battle of wits I faced in those weeks with Muldoon. He knew what he was talking about, and he had serious arguments to raise, even if those were not arguments that I found persuasive. With Rotgut there seems to be no question of settling matters on the merits. What he doesn't agree with, or doesn't know, he simply dismisses as irrelevant. Does he imagine himself, I wonder, taking Muldoon's place, the official antagonist, the devil's advocate, a place vacant now that Muldoon has dropped the course. I don't think so. Or if he does, he has seriously misconstrued what Muldoon offered. Until the very end Muldoon engaged. He didn't perch away on the edge in public silence, speaking only afterward in private. Muldoon would have raised these objections in class. And he was never like this in manner: aggressive, sullen, irrational

Quickly, I try to summon up what the finest teacher I know would do, the incomparable James Kincaid at the University of Southern California. He would, I am sure, say: *John, lay off the kid, let the poor guy follow his own loopy path. Don't try to dissuade him. Do just the reverse. Encourage him. Enjoy it. Get on his side. Over accept. Push him to race faster round and round his fact-fleeing labyrinth until he is forced, without the faintest hint from you, to confront himself with himself. Then, and only then, show him the key to the way out.*

But I'm no Jim Kincaid, so stupidly I keep trying to reason.

"Shakespeare we know was popular, right," Rotgut is saying. Nervously, I concur. "Then he must have been the Steven Spielberg of his day, and it would be absurd to read a Spielberg film so deeply."

Actually, I say, Spielberg, when he tries, can be remarkably complex. But might it not be better to parallel Shakespeare with film makers like Martin Scorsese or Woody Allen, who in popular film set out to challenge prevailing narrative and psychological and moral norms?

He seems not to know Scorsese or Allen but returns to insisting on the superficiality of *Much Ado*. The ending he says disappoints him. The characters compromise themselves, behaving without integrity. That makes the entire play superficial. I remind him that we spent much of the previous class on that argument, which we took up in detail. He cuts me off. He is no longer even pretending that this is a conversation. Was he listening at all last time?

We are at an impasse. The sun is setting. The loggia is suffused by a cold pink light. A dark wind begins to stir. This is very sad. I have not only failed with this earnest, serious and hard-working young man, I have, clearly, and stupidly, contributed to making things worse. We part in silence, he to the villa, I to the villino.

Word comes back that during dinner Rotgut and Beluga had a punch out. It got pretty violent; they had to be pulled off each other. I may be responsible for part of Rotgut's problem. But, clearly, there's something far more significant, and dangerous, at stake here.

Detection

Joanne has left for Rome and the Capolagos. She admits that she has been more or less unwell since she arrived here. I am ashamed. I pushed her hard and she always seemed so cheerful. I apologize but she won't have it. She was only here for a short time, she wasn't going to squander it. But she did have to spend yesterday holed up in the villino, trying to reach her physician in the States. The problem is a pre-existing condition, one that is likely to require surgery when she gets home. She's been astoundingly brave, and my hat is off to her, a clear instance where pretending trumps sincerity by a long shot.

We called Dora who offered to get her doctor in Rome to write a prescription, but he needed to know what the doctor in the States had been prescribing. After much back and forth, and my inadequate medical Italian, it turned out that the drug, requiring a prescription at home, is sold over the counter here. Dora promised to have it on hand when Joanne arrived.

At least Joanne enjoyed a few good days at the start, and of course there were her several romantic conquests in two different cities. Not bad for a first time in Europe.

Now Dora calls to make sure Joanne got off safely. She will meet her at the train. She has decided to tell Joanne everything after she arrives. That seems sensible. How can you hide all this from a house guest and cousin staying with you for five days? But her real purpose in calling is to tell me that she may have found a detective.

However, there are still difficulties.

For three days she contacted pretty much every private detective agency she could locate in Rome. All of them turned her down. Either they said that without a real case, records, evidence, there was nothing for them to investigate. Or the reverse. They didn't want to get involved once they heard the police had refused to handle it. But just when she thought she would have to give up, she got a call from this guy, whose name she can't tell me. He's actually a policeman. He'd be doing this on his own time, illegally.

He heard about Dora through some contacts in Rome talking about a lady who thought the police hadn't done their job. He was intrigued. He didn't say why but Dora thinks it's because he's got a personal grudge against the men she dealt with. She thinks he'd like to get them in trouble. He's also warned Dora that since there are no files, no evidence, no interviews, he's going to have to buy information, and it won't be cheap. He named a probable figure that she wouldn't tell me but which she said was more than she could promise him.

Although Waldo is very generous, indeed indulgent, toward Dora, encouraging her to buy whatever pleases her, he also keeps strict accounts. She has no money of her own. This is something she resents, powerfully. After all, the money that started the Capolago business came from her side of the family, from her father and her uncles who had immigrated to America before the war. Of course, they had been paid back and profited handsomely from their original investment. Nevertheless, she feels that in some way this money is as much hers as Waldo's, a position he decidedly does not share.

Although when we first met the Capolagos Dora seemed an equal if not the dominant partner, I soon came to see it's a completely un-American marriage. Waldo is entirely in charge. And Dora, who lived in the States until she was over thirty, seems to have begun to find that control suffocating, even before they lost Ivo. It's as though her early life is repeating itself. Her very old-fashioned and strong-willed mother had refused to allow Dora either to go to college or to work. She was made to remain at home, waiting for a suitable proposal. None came. After thirty, she was allowed to go to Italy to meet the Roman branch of the family. No possibility of any other travel was permitted. She's told me about getting off the train in Rome to be greeted by the dazzling, handsome cousin only a few years older than she. He was nothing like the American guys she knew. Beautifully dressed, impeccably courteous, formal and yet — she doesn't say it but you can hear it in her voice and see it in her face when she recalls that meeting, sexy. She was smitten before they got to his car.

She never went home again. Since they were first cousins they needed Vatican permission to marry. Stalwartly, Dora stayed on in Rome and waited it out. After her father died, her mother and sister moved to Rome, where they of course still live.

Theirs is clearly still a love match but just as clearly Waldo's idea of a husband's rights, or a man's role, dates from a time and a culture alien to those of the American woman he married. Paradoxically, it was his difference that attracted her; now it's his difference that constrains her. She knows there is no way he would agree to cover the costs of this investigation. Indeed, if she told him about the policeman, he would probably forbid her to meet him again. But she's hooked. The cop told her that even from her brief account of what happened he's convinced Ivo was kidnapped. Of course, that is just what she had hoped to hear. Now she's determined to get whatever she needs to hire him.

I don't tell her how dubious the whole thing sounds to me. I do ask if she and Waldo have started speaking to each other again.

Waldo told Cip on the way back from South America that as long as Dora did not raise what happened that catastrophic day in the villa normal relations would be restored. Dora has so far held to the bargain. Maybe it will be easier for her now that she has Joanne to confide in.

She finishes by insisting that after Joanne leaves I have to come down to Rome, to get the facts I will need first hand. In the meantime she is keeping careful notes about everything. It's fascinating that she never even considered for a moment that I am not entirely on board with her plan for me. I didn't have a chance to say a word.

Maggie Ritornata

Maggie has arrived back from the extended jaunt. And, miraculously, she's managed to lug back with her two cases of champagne, last year's vintage, as well as roses from the bushes planted among the vineyards. Roses suffer from the same diseases that affect the vines, but they show symptoms first. When the roses begin to fade you know it's time to treat the grapes. And in the meantime they make the vineyards even lovelier. She and Kyra spent a day clipping the tender champagne grapes using small silver scissors. The grapes are so delicate each has to be treated individually. Work that is in equal parts back-breaking and intoxicating. It was the owner of the vineyard who once again proposed to Kyra. He does it every year at the *vendange.*

We stow the champagne and head out at once for the 222 and Volpaia. It doesn't matter that it is raining. And I am starting a cold. We are together again, without houseguests. This time for three whole days! I debate telling her about Dora but don't. Why spoil our reunion. I do tell her about the miraculous first class on *Much Ado* and the sad second class with Rotgut. She can't believe no one in the Villa administration is intervening.

Hungry by mid-day, we stumble at just the right moment onto Pietra Fitta just outside Castellina in Chianti. This is by far the best food we have eaten in weeks of very good meals. And it's even more wonderful because it seems a discovery and a gift. We can imagine having lunch at Pietra Fitta every Saturday for the remainder of our lives, and never getting bored. We immediately make a reservation for Thanksgiving when Cecilia will be back, with Douglas Gordon.

After lunch we decide to drive home only using back ways east and south, refusing to look at a map, choosing turns at random, until we surprise ourselves by turning up outside Siena. The good new is promising to become the even better new.

WEEK SIX
October 8 – 14

Up at the Castello, Down at the Villa

Joanne calls from Rome to say goodbye; she flies home today. Not only was she sick for the whole of her stay with Dora, she never slept. Joanne has always been deeply superstitious, frightened by lightening, and terrified of ghosts. Of course, Dora gave her the one empty room in the apartment. Ivo's. And then—how can one laugh? how can one not?—she would bid poor Joanne goodnight each time by saying: "He is watching over you." Joanne claims she sat frozen upright every night until dawn, all lamps burning bright. She couldn't even make herself pick up a book, let alone read.

Poor thing. She wanted an unforgettable Italian holiday. Now I suspect she's got one she's longing to forget.

After she hangs up, I rush up to Piazza Mino to catch a bus for the second session of the "Educating in Paradise" conference. Today it has moved to the Castello di Vincigliata, a battlemanted nineteenth-century folly in the hills just beyond Fiesole. The castle was entirely rebuilt and Gothicized in the nineteenth-century by an Englishman John Temple-Leader, and became one of the Florence must-see sites. Queen Victoria used to do watercolors there. And Henry James, no pushover, loved it. I'm eager to go; I've never seen it.

Chartered buses are scheduled to leave Piazza Mino at 7:45, 8:15 and 8:45. I arrive about ten minutes too late for the 7:45. I board the 8:15. And wait.

I'm alone, except for the driver. This the bus for the Vincigliata? Sì. I continue to wait. It emerges that this bus is in fact the 7:45. I am the first and so far only person to show. At 8:10 a dispatcher decides to send me off in lonely splendor. Twenty minutes later I arrive at the Castello to find maybe half a dozen or so conferees, wandering about in the gardens, though the first session is due to start exactly now, at 8:30. This delay surprises only me, and bothers no one.

At 9:30, the 8:30 session starts. There are to be three consecutive sessions: each scheduled for ninety minutes, the entire program concluding with a talk by a senior figure from our Embassy. Lunch at 1. At 10:30 the organizers warn everyone to stick to the allotted time limits. The Minister Counsellor will only have a few minutes between the end of his talk and his train to Rome. Who will be sacrificed? At the rate we are going perhaps the entire 11:30 discussion, "Special Programs," will take it in the neck.

As it turns out, the entire program concludes—including the Minister Counsellor—at twenty minutes to one. We finish early because many of the speakers simply didn't show. Nor, apparently, did they bother to cancel in advance. (*Oh, Gian, but this is Italy!*) One fellow brought a slide carousel with slides for an hour's talk, though he was scheduled for five minutes. He didn't use that empty first hour to set up the carousel. In fact, he only started loading when it was his panel's turn to speak. Then, when he pushed the button to show the first slide, it wouldn't appear. Unfazed, he told us what we might have seen. Everyone else says it's such a shame I missed those slides. They've all seen them many times before, at other conferences. I gather he has only one talk in him, which he sometimes manages actually to deliver.

Another speaker explains that he had prepared an extensively detailed account of how he manages his very famous historical property turned study center, but in light of the tight schedule he jettisons his prepared remarks and offers simply to answer questions.

There are no questions.

How could there be? He hasn't said anything. When I murmur how interested I would have been to hear about his conservation efforts, Marcello, sitting next to me, confides that he's known this person for years and that there are no details. None. The speaker, notoriously, never prepares. But he is always asked to participate since he represents such a distinguished program, and then he always cites time as a reason for not speaking. I am told I will find him delightful at the lunch.

And indeed lunch is as exquisite today as it was at the first meeting. In Florence we had a buffet on the Terrace of Saturn, a frescoed loggia at the top of the Palazzo Signoria, with an incomparable view down on Santa Croce, the great Franciscan chuirch, which serves as Italy's Pantheon. But today, plates in hand, we wander through the castle and its gardens as we please. Both days start with a choice of champagne, white or red wine, and then move on to cold meats and cheeses as well as a variety of hot Tuscan specialties. My favorites are individual bits of crustacean served on small toasts carved into the shape of the sea creature they bear. Shrimp on shrimp-shaped croutons, crab on crab-ditto. Cream-crammed pastries conclude, as many as you are unashamed to gobble.

The conversation is easy. As a newcomer to the scene I am told sevral versions of what seems a favorite item of gossip. The current pope is actually an actor. The real John Paul II in fact died in the assasination attempt in 1981. For almost 20 years he has been impersonated by a look-alike. The Vatican is now entirely under the thumb of Cardinal Ratzinger. This is widely known, I am assured, but it cannot be mentioned in the news because the Vatican entirely controls Italian media.

Why it would not appear in the international media seems not to be a question to consider.

The graciously nonchalant tone of the entire enterprise bears out the cliché repeated several times on the opening day: Americans live to work, Europeans work to live. (Duke's claim about pleasure re-claimed.) But watcing these academics at play, I suspect that this proposition has a lot to do with where you stand on the food chain. Italian manual workers seem to me to put in very long, arduous days. Not quite as arduous as Kipling's 1911 guys "grubbing weeds from gravel-paths with broken dinner knives." But not a whole lot better.

A timely illustration: repairing the villa's stucco walls. It started almost as soon as we arrived. First the scaffolding men came, a middle-aged father and a young son. The two of them spent the better part of a week laboriously putting up a rough pole and plank scaffold over one half of the south façade. They could only scaffold half the façade because that's all their mini-truck could carry. Then the scaffold builders left, and the stucco experts arrived, again a father and son, this time an elderly father and a middle-aged son. In the States we'd have a crew of workmen for a job like this, and it might take them three days per façade. Our pair has been fully occupied 7:30 AM to 6:30 PM (excluding the intervallo for *pranzo*) and they're still only on the first half of the first façade. Every inch is taken off with mallet and chisel. When they finish this half, the scaffold team comes back to pull it all down to re-erect it on the second half of that façade. And then the stucco men return.

The contrast between these guys and my fellow academics could scarcely be more stark. Last week it was announced by the official statistics people that sixty-five percent of Italian University students fail to graduate. That gives Italy the worst baccalaureate record in Europe, and of course the smallest educated workforce. This is an especially worrisome statistic in the country with the lowest birthrate in Europe. And it also takes Italian students who do graduate longer to finish than in any other developed country.

All this is about to change announces Professor Roberto D'Alimonte of the University of Firenze. In the conference's waning hours he explains that, pressured by globalization and European integration, Italian universities are becoming more American. They now follow, for the first time, a semester system. And, scandal of scandals, professors have been told they must actually meet their undergraduate students, a practice hitherto unknown. Europe is in the process of becoming America East, with significantly better food and much poorer services. That's seems to be the lesson of the day.

Marcello drives me back to Le Balze by way I Tatti. Our very good friend Pietro Marani, the distinguished Leonardo scholar, and Stefano's partner, has offered to try to get us in to see the place this time around. Generally, it welcomes onlyspecialists in the Renaissance and similar cognoscenti. So far, however, Pietro hasn't managed to get us on the list. So I have to settle for Marcello's tour of the externals, which are in themselves not at all bad. Clearly litle has changed here since 1911. Driving on, I offer a little prayer to the genii of the Renaissance to favor Pietro's petititon.

Just inside Le Balze's front gate, I pass our alpha males, Beluga, Benny, Duke, and Ripley, along with the beautiful Orchid, sunning on the south terrace. These are the smokers. They're discussing business pages from Friday's *International Herald Tribune*, checking them against prices they call up on their palm pilots.

I smile broadly. They've just made me a very happy man. Seeing them like this, juxtaposed to the conference, supplies an answer I've been searching for. All along *gli studenti* have insisted they they are here for a much needed break from their lives at home. But now, watching them enjoying their cigarettes, their wine, the Tuscan sun, the Florentine view, *and* the stock pages of the Trib, all at once, I see that they are not breaking from, they are simply adding on. A hundred years ago people like the Cuttings at Villa Medici across the way, and Strong here, and Berenson over at I Tatti loved Tuscany not only because it wasn't home, but because it was in every possible way home's rebuttal. But for *gli studenti* the world is, in the word I learned today at the Castello, "integrated." Which means that the fun of this place, of this program, consists for *gli studenti* precisely in the fact that living here, they don't face a choice, or make a break. They can enjoy the villa, and the view, *and* the stock quotations. Italy provides them not a different sort of life but merely, and richly, additional kinds of pleasure.

What a waste it's been to wallow for five weeks in all this frustrated nostalgia. If the Italy I came here thinking to recreate has dissolved, I've got to use the lesson of the parabola, before it is too late, and find a way to enjoy what I have at hand.

And part of that, I am just about ready to accept, may come from Dora. Certainly that part will have nothing to do with enjoyment. But another part, a major part, will have to come from allowing *gli studenti* to give me what they have to offer.

Grooving in the Grove

Everything in the course is going to change, starting today, not only the how but also, and crucially, the where.

"Let's move into the ilex grove."

This is the garden west of the house, four trees wide, twenty trees long, each tree exactly five feet from its neighbors on every side, walled on one side and open on other to the view of the Arno. We should have met out here from the start. We wasted more than a month squeezed into the stuffy, uncomfortable library. Now, happily, *gli studenti* carry green garden chairs from the terrace to encircle a table made from a large slab of naturally rounded stone. Above us, the evenly spaced trees provide a flawless canopy. Birds everywhere. In the distance, the gardeners tend the beds of dahlia and rosemary. The perfect pedagogic space: the grove, the air, the light, the irresistible charm of green thoughts, as Andrew Marvell said, in a green shade. *With* bird song.

We resume *Much Ado*. What names, I ask *gli studenti*, do they associate with the word prince.

Consuela: "Charles."

Ardita: "Harry."

Orchid: "Will."

Amiable, and in the younger cases, handsome non-entities.

"What name do you think Shakespeare would associate with prince?"

Beluga laughs. "Machiavelli."

Exactly so. And the difference between those two kinds of association opens a new way into *Much Ado*.

"Why don't we make such an association?" I ask. "After all, Machiavelli's fears about power are all over that founding document of our republic, *The Federalist Papers*. Why don't we any longer associate power with tyranny? Is it just because we have a president and not a prince?"

They ponder. Good.

In my last stint here I taught the historian J.G.A. Pocock's magnificent and almost insanely demanding, *The Machiavellian Moment: Florentine Political Thought and the Atlantic Republican Tradition*. Densely but persuasively, Pocock traces Machiavelli's influence on the invention of American democracy, particularly in the Federalists' fear of concentrated power. Both the Florentine and the Federalists saw power as toxic. Machiavelli in particular made it starkly clear, well before Lord Acton, that all power corrupts. And what Machiavelli knew, Shakespeare's theater routinely staged.

As *gli studenti* continue to ponder I am happy to study the grove. It's so lovely being out here with them this afternoon. In part that's because of the autumn glory of the grove. But it's not only being in the grove. Whatever has brought us to this moment, we seem to be on the verge of becoming a genuine community now. And, of course, as soon as I put my mind to it, I recognize what's changed. I liked them from the start; I tried to show that. But now I respect them. I am also trying to show that. I am letting them take the lead. We have revised the plan. Wherever they lead, I will follow, happily. I think they are beginning to sense the difference, and so now they are begining to trust me.

Ripley Snell ventures first, and gets it in one: "We don't automatically associate power with tyranny becuase of the New Deal."

His answer is better than, goes farther than, I had hoped. Clearly, it does pay to be the scion of Park Avenue Republicans. My grin grows, as he explains. The New Deal changed America, not just because it gave us programs like Social Security, but because it neutered the danger in power. *The only thing we have to fear is fear itself.* Madison—like Machiavelli—would have thought that was ridiculous. The Federalists keep insisting that the thing we have to fear is power itself. So put in as many checks and balances as you can invent. But the New Deal changed American culture by making power appear naturally benign, corrupt only when stolen by criminal regimes or lunatic individuals. The Nazis. Later the Soviets. Then Nixon. America used to fear power at home. Now we only fear power abroad.

Miss Haag inserts: "It wasn't that way in the nineenth century. Look at *Huckleberry Finn*. Or anything in Twain for that matter."

Claudia adds: "*Uncle Tom's Cabin*."

Ripley concludes: "Now we fear the power America opposes, not American power itself."

I ask them what we believe instead.

Benny: "Private life should be beyond the reach of power."

Jacqueline: "Power is dangerous only in the hands of dangerous men."

Beluga: "The only appropriate force to drive lives like ours is market force."

Let's then think of Shakespeare as an Actonian before the letter. Always excepting Henry V, is there any man in any of his plays who touches power without being corrupted by it?

Miss Haag: "But not women right?"

"Well, not automatically with women."

Women like Beatrice in this play or Portia in our next, *Merchant of Venice*, can intervene safely in public life. Because they are acting only in and for the moment, power doesn't contaminate them, as it does women who want and cling to mastery, like Cleopatra and Lady Macbeth. For viragos like these, as well as for all of his men, Shakespeare insists power is poison.

So when Shakespeare's audience saw a prince, any prince, they saw a red flag, and heard Danger Alert. When princes were abounding, no one was safe, not even the princes. The people who went to the Globe also knew their way to Tower Hill, and the chopping block. That's certainly a cardinal point in Shakespeare's History plays. But it's also the point of an apparently more benign play like *Much Ado*. For us it's about Benedick and Beatrice, or maybe about both pairs of lovers. But if you look at the play as a whole, from start to finish, it's driven by princes, and their power.

I ask them to tell me back the plot, concentrating on the princes.

Two princes, Don Pedro and Don John, arrive at Leonato's house in the country. Clearly a nice guy, Don Pedro is funny and open and helpful toward the lovers. Don John is, figuratively as well as literally, a real bastard. But as the action develops, the play deliberately sabotages that difference. The good prince winds up doing almost as much harm as the bastard. He woos Hero so convincingly that Claudio is easily persuaded he's been betrayed. Learning nothing from that episode, Pedro then throws his full authority behind John's scheme to discredit Hero, agreeing even to her brutal humiliation at the aborted marriage ceremony. Do they find Pedro cruel?

"No," Judy answers, "just arrogant."

Is that why Shakespeare makes him the Prince of Aragon?

Can *gli studenti* differentiate between the brothers? Doesn't the play suggest by making one legitimate and the other illegitimate, that they represent the good and the bad, or the virtuous and the corrupt versions of the same thing?

Gloria: "No. They both do harm, the only difference is that Pedro repents."

The play suggests that this good prince/bad prince distinction can come down to pretty much nothing. The bad prince manages all his evil through the good prince's agency, while the good prince is so swayed by the swell of his own princely status that he consents to every sort of vice.

But Beluga rightly insists we respect one of the final lines in the play: Benedick saying just before the end "Prince, thou art sad"(V:4, 20). As well Pedro should be. But the unrepentant brother Don John, who early on insists "I cannot hide what I am" (I:3, 12-13), disappears before the finale to foment more trouble. In effect, I can only be, unchanging, the me I state.

I point out that when Kenneth Branagh filmed *Much Ado* he treated it as an inconsequential, frivolous, giddy romp.

About power, clearly, then, we are not of the same mind as Shakespeare, Machiavelli, and Madison. Inevitably we glide past the play's dark warnings because they are, flatly, un-American. It just can't be true what this play insists on: that you can not find a private space that remains impervious to power; that power is always potentially a menace; that no good man remains good if he holds power even briefly. All of which seems to mean that, though Shakespeare may speak to us, he does not speak from or for us.

Time is up but for the first time *gli studenti* don't rush away. Maybe it's the grove, but, maybe, also, in some small part at least, it's the class.

After they've all gone, I linger, relishing the gift of late afternoon in a Tuscan October. It's even made me forget I have a cold. How many more days of our stay can possibly be this perfect? Five? Ten, at the outside. No more surely. But why is this particular hour so magical?

Because there's no noise here. The grove is not silent. But all the sounds are natural, wind in the branches, birdsong, the gardeners pushing a wheelbarrow over gravel. Nothing industrial, scarcely even anything mechanical. No airplane overhead. No cars below. No whirring buzz saw. No sirens. No telephone. No radio. This sun could be setting in 1900. Or in 1600. On this hillside, where we know Galileo once walked, where we think Milton visited, in this garden, it is now as it once was most places. And I feel, solitary and silenced, how high, broad, and perhaps insurmountable is the barricade history has thrown up between *gli studenti* and the past, between their world and the world of this play.

Which is indeed a good thing. *Gli studenti* and I are unlikely to find ourselves in Shakespeare. But if we read him carefully, and respectfully, we can always spot ourselves sharply in the difference.

How foolish I've been not to trust him, and them, and the place, from the start.

Rotgut

What seemed bright and promising yesterday, today has become threatening and dark.

This morning Maggie had a strange encounter with Rotgut. She ran into him outside the villa scullery. Over the past weekend *gli studenti* had all gone to Venice for a tour by the art history teacher. But when Maggie asked him what he had liked most on the trip, he would not answer her. He only smiled back in a way she found weird and upsetting. And then after a prolonged stare he abruptly disappeared. She came back in the villino clearly upset. Up until this point Rotgut has been the student she liked best, the one who seemed most interested in and moved by Italy. Now she says she doesn't want to go into the villa by herself anymore.

Later, when I see her outside painting, I realize she has chosen not her usual favorite place in the orange garden but a spot closer to the terrace below which the gardeners are working.

When I mention this to Marcello I hear that Rotgut's behavior in Venice was indeed genuinely bizarre. During our class in the grove Rotgut was strange. He contributed nothing, just sat at the far edge of the terrace as far as possible from the others, smiling sardonically. But on the trip things became alarming.

On Sunday morning their guide urged *gli studenti*, whether or not they were believers, to attend the aesthetically sublime Sunday liturgy at San Marco. Rotgut became excited when he heard there was a chance of *acqua alta*, the canals overflowing their banks. As they headed to the basilica, he began vividly to detail to the others what would happen if the Cardinal Patriarch accidentally dislodged a microphone into the water, electrocuting the congregation. His relish at inventing the catastrophe unnerved the others, several of whom peeled off rather than continuing with him into the church.

Now fear crackles throughout the entire Villa population. Marcello says that more than one of them has told him that Rotgut's presence is souring their time here. They all find him scary. One or two have even asked about dropping out and returning home early. And one set of parents has already contacted the office back on campus about this possibility. The blithe and harmonious amity that marked the group through September is gone. What I experienced as a breakthrough in the grove seems now not to have marked a beginning but only an interlude.

In the evening Beluga comes to see me. Rotgut has chosen him as the prime enemy. Beluga, though much more fit than Rotgut, says that since their brief fist fight he feels vulnerable and exposed in places like the showers. He's particulalry anxious about the scullery, where Maggie encountered Rotgut today and where, apparently, he now lurks. It's got a wall of long and clearly lethal carving knives. Heidi and Marcello have warned Beluga not to over-react. They insist that Rotgut is merely immature not dangerous. He just wants attention. He won't become violent. (Apparently, the earlier fist fight has been covered up.) And Marcello has also made it clear that, if there is a fight, both guys will be immediately sent home.

That's a cardinal rule of the Villa. Any fighting between students and everyone involved immediately goes home. No exceptions. It has to be. Ten guys cooped up in a small place for over three months. No gym. No courts for basketball, or squash, or tennis. No pool. No playing field. Half buzzed most week nights, blitzed most weekends. Only a draconian ordinance will keep the peace even in ordinary circumstances.

Beluga asks me what I think he should do. I don't want to publicly oppose the people responsible for running the program but I also don't want to minimize the risk. I ask for a chance to talk it over privately with Marcello. In the meanwhile I urge Beluga to try never to be alone anywhere in the villa or in the gardens and above all to stay out of the scullery. .

When I tell Maggie what Beluga has told me, she says we should send Rotgut home immediately, for his own good, as well as to protect the others. Maggie is the most sensible and pragmatic person I know. If Rotgut alarms her, he should petrify the rest of us. But when I pass this on to Marcello he insists that in this crowded environment, everyone living virtually on top of each other, if we show any kind of fear panic will ensue.

An ostensible air of calm and untroubled control, *gran figura*, always outweighs in Italy the pressure for pragmatism and honest action.

Taddeo

It's rainy today, overcast and cool, and my cold is distinctly worse, but none of that matters because at 1:00 this afternoon Thaddeus and Sarah, our son and daughter-in-law, arrive. Rotgut, Dora, Shakespeare, all of them fade from sight as Thaddeus and Sarah lug their things out of the taxi and up into the villino guest room.

They have been married for fourteen months. Sarah is in the middle of her residency at the University of Chicago Hospital. Thad, having left one of the so-called Big Five accounting firms, is in the process of establishig his own company, Redline Communications. He expects to run their first ad the week after Thanksgiving. The idea is to offer small companies the same sort of IT services larger companies manage in house. It's a bold venture and he is enormously excited at the prospect of becoming his own boss. Sarah and Thaddeus met as undergraduates at Georgetown, and now they are here to celebrate Thad's twenty-eighth birthday which actualy happened yesterday while they were in transit. Nothing can be entirely perfect.

The first time he came here he was fourteen, exactly half his lifetime ago. Sarah has been to Florence as a tourist, but she is clearly delighted now to be shown what Thad considers not just a second, but a true home. On the quarter of him that's Italian by blood he's always placed a high value.

When Thad was small we called him the Chief Baby of the Train. He was an astonishingly beautiful little boy, the avatar of Greuze's exquisite *Boy in a Red Waistcoat*. We'd go up from D.C. to my family in Philadelphia and he would happily parade through the cars, smiling and bowing at the passengers, pleasing them and knowing they'd be pleased with him. He's always possessed this extraordinary gift of wanting to please, and the world, flattered, has reliably returned the compliment. When we were here last, the Capolagos begged us to leave him with them.

On the first day of our first stay we were guided through Fiesole by the Villa Resident Assistant Mark Gillen. To kick off his return Thad wants to recreate that memorable trek. So we set off up the hillside, through the narrow winding strrets of cream and custard-colored villas, with their green or burnt orange shutters, until we arrive at our orignal first stopping place, Fiesole's redoubtable *pasticceria*. We stopped here that first time because Thad was drawn to a letter in the window. It's a letter of thanks from an American General to the pastry chef who after the war opened this shop. The chef had been, the letter acknowledges, the General's own pastry chef during the Italian campaign, and contributed considerably to keeping up the spirits of the general and his staff. Thad, a World

War II buff, was entranced. Who knew generals kept pastry chefs? Thereafter the shop became a site of regular and reverent visits. It didn't hurt that the pastry was, and is, superb.

On this visit, just inside the door, Thad notices a photo of oarsmen in a shell on the Arno. Thad, a college oarsman, and afterwards for a few years a coach, insists on nipping back to the villino, returning swiftly with one of his own collegiate rowing shirts as a gift for the baker. But it turns out that the picture is only part of a collection of images of an older Florence. The baker is himself a cyclist, in his mid-fifties still taking every other afternoon off to bike for hours these arduous hills. But he is so touched by Thad's unprompted generosity that he insists he will make Thad the mother of all birthday cakes. He describes chocolate, several kinds, mascarpone, custard cream, whipped cream, candied fruit, and beautifully wrought tiny pastries on top which will spell out *Buon Compleanno Taddeo*

I glimpse the neglected potential of our life here through my son's newly arrived eyes. If the parabola we started when we arrived has now bottomed out, Thad's enthusiastic engagement seems to suggest the opening of yet another, brighter curve.

In the evening we all go to Stefano's apartment for a reunion dinner, an evening where Italy speaks for and as itself.

"Oh Maggie," Stefano exclaims as we come to the top of the narrow stairs—a kiss, then a second kiss—"always the youngest of the young."

He and Pietro marvel over Thaddeus, last seen a boy, now a man, a married man. They are enchanted by the beautiful, blonde Sarah.

They offer us prosecco. In return we hand over a chocolate and mascarpone tart from the superb pastry shop. You never bring wine to an Italian evening party. If you do, your hosts will assume you doubt the quality of what they intend to serve. It's equally incorrect to bring chrysanthemums, which in Italy are seen only at funerals. But you also can't arrive empty-handed. That would be, in Stefano's world, the worst of the worst. What you bring are chocolates of the highest quality, or very good, freshly baked pastry, or flowers. But the flowers must come from a first-rate florist and show that they have been carefully selected stem by stem. No bunches, no arrangements. You trust the taste of the host or hostess to arrange them more beautifully in a vase than any shop owner could.

Stefano is extravagantly grateful to have something from that bakery, he says, because he has not been able to return to it since Maggie and I were here the first time. Fourteen years ago? That doesn't seem possible. Though he works in Trieste he maintains this apartment in Florence and is here regularly. And he has very good friends up in Fiesole. I think he must have gone past the *pasticceria* countless times.

He explains.

In those days, Stefano taught Italian at Le Balze while he waited for a job in Hittite to open within the Italian university system. For Intermediate Italian he had only two of *gli studenti*, a young man and a young woman. The young woman was slightly older, in her mid-twenties, striking looking, a former professional dancer. But she had minimal aptitude for Italian, or indeed any sort of study.

"No, it was a serious problem for her," says Stefano. "She was allergic to work."

He could get her to speak Italian only by allowing her to describe in graphic detail the romance she was carrying on with our pastry maker's Adonis of a son, whom in those days we all called the *fornarino*, punning on the name of Raphael's famous mistress, a baker's daughter, *la fornarina*. The topic of the *fornarino* obsessed her, because, as she made very clear, his virile appearance stood in frustratingly inverse proportion to his virile skills.

"Two minutes, that was his limit, this *fornarino*, she kept saying, *due minuti*. That is the only thing I think she has learned to say in Italian in all her months here. But then after she has been gone away, it was becoming so embarrassing for me to enter into that bakery shop and to see there the *fornarino*. Smiling, laughing behind the counter, flirting with all of the girls, and in my ears I have been hearing her voice saying over and over again this *Due minuti, sole due minuti*. And so I have never again been going into there for my *paste*."

Laura, one of the dinner guests, says the *fornarino* is now her next-door neighbor. Fourteen years later he is still very handsome, and trying hard to become a singer. But his ability to stay on pitch seems also to suffer from the two minute limit. Still, she is happier with his singing on one side than she is with the music that comes from their third neighbor. This is a transsexual prostitute who returns from work at dawn, sleeps till three in the afternoon, and then plays pounding rock until the time comes to peel off down to Cascine next to the Arno for another night of profitable sin.

This is Italy? Incompetent lovers? Transsexual whores? Of course. The bedrock Italy beyond the travelers' villas and the tourists' hotels.

Stefano summed it up succinctly when, giving directions for driving to his house, he said we should just park up on the pavement. "Yes, of course it is against the law, Gian, but this is Italy. In Italy everything is forbidden, and everything is permitted."

We drive back up the hill ecstatic.

Blithe and Bonny

No further word of Rotgut or from Dora. Instead, happily, up in the Loggia, another dazzling afternoon.

I ask *gli studenti* to think about how they might stage parts of the masked ball in *Much Ado's* Act II, scene 1. I think of it as a compensatory gift to Duke. We focus on the short sequence where Don Pedro flirts with Beatrice.

First we review the dialogue. Here's what seems to be going on. Don Pedro offers to "get" Beatrice a husband. Flippantly, she replies she'd rather have one "of your father's getting. /Hath your Grace ne'er a brother like you?"(307-308) And suddenly, he asks a very loaded question: "will you have me, lady?" (311) He thinks he's heard some kind of offer in her teasing question. His teasing response makes his interest clear.

There can be no question of marriage between them. She is the apparently dower-less niece of a local magnate, by no means princess material. He is the prince. Not just a prince. THE prince. And they both know that indeed Pedro does have a brother of his father's "getting." That brother is the bastard John. If, then, "Will you have me, lady" is not, can not be, 'Will you wed me, lady,' and if they both know that princes have other ways of *getting* sons, it's pretty clear what Pedro is getting at when he asks: "Will you have me, lady?"

Beatrice knows that, and she also knows she's in trouble now.

Queen Elizabeth once warned her great minister Cecil, "Little man, little man, must is a word not used to princes." Nor is *nay*, especially from maids to princes.

We see how flustered Beatrice becomes. For once she's at a loss for a witty quip. "I beseech Your Grace, pardon me. I was born to speak all mirth and no matter" (314-315). But this *matter* has aroused his interest. He presses his offer, insisting that "to be merry best becomes you, for out of question you were born in a merry hour" (316-318). Her dowered cousin may be a fit bride for a Count, but *merry* Beatrice who can't *marry* a prince might provide him with *a merry hour*. Given the Elizabethan addiction to puns, and what we know of Elizabethan pronunciation, I have no doubt of the word play. Let others *marry*, "to get husband[s]," they, Pedro and Beatrice, will be content merely to be *merry*.

But clever Beatrice finds her opening in the pun, which she now reverses. In that *merry hour* when her married mother gave birth, she says, "sure, my lord, my mother cried" (319). It is maids who pay with pain, she is reminding him, for a prince's merry hours. And then, before he can reply further, she goes public and hails the newly engaged Claudio and Hero.

The interchange is a miniature miracle of compression, wit, and pathos. I don't expect *gli studenti* to be able to "act" this. Years ago, a *New Yorker* critic said he knew that the then-very-young Maggie Smith was destined for greatness when she produced a sudden drop in tone in the line about the mother without for a second changing the rapid pace of the interplay. You have to be very skilled indeed to play any, let alone, all of what is going on in these lines. But I am hoping that together *gli studenti* will produce a reading of the scene which might respond to its cultural specificity. So, withholding for a while the interpretation I've just outlined, I ask them not to perform it, but to talk about how they would direct it.

The jolly girls in the class, Faustina, Stonewall, and Betty, all immediately volunteer for Beatrice. They like her feisty outspokenness. She is the first Shakespearean heroine this semester with whom they say they can identify. Each of them reads the interchange as "joking." I mention what seems Beatrice's radical change of tone after the prince's ambiguous offer.

They don't hear it.

I point at the sense of constraint and embarrassment in the rhythm of her words.

They shrug.

I read the lines that switch suddenly from merriment to the pain of childbirth. They tell me the notes to their edition suggest that Beatrice's mother must have died giving her birth, which is why in the play she is an orphan. Beatrice is now suddenly reminded of her mother's death.

Fine, I say, but why then does she remember her mother's death at this moment?

Because, Ardita suggests, they have mentioned *begetting* and that always reminds Beatrice of her mother's death. If that's so, I ask, why did Beatrice introduce begetting as a joke?

They are too smart to say she forgot.

I offer them my interpretation. It doesn't wash. Everyone stares down at their pages of script. The wind blows through the trees below. The birds sing.

To cheer things up—they are now on my side, intellectually, I know that; they just don't know how to get there on their own—I have the guys sing (they were told last week to prepare this) the song from Act II, scene 3, accompanied by Miss Haag on the guitar. This the famous song that begins:

Sigh no more, ladies, sigh no more.
Men were deceivers ever,
One foot in sea and one on shore,
To one thing constant never.

The guys do this with admirable good nature. They link arms and sway, or try to sway, in time with the music. They all sing, even, to my stunned surprise, Rotgut, and they sing loud. Some even manage to sing melody. When they finish, I tell them I expect them to perform an encore after the villa Thanksgiving dinner. There are groans, but also smiles of anticipation.

As the guys find their seats again, I ask what connects the song and the little scene we tried to do? As usual, theatrically experienced Willy Voltaire comes rapidly to the rescue. "Men were deceivers ever." "The fraud of men was ever so," the next stanza says.

Knowing that fact is what arms Beatrice in her exchange with Pedro at the ball.

June, who rarely speaks, now neatly chimes in by reminding us that at this very moment Pedro, who has in fact commissioned the song, is using it to deceive both Beatrice and Benedick into falling in love with each other. Beatrice could hold off Pedro the first time, but not the second, when all the other characters participate in her duping.

But why then, I ask, does the song repeatedly advise women:

Then sigh not so, but let them go
And be you blithe and bonny,
Converting all your sounds of woe
Into Hey, nonny, nonny

If men are always deceivers, what have women got to be blithe about? Where's the joke? And why at the end of the play don't the women follow the song and "let them [Benedick, Claudio] go?"

Which is, of course, another way of asking why, if this plays insists on how unreliable are even the best of men, on how far apart *marry* and *merry* can soon become, why is it nevertheless a comedy? Is it just a matter of grin and bear it, for women, of literally *bearing* it?

They don't know, but I can tell that they leave thinking about it.

Boy, I loved it when the guys sang. And so did they.

Since he joined in perhaps this also means the Rotgut problem has been resolved, or at least softened.

Montepulciano
In the midst of all this tourism, Maggie continues to live like a traveler. She adheres rigorously to her morning schedule of painting and needlepoint followed by reading in the afternoon, shifting from the sunny to the shady parts of the gardens as the sun crosses overhead. And to the second half of the afternoon she has added a vigorous, demanding, solitary walk up into the Fiesolan hills. She refuses companionship. She doesn't want to talk or share, she only wants what her own senses offer, and she is very protective of her routine. When I fret about how preparing class prevents me from

doing more to guide Thaddeus and Sarah, she is correctly dismissive. "They have been married for just fourteen months; they don't need a father, worse a father-in-law, hanging around. As long as we give them dinner, they can fend for themselves for the rest of the day. They've got Florence, they don't need us." Of course she is, as always, absolutely right,

And true to this same self-reliance, she decides not to go with us today as Thad, Sarah and I drive to the hill town of Montepulciano in southeastern Tuscany. As she happily waves us off you can see she can't wait to get out her brushes.

In 1987 the whole Le Balze group spent a memorable day in and near Montepulciano, guided by our extraordinary professor of Art History, Christine Smith, who later went on to teach in the Design School at Harvard. The tour culminated in exploring Antonio da Sangallo the Elder's great pilgrimage church of San Biagio. In English he's Saint Blaise. Like all Roman Catholics of my generation, every year I have my throat blessed on his feast day, February 3. He is the patron of those who suffer from diseases of the throat. The blessing is a wonderful ritual, the only one of these ancient rites left in the modern Church. You put your neck between an X of two blessed candles, blessed the day before on the feast of Candlemas, when all the candles for the year are consecrated. The X is held in place by a red ribbon. The priest murmurs a quick blessing. But it's the candles that do the comforting. The apparatus feels vaguely medical, a sort of precursor to the stethoscope. You know what's happening is not medicine but the instrument makes you feel it is not quite superstition either.

Of course, I have good reason to be grateful to Saint Blaise. I know whose intercession saved me from suffocating in 1979.

This part of Tuscany southeast of Siena, the Val d'Orcia, is new to us. Like the Val di Chiana we saw coming back from Cortona, it's mostly and strangely empty. Northward in Tuscany everything looks gray or green or brown. Here it all seems pink, brown-pink, gray-pink, rose-pink. And because the land was deforested by the Romans, and subjected thereafter for almost two thousand years to fierce erosion, there's a vaguely lunar quality to these hill shapes. Or maybe, because of the color, it's more like Mars than the moon, if on Mars sheep might safely graze.

Inside the car things are bonny. With Sarah you can't have bad luck or bad weather or bad temper. She's a California girl, a California blonde girl. She glows, and carries sunlight with her as a birthright.

Thad and I decide this is the ideal moment to teach her how to play the family game, Enrico Schnauzer.

We devised Enrico Schnauzer on the first trip to Italy as a way to amuse young children in the tedious hours of the longer journeys. It grew out of the curious Renaissance penchant for re-naming artists to sound like princes. Francesco Mazzola, such a good, trustworthy name for a grocer, became the very grand Parmigianino. Paolo Caliari, sounding much like a Scorsese hit-man, still resonates as Veronese. But the real charm of the game grew from the way it allowed all of us, but especially Thad and Cecilia, to show off the knowledge of Art History we had picked up from Christine.

As played, it always had a kind of stealth quality. We would be driving along, or riding in the train, or crossing on a ferry when suddenly, without fanfare or introduction, one of us would say "once there was a man called Enrico Schnauzer." And the rest would listen attentively, straining to pick up the key clues, to beat the punch line to the punch.

Here is one of them. All the other stories went much like it. You can skip past it if you choose, but I hope you won't.

The key is to try to guess wihch famous artist Enrico becomes before we get to the end of the story.

The Interpolated Tale of Enrico Schnauzer

Once there was a famous artist whose name at birth was Enrico Schnauzer.

Enrico was born in Rome to a well-off family of terrible spendthrifts. His father, and his uncles, his cousins, and even his mother and grandmother, they squandered and spent, and spent and squandered, until they had gone through everything they had inherited. Then by sponging and wheedling and just plain cheating they went through most of what their cousins and godparents had inherited. But of course, even in Italy where family ties are strong, this could not go on forever. It all came crashing down around young Enrico when he was barely into his teens. All his family was put in prison for debt, where pampered and unused to any kind of hardship they quickly died, principally of malnutrition and exposure, but also of shame.

Enrico himself was taken out of school. Although he was then only twelve years old he was set to work as a laborer in a building business to which his family had owed some of its greatest debt.

This is Dickens, right? Didn't his family get sent to debtors' prison?

Yes, Dickens's family did get sent to debtors' prison but Dickens was not Italian. Remember, Enrico was born in Rome.

Because of his family's debt, for many years Enrico was not paid at all. Everything he earned was garnished by his employers in back payment for what his family still owed. Eventually he did manage to keep a little for himself. But beyond a basic literacy he had been taught nothing, not even the simplest skills. So even after he became a man he found himself still forced to earn his living by breaking up stones at the lowest levels of the Italian building industry.

And yet, whenever he could manage to find the stub of an old pencil and the back of a castaway envelope, he was capable of producing the most beautiful and original plans for buildings, far bolder and more imaginative than any of those he worked on. No one knew he had this gift. So terrified was Enrico of falling into debt like his family, that he made himself his family's reverse, a miser, mean with money, a cheapskate. He had no friends because he would never even share a crust of bread, let alone a jug of wine. And he insisted on living in the worst sort of hovel, where even the animals shunned him because he smelled so bad.

Years went by. Enrico drudged by day, long hard hours, and at night, when he could, he drew, and he still had no friends. Then one day all work stopped. A furious dispute had broken out over the church on which he and his gang were engaged. One cardinal insisted the patrons use his favorite architect. Another cardinal insisted his favorite was the only one to build it correctly. Finally the dispute grew so acrimonious that it had to be referred to the Pope himself for settlement. The Pope wisely refused to state a preference. Instead, he said that by a certain date models of each of the competing plans should be made to the same scale and brought to his private chapel. They would be laid on the altar and the papal court would pray for a sign to indicate which one God preferred.

Is there some architect called Joseph? Or Giuseppe? Isn't there some story about Saint Joseph laying staves on the altar for a sign of who should marry the Virgin Mary?

Yes, there is such a story, but this one is about models, not staves.

So all worked stopped and Enrico started day by day to starve to death, like his family, except that he was starving to death in a hovel not a prison. And all the time, almost delirious, he refined his own plans for the church. He drew and re-drew, and with each refinement his idea became even bolder, more original, and more beautiful.

One afternoon, a very sensible woman, a wife and the mother of six, looked out of her window and saw the dirty, bearded, looney-looking workman sitting in the entry to his hovel, drawing, drawing, re-drawing. "This has to stop," she said to herself. "I don't want my children growing up near a crazy, smelly fellow such as that."

So she went down the stairs, and out through the yard, and bustled up to the hovel, prepared to tell him to vamoose pronto, and to insist that if he didn't leave voluntarily, she would have her husband pull the old shack down.

Then she caught sight of the extraordinary plans for the church.

"What're you doing down here, starving to death, you dope," she said, "when you could submit these plans in the contest for the new church and be a rich and prosperous Renaissance architect?"

Enrico murmured back barely audible, faint with hunger, parched with thirst: "You have to submit a model, not just drawings, but, Signora, I am too poor to buy the material with which to build a model. As you can see, and hear, I am in fact quite close to starving to death."

"'Well, if you can't buy the materials yourself,' she shot back, impatient with every form of self-pity, "why don't you Borrow, You Meany, just Borrow.'"

And she herself offered to loan him the money. Which, I am happy to say, breaking the habits of a lifetime, he did. And in short order he made the model, presented it on the papal altar, and then waited at the edge of the crowd. Of course, everyone who saw it realized this was the one to pick. Even the competing architects, prompted by their cardinals, withdrew their earlier designs.

"But what," asked the Pope, "is the name of the architect whose model this is?"

And then, coming forward shyly, Enrico said, to honor forever after the wisdom of his benefactress, "The name of the architect is, Your Holiness,—Borro-mini."

And that is why for the rest of time Enrico Schnauzer has become known to generations of Art History students simply as Borromini.

Here Ends the Interpolated Tale

There were many of these Enrico Schnauzer stories back in the day, including a particularly good one about Bernini, who behaves very stupidly, gets in trouble with fire, and is then for some reason hailed from the papal balcony with the taunt, 'Burn, you Ninny, Burn.' Thad and I tred to tease each other into recalling the middle of that one, but despite prodigies of invention far surpassing what either of us might have produced fourteen years earlier, we found ourselves at Montepulciano with the middle of the tale still undistributed.

Sarah, still sunny, benignly indicates that this has all been very instructive, but it is not a game she ever intends to play herself, or allowed to be played within many feet of her presence. And it certainly shouldn't be taught to any children she might produce. She then bounds equably from the car to encounter Montepulciano.

Montepulciano is, as always, dazzling, and because we're with smiling Sarah we also immediately, and miraculously, find a convenient place to park. And even though the intervallo has begun, as soon as we pass through the ancient town gate, *Porto al Prato*, we find a modest and welcoming restaurant of better than average food and superb, inexpensive wine. This is after all the Montepulciano of *Vino Nobile de Montepulciano*. And still because we are with Sarah, a source of grace, after lunch the entire city is literally all ours. We have every church, every piazza, every view to ourselves alone. We have been given not only the glorious day but the equally glorious town.

No Dante scholar, I still want to think that he got the idea for Purgatory's seven storey mountain from hill towns like this one. Certainly, walking up its sharply angled, constantly turning main road, the Corso, Montepulciano feels like the *Purgatorio* reads. At each level you encounter a different sort of enterprise, like Dante's different sorts of sin and punishment. Here are the leather workers. Turn, climb and here are the print sellers. Higher up still, the ceramicists. And so on until, as in the poem, at the top you enter the cleared fullness of a consecrated space, the piazza fronting the Duomo, the local cathedral.

Perhaps the *Purgatorio* comes to mind also because at every turn the city speaks of loss. Like the dead who stop Dante, needing deeply to have themselves named one last time, death speak to us from every surface. There are no local newspapers in this still rural world. A death is announced by a family with a black-bordered broadsheet glued to the public walls. The deceased is named. Perhaps even more important for these thickly ramified societies, the principal mourners are named, and their precise relation to the deceased carefully notched, *great-niece to... son of her sister...* And then the hour and the church of the funeral.

It's not that people are expected to attend the funeral. Anyone who should attend the funeral will already have been notified by telephone. It's so that when you encounter your child's schoolmate's parent on the street, or when you run into the electrician in the *frutta,* you know at once to say to that great niece, to that nephew, "I am so sorry about your uncle, your aunt." In towns like these everything works to support family.

When they were built, towns like Montepulciano cared more for defense than the view. There were few windows looking outward. Now, with the ramparts lowered, you can exit the main thoroughfare by mysterious alleys and tantalizing, oblique passages, that lead you out to extraordinary points of vantage, hundreds of feet in the air.

High on one of these ramparts, 2000 feet above the surrounding plain, Sarah and Thad have a friendly marital bicker about what they think they see. For Sarah it's California she's looking out and down on. I see what she means. This landscape could easily be sleepy Sonoma or generous Napa, once you get beyond the interstates. Gentle hills, no trees, many vines, monochrome and yet constantly shifting shades. Thad insists he sees something older. He points to the ruined castles and fortified villages dimly visible on the far ridges of the horizon. He claims a knight will emerge momentarily from one of the castles, horse and rider thickly caparisoned in black and white diamonds, couched lance at rest, just as an opposite number, in maroon and purple stripes, emerges from the village walls on the other side of the valley. Slowly these panached centaurs will approach on the empty and available, pink and quilted plain, steady, utterly at ease with the fact that only one of them will return. "Just settle in," he says, "and wait. You'll see." Probably because I only visit California one week a year, Thad's story wins for me. Of course, Sarah says, where she sees peace and plenty, guys will choose to pick a fight.

Back at the car, despite the fact that it is getting late, we decide we will walk to San Biagio. Sarah can't be allowed to miss it. This is one of my there's-still-another-church-around-the-corner-not-far-from-here-that-may-have-a-Rubens efforts, which Maggie the traveler—dismissing me as the Nazi tourist—no longer tolerates. But Thad wants Sarah to see everything that he treasures, and so off we trudge.

At once we are lost, this time because we are constantly and consistently misdirected. Italians, if asked directions, will never say they don't know. They will instead invariably and courteously point you the way they think you should go, whether or not it has anything to do with where you are heading. Since we can't believe the *Montepulciani* can't know how to get to the most beautiful object in their universe, we keep on plodding till we have gone miles out of our way. Something we learn only after a gentleman overseeing construction on his new driveway gives us the most elaborate misdirection yet. Directions that are corrected only when one of the African laborers, seeing the *patrone* safely out of the way, rushes after us, and tells us in perfect English exactly how to retrace our now several miles out-of-the-way way.

This time we get the car first. And so we come comfortably to the church just before closing but still with enough time to see it thoroughly. Sarah is stunned. We told her it was among the most perfectly beautiful buildings in the world. But no words can prepare anyone for San Biagio. It's St. Peter's in Rome miniaturized and perfect in scale, the St. Peter's Michelangelo imagined, before its nave was distended. It's laid out as a Greek cross, each of the four arms equal to the others, and though I can't give the measurements, the height seems also perfectly equal to the other dimensions. Outside (and inside) it's all a sort of honey colored travertine. In this late afternoon October light it seems like living amber. Isolated on its large green lawn, its outlines crisp against the still blue sky, it's so perfect it does not seem built. It seems bestowed.

We spend a long time inside, where again we are alone. Thad teaches Sarah to see what Christine years ago taught us to see. He says something like: *this is a space where architecture and sculpture dissolve into each other. It isn't extravagant or excessive as in the Baroque that follows with Sangallo's son (or is it nephew). It still shows the Renaissance emphasis on restraint and proportion. But look. There's no still surface, no mere background against which a column or a statue is posed. All the surfaces undulate, concave alternating with convex, so that the entire interior, all twelve of its vertical surfaces, becomes sculpture. The whole building is like a single seamless sculpture, entirely at rest, and vividly in motion.*

Several times we decide we have to leave. It is late. There is the long drive back. But each time we settle back down again and gape. We know we will see many beautiful things in our different futures but we all know we will never see anything lovelier than this. How can we surrender it?

Driving home, as Sarah sleeps in the back seat, Thad and I talk about his life, their marriage, Sarah's residency, the new business. The plains are orange now, the distant hills violet. I know the way back. We don't get lost. Clearly, he knows his way too.

When we arrived in Italy the first time, when he was fourteen, he hated it. He had never spent any time abroad. He had been yanked out of school, separated from all his friends. He spoke no Italian, and found himself forced to live almost entirely in the company of his parents and his eleven-year old sister. Nothing about that experience seemed endurable to him, let alone promising. But after a few weeks of solid moping, he was persuaded to give it one good try. Without telling us, he found his way, by the Number Seven bus, down from Fiesole into Florence. He got off near the Duomo, and started to walk the streets. Down the Via Cavour in front of the Palazzo Medici. Around the Baptistery. Into the Piazza Signoria, and up toward the Bargello. Alone. Without a plan. Without even a map. He wandered around for the better part of an afternoon, never going inside anything, never even pausing. And then, unexpectedly, he had that epiphany about which he later wrote: *the feeling you get the first time you eat something, and you know immediately that from now on this will be your favorite food.*

By the time we were ready to leave Italy, he was testing himself and his new Italian by hitchhiking out of Fiesole, pretending to be Italian, seeing how long real Italians would take to figure him out. With some new Italian clothes, his own olive skin and thick dark hair, he would brag that he could sometimes go the whole way without being spotted. —How generous and indulgent Italians are to children. —And he would come back thrilled.

I am just as thrilled this evening to see how much Italy has contributed to the man he has become. All the things we shared here when he was a boy, respect for and love of the past, a passion for architecture, delight in anything new, different, and original, with the eager openness that comes from that delight, they've all matured in him, rooted just as immutably as golden San Biagio is rooted in this perfect landscape.

What a gift.

Friday, October 13
Ominous date
Thad and Sarah leave early for Lake Como to visit Sarah's parents, Ginny and Bick Hooper, who are staying there for a conference. They will return next week. I miss them at once.

Sadly the Rotgut problem has not been resolved. Heidi and Marcello invite me to join them in a talk with him. I refuse. Several people have now told me, both students and staff, that he considers me part of his problem. In September he treated me as a sort of mentor. I have no idea what changed. Whatever the cause, I am certain my participation at this point can only make him feel even more persecuted. Especially since my instinct is to say: send him home, quickly. Don't you see: he's disintegrating before our eyes. But I know this is not the message the Villa wants to hear. So I keep my distance.

Freud's nephew
Thad and Sarah took the good times north when they left. Here

we've returned to non-stop, hard-driving rain. Maggie does not complain. These days the only landscape she cares about is the one within her. Since she can't go out to paint in the garden, she arranges some pears as a still life on the dining table. And then, since it's raining, she hauls on a slicker and heads back to the hills. I envy her this serenity. I'm fine when I'm with her or Thad or even—these days—*gli studenti*. Then everyhting seems to be working, but on my own all my goblins return, with garnish.

For a while I try preparing that daunting masterpiece *The Merchant of Venice*, our play for the next two weeks, but my thoughts keep coming back to Dora and Rotgut. Dora is waiting for me to call, I can sense that, but I feel I can do nothing for her except listen. Rotgut refuses to talk to me, but for him, perhaps, there is something I could do, if only he would listen. At lunch, when I try to explain all this anxiety to Maggie, she dismissively explains how entirely wrong I am. Once again I have been playing what she and Thad and Cecilia call *Freud's nephew*.

The family joke is that because I am fairly good at interpreting texts I have convinced myself that I am an equally good interpreter of lives: hence, the not entirely friendly nickname *Freud's nephew*. But life, Maggie has been warning me for almost thirty years, does not work like a novel or a play. Life is altogether cruder and more basic. When I try to remind her that I did once teach a course in Blake and Jung, she reminds me that I taught the Blake, the Psychiatry department taught the Jung. And when I go on to remind her that the course was a great success, she reminds me that it was the end of the 'sixties, when Freudians and Jungians were doing everythuing they could to seem relevant to an emerging world of pharmacology. And don't forget, she can't resist pointing out, that course was never repeated.

As she clears away lunch, Maggie also tries to dispatch my difficulties. Dora has lost her son in a way that is not only terrible but evil. Rotgut is having a breakdown. Dora needs a priest, Rotgut needs a therapist. If I really want to help them, I should get Dora to the one, and Rotgut to the other.

After that she goes out into the downpour for her walk, apparently blissful.

At least Dora hasn't called ths week. That's something. Does it means that I am at least off that particularly painful hook?

WEEK SEVEN
October 15 – 21

Cip

The rain continues. It is supposed to clear by late afternoon. Maggie urges me to stop moping about Thad and Sarah not being here. Find another new place to visit, she insists, someplace close enough for a drive after the rain stops. A challenge. I want Thad's magic to transform this gloomy afternoon, and I want to cling to my resentment that he's not here to wield it. But I know Maggie is right so I shelve *Merchant* and take down the guidebooks. What is there both new and nearby? There's Barga, in the mountains to the north, the dark Garfagnana. We've been told the area's so inbred it's not uncommon to find people with eleven fingers. Nearby you can visit a lake with a sunken town visible beneath its surface. When the wind disturbs the water's surface, the bells in the drowned church-es toll. Sounds just right to conclude this sodden weekend.

But the rain doesn't stop. Finally, around four, Maggie throws on her foul-weather gear and boldly sets off on her hillside walk. Which means I am home alone, when Cip Capolago calls.

I have met Cip only once. I had a short private conversation with him. This second one does not start well.

"Stop encouraging my mother."

I'm speechless.

"I know she's told you about this cop. The next time she calls you I want you to tell her he's a liar and a thug. And I don't want you to offer her money."

The idea that I would be in a position to offer money to any of the Capolagos is so absurd I get my wind back.

"The only thing I know about the guy, Cip, is what your moth-er's told me."

"I had him checked out. Everything he said to her is a lie. All of it"

"You're her son. He's a complete stranger. Who is she going to believe?"

There's a pause.

"John, my mother is a desperate woman. You've seen the statue: the she-wolf suckling Romulus and Remus. Every Italian mother is that wolf. She couldn't save Ivo, but she won't stop at anything if she thinks she's saving his name."

"All your mother wants me to do, Cip, is listen. And, really, that's all I can do."

I am glad Maggie is out. This is just what she's warned me about: getting involved where involvement cannot be distinguished from interference.

"He came out to the field three days ago, where I keep the plane. How the sonavabitch knew I'd be there, what time I'd be landing, how he even got through security I don't know. But there he is. I'm crouched down, checking one of the wheels; I look up there he is, this big bastard, leaning on the wing. As soon as I got a look at him I knew he was the guy my mother's been after me about. And what's with the sudden show? Am I supposed to feel threatened? Impressed? He can go where he pleases; he knows everything about us? Whatever it was, I told him to get the hell out of there, or I'd have him arrested.

"Since then I've been checking him out. All lies. All of it. He was a cop, but got thrown out of the police a couple of years back. For corruption."

I consider lightening the tone by asking what kind of corruption gets you kicked out of the Italian bureaucracy where corruption is only business as usual. But Cip is not going to take that as a joke.

"The guy's completely bent. He's a swindler. A blackmailer. Even the crooks think he's a creep."

"Cip, do you believe that Ivo was kidnapped."

"My brother didn't kill himself."

"Was this guy in on it?"

Nothing.

"Maybe."

Cip doesn't want to share. He certainly does not want me to be his confidant. He wants to order me off the premises so he can close ranks and protect his parents. I'm not real family. I'm a foreigner. As far as he's concerned I've got no business knowing anything about any of this. But his mother has included me in it, so he's forced to compromise and let me in, at least a little. But he will hold this against me and as soon as he can he will do me damage. I know that.

"It's one of two things. Possibility number one: this guy was in on the kidnapping. Something went wrong. They lost their grab for the ransom. Now he's going to squeeze us for it, at least part of it, pretending to find out what happened. Possibility two: this is all part of a larger scheme to bring us down, the whole family."

As Cip outlines his possibility two, I recall that when we were here in 1987, until Waldo hushed her, Dora talked about how the Mafia had been pressuring him for a share in the business. They made threats but Waldo wouldn't back down. Waldo was well connected politically in those days, and he used his connections to scare off the crooks. Now Cip tells me the threats never really died out. And Waldo's friends no longer hold power.

"Maybe a threat was made to my father. He shrugged it off. Then Ivo was killed. Maybe that's why he won't talk about it, any of it, even with me. Because he feels responsible."

"Is that what you believe?"

A much longer pause now.

"Cip?"

"My mother wants you to write about this. I know. I don't. So what I tell you now, whatever she tells you later, it's just between us. Right?"

My book and the Capolagos, these are two entirely different stories; I can easily agree to his condition.

"I think what's happening now is step two. The first step was killing my brother. Now they're trying to entrap my mother. They know she doesn't have access to the kind of money they're asking for. They want her to do something maybe not even illegal, just fool-ish, but something they can use to get her in trouble. Then my fa-ther, to protect her, — you can see the dominos. Step by step, they've got a plan. We wouldn't share with them, and so now they're going to bring us down, all of us, one by one. That's why you've got to help me keep my mother away from this so-called cop."

Before I can answer, two things happen. Maggie comes in from the rain, and somebody at his place calls out to Cip. Quickly, he says he'll call me again later in the week, and hangs up.

Who came in? Dora? Waldo?

I suddenly see their apartment clearly, the three of them sharing the space, each cut off from the other two in his or her own secret story, secret shame. By the time Maggie's out of her wet things, I'm in the study poring over *Merchant*. This is not a conversation I feel prepared to share.

But it's now way too late to drive to the Garfagnana. We settle in for the evening. Thad calls to tell us that Lake Como has overflowed its banks, flooding them out of the hotel dining room in the middle of supper. The hotel is trying to find someplace else to put them up. Even Thad's magic seems on hold.

Getting to the Ort

The rains end. It's cool and clear, not too cool for class in the grove, but for the first time I see sweaters all round. After last weekend *gli studenti* abandoned their visits to the Italian beaches. They began instead to head north, mostly for the Oktoberfest in Munich. You can get from here to Bavaria pretty easily on an overnight train. For the Fall Break—it begins in ten days—they are planning to go even farther afield. A large party will fly to Spain and Portugal, Clyde as usual roostering his flock of seven females. Ripley is going to Dublin. Willy Voltaire to London. Judy's venturing up to Krakow. Beluga's even returning to New York, for the World Series. But when I ask why these choices, the invariable answer—except for Beluga—is: to see other Georgetown students studying abroad. Their excitement at this prospect is palpable.

The limited company they keep here is becoming pretty predictable.

The brisk air helps them to settle down quickly to *Merchant*. Intellectually, it's a minefield. If I start off wrong-footed here, we may be back where we started. Some people argue that, like Wagner's operas, *Merchant* should no longer be performed. Read, perhaps, and certainly studied, as a powerful document in the ugly history of anti-Semitism, but never performed for pleasure. Others would argue that it *must* be performed, but only as British theatres have done several times, notably with Laurence Olivier in the late 60s and again with Anthony Sher in the late 80s, with anti-Semitism foregrounded in all its deplorable brutality. It's not a text that invites or even allows you to seek common ground.

Rather than framing the text myself, then, I decide this is the apt moment to introduce the *ort*.

In German *ort* refers to an opening or a place. There's an English word ort, now rarely heard, which means the bits of food left over after banquets and picnics. But the German word seems to have nothing to do with that. The German comes closest to our word for *a space, an opening, a clearing*. It's a key term in the work of the controversial twentieth-century philosopher Martin Heidegger, who uses it to describe the experience of reading, *really* reading.

Reading, for Heidegger, reading that is lively, engaged, productive, resembles a Sunday walk in the woods. And by woods Heidegger means Woods! He lived near, and walked regularly in, the Black Forest. Thinking of that sort of thickly wooded dense forest, he says that on a beautiful day, you walk along, you hear the birds singing, you see the sun shining. You think you are paying attention. Actually, you are responding to all this beauty with only half your mind. The rest of you has surrendered to a reverie, a daze, a walking daydream. That half-aware experience, Heidegger claims boldly, corresponds to what most people mean by reading. Half your mind, probably less rather than more, you are giving to what you read. The other half, probably more rather than less, you actually have focused in on yourself. You aren't thinking about what you are seeing on the walk or reading on the page. What you are doing is more like responding to a Rorschach blot, setting the mind off on its own self-propelled divagations.

Then, unexpectedly, the walker finds him or herself stopped in the *ort*. You realize that in this mindless stroll you've arrived at a place you don't know, a place you've never seen before. You are lost. You recognize nothing around you. And now, Heidegger says, now, for the first time, you actually begin to pay attention. Immediately, everything needs to become, and therefore does become, a potential clue. Are those man-made sounds? Are they coming from the left? Or from the right? How far off? Where is the sun, and how can I use it to improvise a compass? Can I see anything though those leaves? Is that a path down there? Who or what else is out here with me?

Paradoxically, you begin to notice where you are only when you realize that you don't know where you are. And of course that is exactly what has happened to me over the course of the past six weeks. Gradually the familiar, the expected gave place to the strange, the bewildering.

Le Balze is my *ort*.

Heidegger insists that a similar sense of discombobulation marks the moment pseudo-reading becomes real reading. We begin to read when we stop *merely* recognizing. At that moment we begin to pay attention to something for what it really is in itself, and not as a version of what we already feel or think or know. The moment of the *ort*, then, arrives when we admit we are encountering a genuinely other point of view, another voice, another mind. When we move from an agreeable and easy *yes, I see; of course; I agree; how interesting* to something we didn't think, wouldn't think, couldn't think. *Can that really be true? What is he or she saying! I don't think so.*

In that moment, Heidegger insists, you start to read.

Concentrating on the *ort*, the place of incomprehension, frees us, gets us to hear something new, challenging, potentially even mind- or heart- altering. As the remarkable British novelist Barry Unsworth says someplace in his gorgeous comic novel *Losing Nelson*: "Cardinal error, looking for what you hope to find rather than looking at what is there before you."

So we are going to make student-generated orts the starting point of every class.

Of course from the start of our time together I've been asking the students to talk about the fissures and the gaps, the historical and cultural differences that separate us from Shakespeare. But I've always provided the starting point and the surrounding context. For six weeks it's been my agenda that's shaped the allowable questions. I haven't let their issues lead. But that's over now. From now on, I tell them, they are in charge. They pitch, they bat, they field. I referee. We build each class out of the orts they suggest.

Not only do we begin with what they individually and as a group don't understand, it's their bewilderment, and not anything I contrive, that grounds the subsequent discussion.

To begin this new regime, after explaining Heidegger's idea and how the ort will work in practice, I invite them to spend the remainder of the class writing a short paragraph that begins "The thing that vexes me most about this text is... " The only rule is that they locate their "problem" in at least one specific passage in the script, which they go on to elaborate in a few sentences that clarify why the issue bothers them. We will use these orts to guide the remainder of our time with *Merchant*. And, if all goes as well as I hope, with the scripts that follow, *Othello* and *The Tempest*.

At first they are surprised that they are to do nothing this afternoon but write, and not only write but write about what they don't understand. But then as they start writing I can see they begin to enjoy what they are doing. Orts are always liberating. Having been trained from the start of their scholastic careers to pretend to know, it's an astonishing moment to be told it might be even better to acknowledge what you don't know.

After they leave, I quickly page through the pile. Freed up, and encouraged, *gli studenti* have produced a lively, extensive list of the issues that vex them. When I total all the questions I find they've covered pretty much all the significant features of the entire script. Individually and as a class they have forcefully *thought* about the script. It's going to be fun, and frustrating, figuring out which one to use in the next class.

Frutta

Thaddeus and Sarah returned last night from Como. Their flooded hotel did finally find them a much-less-nice place to stay. But the entire visit was a drag, since it did nothing but rain the entire time. The water at Como is supposed to flow below not around you.

Our gloom lightens, however, when Maggie returns from shopping to tell us they've accepted her at the *Frutta*. This is an astonishing achievement. Not simply an achievement but a tribute. Keeping to the vegetal motif, I find myself green with envy.

Frutta is the vegetable and fruit seller in Piazza Mino. I'm sure it has another name but we only know it from the sign outside. Since we arrived, Maggie has been shopping there three, sometimes four, times a week whenever she's been in town. In Italy you buy everything in small and incredibly fresh quantities on almost a daily basis. But until this week she had received from the owners and her fellow shoppers nothing more than the most correct politeness. Which would mean nothing in the States, but which here deliberately marks your outsider status. Virtually everyone else entering or leaving a small Fiesole shop is hailed by name, kissed or shaken hands with, and has the health of all their extended family asked after in detail. Maggie, however, barely managed to get *Buon giorno, signora*, although I tried to persuade her that even that was better than the curt *'giorno* the occasional, wayward tourist receives.

But today all that changed. Perhaps there's some secret quota of purchases. Perhaps it's her innate kindness and warmth. Perhaps it's just her steadily improving Italian. I think it's a sign of her already marked recovery. Whatever the cause, she was recognized, publicly, and it is an accolade of which she is, rightly, quite proud.

Here is what happened.

She pointed to a pear in a basket. At the moment pears are exceptionally beautiful. She could only point. In Italy only the most ill-bred person would touch a piece of fruit she or he had not yet purchased. But the young woman who manages the store dismissed her choice with a firm *niente.* Then, reaching beneath the display, like a new and smarter Eve, the manageress brought out a pear she plainly thought more suitable. At that point, as though to confirm the moment, an older woman shopper spontaneously explained to Maggie, in voluble Italian, precisely how she herself would cook for lunch the baby artichokes already in Maggie's basket. Chopped, battered, quickly fried and eaten hot with plenty of salt.

A precious gift as we realized later in the day at lunch.

Maggie is still basking. It's as though these canny women recognized something in her and were happy to salute its appearance.

A warning: I don't think you can find these little artichokes in the States. At least not on the East Coast. Slighter larger than AA eggs, violet and pale apple-green, younger than springtime. We may grow them but if so, our farmers, wisely, never let them leave home.

A bust beneath the jasmine

This pause in the rain means the gardeners can attack the wall of jasmine over which Jane Harvey felt such despair. They need to get it down so that the stucco repair, almost finished on the exterior of the house, can move on to the garden walls. Within a very few minutes these three very strong men, Ruggiero, Alessandro, and Andrea, hacked an entire wall of greenery, twelve feet high by thirty feet broad, down to a few woody slips. The toppled jasmine lies in a sodden heap, but even uglier is the wall revealed by this surgery, large scrofulous patches, in some spots exposed even to the brick inner core. And what was a flower bed in front of the jasmine wall, all purples, and blues, and yellows, is now a muddy hump. This must be what the whole villa looked like when it was abandoned in 1945, looted and mined by the departing Nazis.

But we also discover, high on the wall, hidden all these years, the stone bust of a lady, a bust rather too small for the scale of the garden, on a bulbous, very ugly, marble plinth. Her nose has been broken. Shot off I suspect by a Nazi thug. And the bust itself was once decapitated, the head now reattached by a thin line easily traced. Even so defaced, however, one can see that it is a portrait, unlike any of the other floridly pseudo-classical statuary in the gardens, all of them bought in a single lot from a Milanese stoneyard in 1913. The other statues are undistinguished and generic, god, nymph, goddess, thinker. This is a person.

She is not classical. She is most emphatically Edwardian. Her upswept hair she's topped with the kind of floral tiara typical of Edwardian evening dress. You see its like in thousands of period portraits and photos. And there's a suggestion of drapery over the right shoulder that hints at a dress by Worth or one of his many, less talented peers. She is by no means beautiful, but she has a charming smile that transforms somewhat ordinary features into a face of real and individual warmth, a warmth that transcends decades of neglect and brutality.

Also she has one breast exposed, the left, with a carefully carved and quite credible nipple.

I think she is Bessie. Elizabeth Rockefeller Strong, the wife whose money built Le Balze and whose death occasioned it. Why else put this odd statue in this particular location? The bust is entirely out of proportion to the space; it has nothing to do with the rest of the ornamental scheme. It's the only statue in the secret garden, indeed it's the only ornament of any kind. The other gardens teem with bodies in stone and busts in shell. But the key piece of evidence is how she's placed. Oddly high up on the wall she looks directly across to, and is in turn looked back upon by, the private loggia opening off the widowed owner's bedroom. I think I understand now the secrecy of this garden, inaccessible from any of the public rooms, unavailable to any view but the master's. At every hour, day or night, he could look across to her, across the voided space of the garden, across the void of time, and find her still there, smiling back.

The moment feels like an ort. I am in a space I thought I understood but now I realize I've misread it completely. Until this moment I considered Le Balze, the Strongs' Le Balze, perverse, an escape, a tomb. I see it now as a memorial, a shrine. The improbable entrance with its frivolous shell work and excess of stony sponge, is merely a façade, a decoy, a way to keep the infrequent guests entertained so that they didn't ask to look behind the garden walls, into the Villa's hidden core, into the hidden space of the heart. Le Balze is not the dead space I thought when I arrived, but an altogether different sort of space, a space consecrated to keeping something alive.

I think I now understand why Strong refused stalwartly to get away as the Germans took over Italy, though, with his Rockefeller connections, he was such a target for capture and ransom. Like the members of the royal house of Savoy stranded in the north, he could easily have managed his way into Switzerland. He insisted nevertheless on staying, urging all the while that his secretary and his wife get away. As they did. But Strong stayed on. Flight would have put death in full possession.

Is it Bessie Rockefeller Strong and not Ivo Capolongo about whom I should be writing? I am not in Rome, but here at Le Balze, her place, her story, her hidden story. I could easily start right away by writing to Kykuit in Tarrytown, to the Rockefeller archives, to see if they can produce a photograph of Bessie, to match against the bust. The face on the garden wall. The bust beneath the jasmine curtain.

I ask Heidi what she thinks. I will need her to make the first contact with Kykuit. She is non-committal. Her real concern is that I reassure Jane Harvey that our three gardeners did the best they could, given the decayed condition of the walls, and that the jasmine will soon flourish again in all its winter glory. She does not want to find us one day featured prominently in a horticultural magazine: "Depredation at Villa Le Balze".

I have a sense she is subtly suggesting a deal: she will write to Kykuit if I calm Jane Harvey.

But as I leave Heidi's office in the villa, I have an afterthought that takes me to a very different place: shouldn't we, when the stucco is restored and the jasmine grows back up, allow it once more to veil that face. Isn't that now what's fitting?

Jazzing the Ort

After breakfast I see Thad and Sarah off on the number 7 bus down to Florence. I am increasingly conscious that they are here with us for only a few more days. I want to spend as much of that time with them as possible. But the more responsible part of me understands this is their time together, and they don't need me for guide or chaperone.

Then back to the villino to finalize which of the orts to use as today's starting point. Predictably, many of them wrote about Shylock. But I decide I will start off with Beluga's: on Bassanio, the play's ostensible leading man. It seems better to let them get used to the ort-based method first, and then we can take on the play's nuclear warhead.

Beluga points to the swing-moment of the play, where Bassanio picks the right casket.

Bassanio clearly wants the money that comes with Portia. He's happy to get the lady also, but it's the bank account he seems truly to prize. In this plot Shakespeare seems powerfully to capture contemporary Venetian class dynamics.

Here's the relevant background. As the Ottoman Turks came increasingly to dominate the eastern Mediterranean, Venice could no longer generate the great sea-built fortunes its older aristocratic families had amassed. During the sixteenth century the richest and most powerful of these older families, departing from tradition, began to buy and build on properties outside the aquatic city, for the first time investing not in the sea but on the land. The greatest of these families created the estates on which, in the mid-sixteenth century, Palladio built his fabled villas, estates like Portia's Belmont, setting new architectural standards not only for the rest of Italy but ultimately for the rest of Europe. The lesser aristocrats, of which Bassanio seems to be a representative, were distinguished by birth but not wealthy enough to buy land. They now found themselves therefore cut off by lack of wealth from the newly landed aristocracy and by pride of birth from the non-aristocratic merchants, like Antonio, the play's title character, who still traded on the sea but in ventures—as the plot makes clear—that had become increasingly risky. So risky that, in this new, weakened, and profoundly de-stabilized Venice, Antonio—and Bassanio with him—must finally rely on the wealth of Shylock the Jew. It's the only way to wed the landed heiress who can re-establish Bassanio's position in the world.

In the ilex grove (we should be in the loggia but I cheat; it's so wonderful out here) I ask the handsomest pair in the class to read the scene in which Bassanio picks the right casket and gets the girl: Benny as Bassanio, Claudia as Portia. It's the closest I can come to type casting. It's a long and complicated exchange and they surpass even my expectations. Benny automatically hits just the right mix of sexual swagger and intellectual anxiety. Claudia's Portia is all charming distance with a hint of something that may be shyness but could equally well be disdain.

When they finish and we applaud, I (without attribution) read Beluga's question. Why should a mere fortune hunter, Bassanio, be the guy who gets the girl?

Beluga's *ort* asks if the play is really saying something like: successful romance always covers up what is essentially materialistic self-seeking. That question rings not merely a bell but a carillon with the class. All *gli studenti* chime in, sharing their anxious discomfort with this dark and troubling romance that seems so frankly and subversively to intertwine the erotic and the materialistic.

Of course, they are all consumers, and proudly such. The good things in life, they believe, are out there to be (first) earned and (second) consumed. But they also have been taught to believe in, to hold back and protect, something they unabashedly call True Love. (This is of course also what set them against the "contrived" marriages in *Much Ado*.) *Merchant* seems stalwartly to refuse any such hard and fast distinction. The heiress, Portia, can fall for the good-looking fortune hunter, Bassanio, knowing that's exactly and all that he is. And the fortune hunter can make love to the girl and her ducats, without having to make a significant distinction between them. That lack of distinction makes the play seem to *gli studenti*—this is their worst term of censure—cynical.

Of course, experience will soon teach them, far more effectively than I, that, in every class, in every age, money and marriage are inseparable. That's not my job. It's enough for me now simply to suggest that Shakespeare in this play does indeed seem to be tracing the outline of a new age. It's not that the late sixteenth is the first century to know that nothing, marriage, love, reputation, happiness, is inseparable from cash. Money had been managing Europe since roughly the year 1000. (As anybody who ever tried to found a monastery or convent, and then keep its doors open, knew.) It's just that earlier moments in Western culture could also tell convincing stories that claimed to dissociate money from chivalry, or piety, or the like. Shakespeare's world is definitively, even aggressively, post-chivalric.

For Shakespeare, in the Forest of Arden, in a midsummer night's dream, lovers can love for love's sake, but love in a prince's court or a city, particularly in a great mercantile entrepot, inevitably engages the cash nexus. But I don't say a word of this. I have learned my lesson well. It's not my job to intervene. Instead I take them back to Beluga's ort and ask: why do they dislike Bassanio so much? Maybe there's not much in him to admire, but does he really deserve such hostility?

They go at and around this question for a bit, and then Willy, quiet but always canny, notches the consequences higher. Bassanio vexes our class, he thinks, because "we've been taught to have our heroes single-minded."

The others begin to tease out what this means.

If you are in love, Orchid explains, you should only be in love. Nothing else about a person you love, position, wealth, family, should matter.

No, says Willy, he understands that, but that's not his problem with Bassanio. His problem is that Bassanio is so crass. *All* he's after is the money. He gets her and then immediately forgets her, rushing off to his buddy Antonio trapped in Venice. Portia is only for him what he calls her, *the Golden Fleece.*

"And he," Clyde slyly interposes, "is only out to fleece her."

"Exactly," says Betty. "He is just not worthy of Portia. Portia is funny, and generous, and good. Bassanio is none of the above."

"He's not even smart," Beluga adds. "Portia has to give him unfair hints before he can figure out which casket to pick. While he deliberates she orders the song in which the entire initial rhyme scheme, *bred, head, nourishèd,* leads to lead."

"That is so unacceptable," Duke insists. "That was like the moment I lost all respect for Portia."

"An acceptable romantic plot," Faustina announces, "has to give us—whatever else is at stake—a guy and girl worthy of each other."

"If we are going to buy the happy ending," Judy sums up, "the writer must make us believe this pair has a good chance to end up happily."

But Shakespeare, they all agree, seems to be going out of his way to make just the opposite point. "When he wins," Ripley quotes, "even Bassanio admits he's in over his head:

So, thrice-fair lady, stand I...
As doubtful whether what I see be true,
Until confirmed, signed, ratified by you (III:2, 146-148)

"What's more," Miss Haag adds, "Portia shows she knows his limitations. She immediately starts giving him lessons in how to behave. And it's because she so clearly sees his shortcomings that she devises the final plot of the play, the ring plot, to teach him how properly to value her *and* their union."

"But even by the end of the play," Jacqueline sadly observes, "he doesn't seem really to get it." Jacqueline is a tender-hearted, generally quiet, young woman who clearly hates to speak ill of anyone, even of someone in a fiction. "We know," she says—her eyes tearing—"that he will disappoint her again, in the future, probably more than once."

"And then," this is Duke again, "she'll reach for other stratagems. And be disappointed. Like, how can you respect her, knowing that?"

"Nevertheless," Willy asks, rounding it all off, "the play is called a comedy. How? Why?"

The *ort* has done its job. It has made *gli studenti* grapple with something central to the play, something that is not only exotically strange but deeply alienating to them. They are struggling with and against one of the many ways in which Shakespeare's mind and world do not work like theirs. And on that note, we run out of time.

A strong *ort* can make a class, a good class like this one, feel something close to jazz. The *ort* sets the group a theme, and then the individuals take off with it: call and response. If you are lucky and in tune, the students make it their own, improvising, inventing, extending, sharing the time but reshaping what they're handed. And after a class like this, I realize I don't want to do anything else with or in my life, ever.

But then, leaving the ilex grove and about to insert my key in the villino lock, I remember that everyone in the class spoke—it's a first—except Rotgut. He sat silent throughout, at the outer rim of chairs, watching and voiceless, merely smiling.

The Detective's Theory

Thaddeus and Sarah were up before dawn this morning to catch the train to Venice. They will be back tomorrow for their last day with us. It's a long way to go for just one day but Thad is adamant that he's got to share Venice with Sarah. In 1987 the four of us spent a week in Venice. We found a poor and obscure convent just off Saint Mark's piazza which rented out rooms. The sisters gave us one long barren room to share, with four Spartan cots and no other furniture not even a single chair, and one of those difficult Italian bathrooms where the shower has no curtain or doors, which of course means that if you are well over six fee you inundate the entire room before you are done. We'd leave the convent early in the morning and spend the entire day rushing from canal to canal, fueling up in working men's fast food (fabulous fast food) eateries. We even took the *vaporetto* (water bus) out to San Michele, the island where the Venetians bury their dead, to venerate the graves of Diaghilev and Stravinsky. It was in Venice that Thad discovered his passion for Palladio, with Michelangelo one his two super-heroes. All of this he wants, in a day, to recreate for Sarah.

In any case I would envy them a trip to Venice but especially today since I am due to have lunch here in Fiesole with Dora. She called last night and insisted that I meet her at a restaurant a little beyond the town. There was no getting out of it. Maggie, who now knows all, thinks I am, and I quote, a "thorough dope" to agree to it.

Shamefaced, I leave Le Balze just after noon and head up into the hills.

All kinds of fruit, not just pears, are glorious here at this time of year. But for me, raised in the American mid-Atlantic, an Italian October feels slightly melancholy. When it isn't raining, the light, it is true, is golden, but little on the ground turns red. Nothing turns orange. And where's there's gold it's old, not spun, gold. Instead of woods growing vibrant in the crisp air, here you find here only a slow, gradual fading. Yellowish greens become greenish yellows. Occasionally, there's a fleck of something cinnamon, but it's not easily distinguished from brown. Over all the walls drape the fuchsia-red vine I chauvinistically call Virginia creeper. But that's pretty much it for color. And of course no chrysanthemums, since mums here are the flowers of the dead

When the sun shines, the orange-peach stucco, standard on every Tuscan wall, can glow like hothouse fruit. And then the berries and creeper along its sides gleam. But even when the eye is pleased, the rest of me misses the cool snappish breeze that spells autumn at home.

At first I don't recognize the woman signaling me from her table. Dora has thoroughly transformed herself since our meeting up in the cloister. She's wearing the same black suit. (Doubtless she will wear black for Ivo for at least a year.) But everything else about her is different. This is the Dora we first met fourteen years back, now only very slightly aged. Her hair has been colored. She's wearing discreet make-up and real jewelry; on the table carefully arranged are gloves and purse, matched miracles of Italian leatherwork. Every inch of her proclaims the confident, pampered matron of the European upper bourgeoisie. Not until she speaks English would you ever guess this Dora to have spent the first three decades of her life in Philadelphia.

Even as we settle to the menus she tells me she knows Cip called me. But Cip doesn't know she's here with me now. I can tell him if I want to. It doesn't matter to her. Everything he told me about the detective, the detective himself had already confessed to her. So much for Cip, whom she now lightly dismisses with a small rearrangement of gloves and purse.

Yes, the detective lied. When confronted he told her he didn't

think she would trust him if she knew about his past. He was probably right about that, but it doesn't matter to Dora now. What he
should have told her from the start is that he's known about the
cover-up since the day after Ivo died. That's what led him to Dora.
He's all about revenge, not hers, his own. The police involved in the
cover-up, he claims, are his former colleagues, men who—a year or
so before—sold him out to cover themselves. He doesn't pretend to
be innocent. He's about as bent as you can be. But he's now hell-
bent to ruin these guys just as they ruined him.

"Has he offered you any proof, anything to back any of this
up?"

"He doesn't have to. I know he's telling me the truth."

She doesn't have to add anything about the instinct of a mother.

"But you thought he was telling you the truth the first time."

"He was. He was telling me the truth about Ivo the first time,
but he had wrapped it in a lie about himself. Now he's unwrapped
it. I can hear that in his voice. We both want to destroy those men
who destroyed my son. We want it for different reasons but we
both want the same thing. What do I care about his motives? His
reasons don't matter to me as long as he gets me the truth."

Our food is served. Fourteen years ago this was both a good
and a fashionable restaurant. Now it is neither. Dora takes one or
two bites, and puts her fork aside. If this lunch were about the food,
there would an explosion. But the food is only a pretext. She seems
almost relieved that she doesn't have to pay it any further attention.

I ask about the money, the guy's exorbitant demands. Not a
problem now. The detective will cover all costs himself, and at a
much lower figure than he originally proposed. He admits he was
trying to milk her with the first deal. In return, when he has proof
she can bring to Waldo, she's promised he'll be compensated for
anything he's shelled out, with a bonus. Waldo won't balk when
the truth becomes obvious. Her assurance about all this is impreg-
nable.

She summarizes the detective's theory. Not theory. For Dora
now this is Gospel.

Ivo was kidnapped on Friday. Something went wrong. The ex-
cop doesn't yet know what. The kidnappers wound up killing him.
Maybe Saturday night, maybe Sunday morning. The police knew

about the killing even before Waldo and Dora discovered the body. That's why they got to the villa so quickly. They were waiting for the call.

"What would have happened if you and Waldo hadn't gone up to the villa?"

She doesn't know. She didn't think to ask. But the police were prepared. Even the priest may be part of it, the ex-cop told her. It was an airtight box ready to lock down as soon as they could plausibly access Ivo's body.

"And he thinks he can prove this?"

The meal is over. Triumphantly, she gathers her things and stands.

"He's positive he can." Dora asks the proprietor to call her a cab.

Now comes the part she says that she really came here to say.

I should move to Rome. A good friend of hers has to go home to the States to care for an ailing parent. Her apartment close to Dora's will be empty starting next week. I can move in there and come back up to Fiesole for my classes. That's only two times a week, right? She's done her homework. If I want to, I can spend the first couple of days each week at Le Balze, the rest of the time in Rome with Dora and the investigation.

I start to explain about Maggie, the garden, her painting. Dora cuts me off.

"You will both be better off in Rome. We can protect you there. Here, you're completely vulnerable. I've told him about you. Nothing stays secret in Italy. It will get out that you are writing this up. If only for your wife's sake, you should come where we can shelter you. These are terrible men, vicious men. You know what they can do."

The cab has arrived. She pauses before she gets in.

"Believe me, John, once they know that you are part of this, they will stop at nothing. They will never let your write this book. Italy is a much more dangerous place than tourists ever realize."

She is gone.

I'm stunned.

Luckily, it's almost an hour's walk back to the villino. It's going to take me at least that long to work my mind around this completely unexpected, entirely bizarre proposition.

If I did decide to write her book, sure, I could commute, staying up here for the classes, seeing *gli studenti,* and then spending the rest of the time in Rome. Actually, there's something attractive about that split. Who wouldn't want to divide his time, rent free, between Florence and Rome? In a lot of different ways it's actually a fantastic opportunity, a kind of bonanza. If it's like Dora's, her friend's apartment is bound to be spacious and probably at least close to gorgeous. And what a chance for Maggie and me really to get to know Rome.

Fiesole is wonderful but it's probably already done for Maggie everything it can. Maybe the smart thing, then, is to see that Fiesole has provided just the first half of her recovery. For all its charm, it's narrow, it's familiar, it's repetitive. But Rome, Rome is the greatest city in Europe. It's got two millennia of history; you never come to the end of Rome. We certainly would never even be able to scratch the top of its A-list. This may be a once-in-a-lifetime thing.

But, really, isn't this crackpot, literally unthinkable? I've signed on at Le Balze for the semester. That semester is only a bit more than half over. We've got a life here. They now love Maggie at the Frutta. We have people coming to stay, people who are planning on a visit to Tuscany. I have responsibilities, a working routine.

And now there's at least the possibility of the book about Bessie and the bust. Something I would really like to do, while I am somewhere between repelled and terrified at the idea of immersing myself in Ivo's horrible death

On top of all this, I would be agreeing to write Dora's book, not mine, only Dora's book. Once we moved to Rome she would insist that Ivo's story is the one she wants told, whatever else I might discover. Do I really want to become Dora's amanuensis?

One thing's clear: I can't just decide yes or no on the basis of an hour's walk.

At Le Balze I find a very dejected Thaddeus. In Venice the *acqua alta,* threatened during our students' visit, finally has risen. The city is closed off. There was no train to Venice from Milan.

Sarah tries to make light of it. "We're living in a villa outside Florence. Is that something we should complain about?"

She has a point.

Remembering Mark Gillen

The failure of the Venice junket means that we have a full day to share with Thad and Sarah. He is over his disappointment and now refuses to allow the repeated frustrations of this week to matter. He is determined to show Sarah a wonderful time. The magic is back. Copying his strength of will, I decide to postpone all thoughts of Rome until after he and Sarah go home. On my own I couldn't manage this, but buoyed by his good cheer, much to my surprise, all my anxieties dissolve.

The four of us spend the day down in Florence where Thad not only scouts out a store that sells Halloween decorations—he insists we have to decorate the villino—but also a bakery that makes genuine doughnuts. Genuine with an Italian catch. They are available only once a day, at 4 in the afternoon, served and eaten hot. The Italians are plainly scandalized that we refuse forks. And soon we discover why. This chocolate glaze does not harden. Within minutes we are each a mass of delicious goop, oozing over skin and every other surface. It's heaven.

We cap the day with a grand farewell dinner at Fiesole's remarkable, too little known restaurant, 145 Piazza Mino, just as we did the night before Cecilia left, in what now seems our faraway first week. We are seated at the table, entirely alone in the dining room because it is seven o'clock at night and no Italian enters a restaurant before nine. The waiter who brought our wine has vanished to chat in the kitchen with his cronies, until work proper will start. Thad is taking the opportunity to explain how correctly to drink white wine.

He has decided, on the basis of a book he was given before he left Chicago, that he is now an oenophile in training. With white wine, he shows us, the glass is first tilted forward until the bottom of the wine appears a rich yellow while the top crescent against the curve is transparent above the white tablecloth.

The waiter suddenly materializes at his elbow. The tablecloth, he apologizes, had a pale pink thread in it. Who knew? It is indeed very pale. "*Piacere*," he murmurs, and with that apology slips a pristine white envelope onto the table below the glass so the Vernaccia can be inspected exactly so.

Thad is thrilled he has been doing it right, and the waiter is even more pleased to quietly show how it could be done better. Ah, the impeccable, incomparable savoir faire of Italians.

As I watch this exchange, I realize that none of this, not just tonight but these days together, could have happened had we not found, waiting here in 1987, Mark Gillen. If with the genius of Pygmalion we had tried to invent a role model for a sulking, lonely, esteem-compromised fourteen-year old, we would have still fallen short of the marvel that was, and pray God still is, Mark.

In 1987 Mark had just graduated from Duke where he had starred on their nationally ranked Lacrosse team. He embodied the old Study Abroad model, literally besotted with Italian art and life. The year before he had visited his older brother, a Georgetown student studying at Le Balze. Mark was hooked. To get his own year here he took the virtually non-paying, thankless job of Resident Assistant. He even broke his leg clambering over the villa wall when he arrived, because he had decided to come a week early, before anyone arrived to open the place for the semester.

Almost as soon as we arrived, Mark took one long hard look at Thad, said something like, "This one's mine," and spent the next four months expunging every lingering trace of adolescent misery. Of course, Mark made it clear, art was not only a privilege to study, it was a pleasure. Thad could soon discourse, knowingly, on the differences between Brunelleschi and Bramante. Of course, complex ideas mattered, and knowing things counted. Thad read Machiavelli, unprompted, and told us about it, equally unprompted. And of course jazz was to America what painting had been to Tuscany. So Thad tagged along to Toots Thielman's concert in Florence, and even learned to play the jazz harmonica Mark gave him as a gift.

Had Thad arrived sulky? Surly? Suspicious? You bet. As we boarded the plane for Italy he said, through bitterly clenched lips, "Just remember one thing: I'm not going into any museums."

Why not try, Mark suggested? So Thad developed curiosity, and then an edge. Irony, with all its joys, opened before him. And, of course, to carry off all the above without being a prig, you had to be in shape. So Thad ran with Mark, up the devastating Fiesole hills, Mark smacking his ankles with a switch whenever Thad fell behind.

For Thad life had never been more glorious.

Last Christmas, at lunch, the conversation turned to each person's most influential teacher. Thad without hesitating a tick said, as though of course, "Mark Gillen."

After dinner, walking slowly back down to Le Balze, recalling all the funny family stories involving this strenuously demanding slope, I begin to realize that, in our reminiscence of Mark Gillen, the evening has brought us full circle. Talking of our beginnings makes me see, and accept, that I am facing not an ending, a completion, a closure, but a crossroads. I have no idea which of the possible paths before me I should take but I am sure of one thing. The path ahead is going to depart radically from the path that brought me to this point.

Le Balze has done its work.

WEEK EIGHT
October 22-28

Archery

I get back from driving Thaddeus and Sarah to the airport just in time to open the door to our new houseguest Judy Throm, arriving from the train. For thirteen years Judy was our next door neighbor in Washington. She is the children's de facto grandparent, and by all criteria a member of the family. Thad is the first to admit that during his trying early teenage years he survived because he could duck silently into her house and shelter there until the storm of the moment passed over.

Though she is clearly wiped with jet lag, she is eager to get moving and see things. Trained as an Art Historian, in fact as a medievalist, she knows all about all the best stuff, but this is in fact her first visit to Italy. She will be with us for two weeks, and since there is so much she is eager to see it would be criminal to waste even one of her days. Luckily, being a proud daughter of Kansas, she also does not know the meaning of tired. And, quite selfishly, I need distraction. I'm already missing Thad, whom we won't see again until spring. How hard this American thing is, raising your children repeatedly to leave you.

We decide to drive down to Montalcino, another new place for us. It's a hill town about 30 miles southeast of Siena. Maggie read about an archery festival there today, where the men of Montalcino compete at the crossbow. Should be ideal for a medievalist.

It's quiet in the car during the long drive south. Judy's shut her eyes; Maggie's doing needlepoint. I ponder the curious way in which our time seems now to have two completely alternative vanishing points, the spot theorized by Renaissance painters at which all other lines converge. From one perspective everything points to death. Ivo and Dora. The stripped bare *Celle* instead of the church at Cortona. Bernabei's execution. The dark, murderous woods of the Casentino. The repeated rains, the rising floods. But from another standpoint everything emphatically insists on recovery and renewal. Maggie's increasing strength and ease. The now reliably successful teaching. The 222 and Volpaia. Montepulciano, indeed all of Thad and Sarah's visit. Which is the real one? Which is the one that matters?

Obsessing over this question, I almost miss the turn for Montalcino mistily capping the hill a few miles ahead of us. We encountered almost no traffic coming along the 2 from Siena. But now it seems almost everyone else in Tuscany this Sunday afternoon has also conceived a sudden passion for the crossbow. Cars are parked bumper to trunk at every possible, and some impossible, shoulder of the road, all debouching foot traffic heading up toward the town.

Reluctantly, I U-turn and go back a mile until I find a possible parking space, or what with a great deal of maneuvering, and several near slides into a threatening ditch, I turn into a possible parking space. We leave the car and start to trudge.

We have three miles to walk to the city gate, much of it vertical. The road ribbons sometimes toward, sometimes away from, Montalcino, but always steadily climbing higher. Sometimes steeply higher. We have no food. No water. And we are wearing the wrong shoes. But the landscape, even in mist, is riveting. Montalcino produces the most prized of Tuscan wines, the incomparable Brunello di Montalcino. And we are walking now through its birth space. Vines to the right and to the left, ahead, behind, at every angle, sometime dangling above perched on what seem impossible planes, and then unexpectedly the entire hillside sheers off and we see chutes of vine, miles of them, checker boarding below. The grape harvest is long over. Only the bronzed vine leaves remain. Happily, I dismiss all thoughts of Ivo to do what the poet Gerard Manley Hopkins would call hurrahing in harvest.

Until we get to Montalcino.

Want to know what Montalcino's like? Start by imagining enchanting Montepulciano. Then subtract everything from Montepulciano that is beautiful, interesting, welcoming, warm, rich, complex, or important. When you're rid of all those qualities, then you say: *Ah, look, we're in Montalcino.* Nothing up here turned out to be worth the tough climb. Not the squares. Not the buildings. Certainly not the costumed citizenry. It's so blandly empty of interest, it could easily pass for someplace in the Australian outback, if men in the outback wore pink tights and purple plumes.

As to the archery, who knows? It took place inside a gigantic fortress at the top of the rock. I got no further than the entry. I've been to plenty of homecoming tailgates. I didn't need to inspect the Italian version.

I go back for the car by myself. My companions are spent, even the impossible to tire Judy. I trudge the three miles. Happily, it's a hell of a lot easier going down. Forty minutes later I'm back. Plenty of parking now available next to the town gates. Apparently, others also have found Montalcino a bust.

And so wearily we head back toward Fiesole, and it would feel as though we had cheated poor Judy except that we decide to drive home through the nearby area called the Crete, which we've never seen before. We thought we had fully explored Tuscany when we here fourteen years ago. But this time round I am beginning to realize that we saw only a small part of it then, the part that rims Florence. San Gimignano, Lucca, Pisa, Arezzo. All lovely but Tuscany is actually much larger, much richer and much more various than the northern quadrant. In fact the north is entirely different from this hauntingly beautiful southeast.

Le Crete is the territory below Siena that is bounded roughly by the 322 and the 326. When the angels, after announcing Christmas to the shepherds, said *time to head home,* by home they must have meant the Crete. The Val di Chianti, compared to the glories of the Crete, now seems merely an appetizer. Rosalind to Juliet. It's lunar if the moon's mountains were made from sand-shaded velvet. Why didn't we discover these splendors in September? Why couldn't I, one Saturday or Sunday, have just pushed on past Siena during a casual weekend drive? Alas, I didn't, and now I feel hard-pressed. We don't have much time left before October turns into November, before the light goes and the weather changes. We've got to make the most of the time we have left, to explore as many as possible of the nooks and crannies of this new space. And who can tell what there might be besides the Crete still to discover?

Interpellations

This may be our last class in the ilex grove. Though it is still warm enough to sit outside, I suspect the light may start to fade before we are quite through the session. And when we resume class after the Fall Break, and Daylight Saving ends, it will be too dark even to begin out here.

I've decided to use June's ort. Though she's one of the quietest of all these quiet women, she's also got one of the two or three most acute minds in the entire group. She asks about Shylock's forced conversion. *Does the play intend its Christian audience to endorse the conversion to Christianity that literally makes Shylock sick to death?*

I remind *gli studenti* that *Merchant* marks a big swerve in the Italian scripts. In the work we've read so far an English audience watches Italians in action. In *Merchant* there are, of course, still Italians, but now there is also Shylock, the Jew. And not just Shylock. There are also his daughter, Jessica, and his friend, Tubal. Shakespeare begins here to represent Italy as an intermingled world, indeed a world that becomes, through the marriage of Christian Lorenzo and Jewish Jessica, not only mixed but mongrel.

And, remember, I urge, there were no openly practicing Jews in Elizabethan England. Certainly no English Jews. The Jews had been violently exiled from England by Edward I in 1290, three hundred years before Shakespeare's play. Nothing could be more exotic, then, for the English audience than the fact that in Venice that radically *Other* figure, the Jew, lives nearby and does business practically next door. Not only does he live next door, he now has real power over your life, and the lives of those you love. You need him to finance your marriage. His daughter can run off and marry your son. He can bring you to court. He can ruin you. He can take your life. In an England where even small differences within the Christian cult can condemn you to the stake or the block, this mongrelizing makes Italy not only different, but strange and even terrifying.

"How relevant is any of this *background* stuff," insists the skeptical Duke, "the point is: who are we supposed to side with here?"

June backs him up. True to her *ort*, she insists that whatever the background, inside a theater we have to feel horror and pity as we watch the badgered, stunned Shylock implode under the Christians' merciless *mercy*.

"And yet a couple of minutes before," Jacqueline adds, "that's exactly what we felt for Antonio when we saw him bare his chest to Shylock's knife."

Duke again: "Exactly my point: who does Shakespeare want us to side with here?"

And then unexpectedly Rotgut, bitterly, from the edge of the group, speaks the first words he's offered in weeks. "According to you" [*that is: me*], this guy," [*that is: Shakespeare*], "this guy doesn't believe in anything. No wonder we can't decide who he want us to side with."

He's rigid with contempt, for Shakespeare, for me, for the course.

This time I decide I *will* try to be Jim Kincaid.

"Well, who's to say Shakespeare isn't anti-Semitic. He was shaped by a profoundly anti-Semitic culture. Why should we expect him to have escaped its toxins? In other courses you've taken have you come across the term *interpellation*?"

Miss Haag has. She defines it as a process that gets you to become a functioning member of a group or larger society, so that you make your own the community's values, its ways of expressing value.

Rotgut sneers. "So it's a fancy term for brainwashing?"

All I know about brainwashing, I reply, is what I saw in *The Manchurian Candidate*. Laurence Harvey, the victim, was made robotic by his nasty mother, Angela Lansbury, turned into a killing machine without self-awareness. If that's brainwashing, interpellation is its reverse. It's brain-writing. It encodes all the systems, protocols, programs that an individual would need to thrive in a specific social setting. Interpellation is amoral and ubiquitous. All societies, and sub-societies, depend on it for their continuity. It's a version of learning the rules of the game, learning them so well, you never question them but you also know immediately what to do next. Without interpellation we'd all always be returning to Go. Or winding up in jail without a get out free card.

His interpellation—bourgeois, patriotic, ethical—is what had to be washed out of poor Laurence Harvey's brain so that he could carry out the assassination plot.

So let's work from the realistic possibility that Shakespeare too was interpellated into his society's basic values: that regicide was the worst of crimes, that aristocracy was the natural order, and that Christianity was the only path to salvation.

Beluga will have none of it.

"You've spent almost two months re-constructing Shakespeare's theatre as—these are your terms—a *supplemental site of contestation*. In play after play you asked us to see how he dissects and subverts his society's normative claims for order. All of it. Gender. Rank. Morality. Now you want us to jettison that? You're reversing everything we've done? Now you want us to see his theater as some kind of machine for this process you're calling interpellation These plays don't question the reigning order, they actually re-enforce it.? I don't buy it."

"But you think the process is there? Shakespeare aside for the moment, can you accept the notion that all societies interpellate?"

"Of course, they do," Ripley Snell thrusts in, "it's cheaper than relying on an army."

I ask him to explain. He offers in response a paraphrase of the French historian Michel Foucault, a crude paraphrase but none the less reliable. Interpellation means a society doesn't have to rely on force. Force is always expensive. It's risky. And dangerous. As the last Tsar learned, your army can always turn against you. So rather than rigorously policing all behavior, it's more efficient to frame the behavior you desire with conspicuous instances of outsider behavior, instances that are routinely scorned, degraded, deprived and punished. Seeing the drastic consequences that befall someone who has refused interpellation, the majority, in effect, police themselves. They assume without apparent coercion the norms society requires to function.

I can feel a stirring in the grove. I can't tell but I think they are coming on board.

"Which brings us back to Shylock, right?"

An outsider is interpellation's key product. Don't we see this everywhere we look? All communities, large and small, station at their boundaries degraded instances of non-assimilation. I ask them to look at the society they know best: high school. Didn't it depend, literally, on creating outsiders, the *strange*, the *weird*, the *oddball?* And the same thing they will find true for adult communities. They are defined by the figures that exclude. Those outsiders can be actual human beings, housed in the ghetto or the slum, shunned, criminalized, made objects of fear. Or they can be their virtual representations in the stories we exchange and consume. Hollywood depends on this structure as a staple: *Jaws, Alien* and their ilk. You can rank these outsiders on a scale, from the relatively harmless, the *goof off*, to the higher stakes categories, *faggot,* to the highest, the ones we call *heretic* and *traitor*, all the way up to the most extravagant form, the *monster.*

One thing does seem to be true for all: as societies experience crises, their need to mark out and punish outsiders escalates. Confident, stable and prosperous societies tend to be relatively, though never entirely, tolerant. But societies in crisis need to define and punish not simply individual oddities but an entire monster class, those who by definition can never be interpellated.

Ah, see the monster; watch him grovel!

And isn't that what we are seeing in Shylock, and the ugly anti-Semitic stereotypes that background him? Be wary, Londoners, don't go Italian, don't mix, don't be tempted to mongrelize, don't let down your guard. You see what you could be raising in your midst.

The dark has come on, and it is past time for us to leave the grove but *gli studenti* are curiously slow to move indoors. Something in this discussion has troubled them. These past weeks usually they rush off, to get up to Via Vai, the travel agent, before it closes, to arrange next weekend's trip, or to resume emailing with their extensive network of friends abroad. But this time they hang around, as though waiting for an epilogue, a further moment of clarification, which will frame things, set them in context, set them to rest.

I know I am expected to add something. I just don't know what it is. And I've alreayd said much than I planned to, or wanted to.

But as I start back to the villino, Willy Voltaire takes me aside, and lets me in on what I just missed. Smart, sane, temperate, he's someone I always listen to carefully. And he quickly makes me see where and how I mistook what just went on in class.

I thought *gli studenti* were disturbed by the interconnection of interpellation and Shylock. But it turns out their unease sprang from a much more immediate source. Did I time this introduction to interpellation deliberately, Willy asks, as a way of talking to the class about Rotgut? And if so, what is it that I want them to do?

Of course I did nothing of the kind.

But this afternoon, as we discussed monstrosity, I could see the exchange of glances begin, the eyebrows raised. I even saw that

Rotgut, who always stations his chair as far to the rim as possible, started at one point slowly to undo the braid of his thick, shoulder-length black hair, running his fingers up and down it against the fading light, accepting, advertising his status as cynosure. I saw that he was reading himself into Shylock. What I didn't get was that the entire class was doing the same thing, wondering whether this had become a class about itself.

And that's what Willy now insists I clarify before he goes back inside. If I can explain to him what I intended, then he volunteers to explain it to the others, and defuse the discomfort now clouding the place.

I assure him say that I was not thinking of Rotgut when I was teaching, though of course I can see how the identification applies. But I would want Willy and the others to consider whether any group can work and live together for any length of time without interpellating someone as its outsider? It could just as easily have been me, I suggest. With my strange, theoretical language, and my insistence on reading these scripts against the class's expectations, I could by this point have become the scorned and spurned one. Except that Rotgut so swiftly, and with such relish, seized the role at the crucial moment when Muldoon disappeared.

Shaking his head, Willy wanders back into the house. He still thinks I did it on purpose.

Rotgut's crisis
Here's what I didn't know when I was teaching yesterday. What was behind Willy's anxious questions.

Gli studenti were in Orvieto this past weekend, staying with Italian families. Orvieto is a hill town close to Rome, a former papal city tightly enclosing a Duomo with remarkable frescoes by Luca Signorelli of the dead rising for the Last Judgment. It also produces a much admired white wine. The town is small and the community close, which means that *gli stude*nti have at least one chance to experience ordinary Italian life. From all reports, they adored it, except Rotgut. He returned denouncing the household in which he was quartered.

His anger spilled over yesterday into his Italian class, the class that meets just before mine. They were using the Orvieto visit for conversation practice. Suddenly, enraged, Rotgut hurled a pencil across the room, and began tearing pages out of a book, as he excoriated everything about the home stay. The gentle and very kind Italian teacher was unnerved, and then, when she could not get him to stop, frightened.

So now the entire faculty is asked to meet in the *salone* of the villa to discuss what action to take. Maggie urges me to beg off. It's my birthday. She and Judy have planned a festive evening.

If something practical could emerge from this meeting, she'd agree to my going. All along her line has been that if this place were run by professionals we would have squelched the Rotgut crisis before it got to be anywhere near this serious. But now she is convinced that anything the Villa decides will be mummery. I know she's right, but I just don't know how to get out of this meeting.

All the faculty and administrators gather in the salone. There are wine and antipasti. I get to meet a few people I haven't seen yet because their teaching schedules are the reverse of mine. It could not be more civilized. We spend an inordinately long time on the social stuff. Clearly no one wants to strike the first blow. Finally, Marcello gathers us into a single group and reluctantly raises the reason we're there.

Everyone who teaches Rotgut speaks with respect and even some affection about his undoubted enthusiasm for learning, his sincerity, and his curiosity. There's general consensus that he is the most committed student in the program and that, were the classroom all, we could manage to see him through the semester. I don't agree with some of the praise but sensing my minority status I say nothing to the contrary. I don't have to. Those who oversee Villa life say the other students are now so frightened they want to present a petition, signed by them all, asking for his immediate removal. The administrators have prudently forestalled the petition. But they know, and insist, that we have to act now and decisively before the entire program begins to unravel.

I make a plea for a competent psychiatric analysis, one that will make it clear to his family, and even if possible to himself, that we are acting in his behalf. I am told that there is in Florence a consulting psychiatrist that all the American programs use, and that she will certainly be contacted.

But that is not anywhere near the conclusion.

Instead there follows a lengthy discussion and in that discussion you see the best and the worst of Italian ways. The best is the genuine kindness. Prodigal sons are sons nonetheless, perhaps even more to be cherished because they are needy. Back at Georgetown we would be talking about how to effect the severance. Here they talk for well over an hour about how to avoid it, seeking some kind of modified response that might permit him to remain. How can they, they ask repeatedly, conclude this in a way that manages to please everybody? This is, after all, Italy.

Here's the worst: when all of these attempts to save him fail and we concur, reluctantly but unanimously, that he must go, whatever the psychiatrist might say, there is no sense of due process. No awareness that he has rights here. That there are ways in which schools usually make such choices so that the least damage is done, especially to the student. That he may very well be in danger of a breakdown with long-lasting consequences. It's simply to be left up to Marcello as director to carry out his exclusion when and how he chooses.

I think of Stefano: everything forbidden, everything permitted. Italy is the same everywhere, at every level. Permissions required, rules restricting every option. You never even enter a room without first murmuring *con permesso?* — may I?, with your permission. But at every turn, you also encounter mere caprice and altogether arbitrary application.

Marcello leaves the meeting looking like Abraham bullied into exiling Ishmael. He is incapable of inflicting pain. How can he, then, be the one who banishes into arid, solitary exile, this sad young man who came so intensely ready to fall in love with Italy?

Returning to the villino—and what may remain of my postponed birthday celebration—I wonder what would happen if I were to bring into class tomorrow a transcript of the meeting that just ended? (I can't; no one took notes.) And what if then I asked *gli studenti* to compare what we've just said and done here to *Merchant*, Act Four, the great trial scene? What would they see; what would they say? They'd certainly spot differences, many and significant differences, in how the two *monsters* get treated. But would they also see the common thread: not just the forced exclusion of someone no longer tolerable but the force in both situations of what in Italy Portia means by mercy?

Italy prizes mercy because it can't provide fair play. Fair play assumes everyone is or should be treated as equal. But equality is anathema in a world where each individual insists on being treated as unique. A world routinely arbitrary and capricious, fiercely resistant to any sort of organization, since organization demands system and system in turn requires self-suppression. Italians prefer to live scoff-law, moment-by-moment lives that ride regularly, unsteadily, the rim of chaos. They are often brave but rarely disciplined; hence the serio-comic history of their military adventures. Most of them are charming—or can be; but few tell the truth. Where's the individuality, the style in truth? Anyone can tell the truth. All Italians are instinctively generous, but they are rarely just. They mock law but feed on revenge, willing to pay with constant corruption for the privilege of undiminished self-assertion. They love beauty in all its forms, but the only two things Italians truly respect are cunning and force: physical force, force of personality, the force that comes from family or connections that stand up for family. And the cunning that—arbitrary, unpredictable—Portia, guying law, calls mercy.

How remarkably well Shakespeare read his Italian sources. He may have missed out on the *terrible* Italian mother, but on most everything else he gets Italy dead to rights: ad-hoc and atomized, unsupported by morality, unconstrained by law, narcissistic, erratic, lethal. And now I also see, framed from Rotgut to Shylock, how it's precisely these same concerns that shape the movies I love best, Italian films of the 50s and 60s, from the sublimely homicidal comedy, Germi's *Divorce Italian Style*, to the epic of imploding family in Visconti's *Rocco and His Brothers*, to the master film of high modern anomie Fellini's *8 ½*.

And I think I also finally get just why Dora is so insistent that I write about Ivo. There's no justice to be found for his killing, but a book, a book could be a kind of mercy.

Our Belmont
We finish the last of our four meetings on *Merchant of Venice* up in the Loggia. To prepare for it I assigned at the end of the last class a tricky passage for everyone to tackle as ort.

It's the opening sequence of Act V. The play's young lovers, Jessica and Lorenzo, newlywed, have fled to Portia's Belmont where they await her and Bassanio's return from the trial. While they wait they playfully—or not—taunt each other with a famous exchange of Classical allusions: "In such a night/ Troilus methinks mounted the Trojan walls/ And sighed his soul toward the Grecian tents/ Where Cressid lay that night" (3-6). "In such a night/ Stood Dido with a willow in her hand/ Upon the wild sea banks, and waft her love/ To come again to Carthage" (9-12). And so on it goes until they finish with themselves: "In such a night/ Did Jessica steal from the wealthy Jew/ And with an unthrift love did run from Venice/ As far as Belmont.... In such a night/ Did young Lorenzo swear he loved her well,/ Stealing her soul with many vows of faith/ And ne'er a true one" (14-20).

I've asked *gli studenti* to work out as many different ways of playing this scene as they can.

Clyde and Judy start off. They do two people rapturously in love who hardly know what they are saying.

Then they do cool and contemporary, playing at having a fight, verbal fore-play before foreplay.

Then they do Lorenzo in high spirits but Jessica melancholy, because she is beginning to understand that in his world she will always be the Jewess, the pretty Infidel as she is called.

Then they do mutual disenchantment, the wild spending spree over, each beginning to discover the not so welcome consequences of their madcap plunge.

They make an attractive couple. Clyde, lanky, coltish, at 21 still suggesting the high school basketball star he probably was. Judy, blond, blue-eyed, pretty and petite, saved from mere conventionality by her surprisingly edgy self-awareness. Clyde is quite the best actor in this group and he seems to strike something in Judy to match his more practiced ease. She makes her angry, cold Jessica particularly plausible. Who or what is she in fact remembering? The others respond enthusiastically to every interpretation they produce. Some prefer one reading, others prefer another. Clearly, we've found no best or even better way to do it. Just as I'd hoped. They see that now: there are good readings, and very good readings, but no one reading.

By the time we have played and weighed all these different ways of doing the scene, the light on the loggia has begun to go. We have to hurry before we lose both light and time. And this is also the final class before Fall Break. The interval will be too long to reconnect to this moment when we get back.

So I return them to the ort from the last class, to Shylock's forced conversion. I ask them this time to look at the speech in which Shylock justifies himself to the Venetian court. Oddly, it's not much cited when people talk about the play. Every Miss America candidate can—and showing no mercy does—perform Portia's "quality of mercy" aria. And even people who don't know the play know Shylock's unanswerable great appeal, "Doth not a Jew bleed?" But this other fourth-act speech, perhaps because it is more rational than emotional, tends to be overlooked. And yet, I think, it may be the key speech of the entire sequence.

> What judgment shall I dread, doing no wrong?
> You have among you many a purchased slave,
> Which, like your asses and your dogs and mules,
> You use in abject and in slavish parts,
> Because you bought them. Shall I say to you,
> "Let them be free, marry them to your heirs!
> Why sweat they under burdens? Let their beds
> Be made as soft as yours, and let their palates
> Be seasoned with such viands"? You will answer
> "The slaves are ours." So do I answer you:
> The pound of flesh is mine, which I demand of him
> Is dearly bought, and I will have it.
> If you deny me, fie upon your law!
> There is no force in the decrees of Venice.
> I stand for judgment. Answer: shall I have it? (IV:1, 89-103)

And what answer does he get?
None.
And in that none official Venice concedes that he's got them. It's one of those utterly silent moments on stage of which Shakespeare is the great master, when the silence speaks more powerfully than even the most memorable lines. The Doge can only then answer

briefly: that he will dismiss the court now, unless someone else, some outsider not yet heard, can come up with a way to respond. Which brings on Portia in disguise.

My question to *gli studenti* is: what does Shylock claim in this speech, what do the Venetians hear in this speech, that so completely silences their hitherto clamorous opposition?

Like Shylock I also get only long silence. I'm not surprised. Readers may feel sorry for Shylock but they rarely take him seriously as a thinker, despite the fact that he is clearly the only truly intelligent *man* in the play. (The women are, of course, all crackerjacks. This is Shakespeare.) *Gli studenti* have to go back and read, really read, read hard, that speech over which they've previously glided. After they've reread it, I make my question simpler. Not why does he win, just what is his claim?

Duke: "Is he saying the Venetians keep slaves?"

Yes.

Beluga: "So then he's claiming there's no difference between what he's doing and what they're doing, the Venetians. Both buy human beings."

Why is there no difference?

Ripley Snell: "He says: 'You guys, the Venetians, *use* the slaves, who are human beings, the way you want, because you *bought* them. I *bought* Antonio, so I can *use* him any way I want. Just like you.'"

Faustina: "That's what he means about *judgment*. I'm doing nothing wrong under your laws, because I'm doing just what your laws allow you to do."

Judy: "I don't know what "fie" means."

In the context what do you think it must mean?

June: "It's dismissive. It's like Mercutio saying: 'A plague on both your houses.' Your laws make no sense, he's saying, if they allow you to do one thing, but they don't allow me to do the same thing. What kind of law, or 'judgment,' is that?"

Willy Voltaire: "This may be way off the mark but this kind of reminds me of Mary Shelley's *Frankenstein*. I had to read it in a "Romantics" course." (God forbid a student would ever admit in front of other students that he or she has actually read a significant book on his own, for pleasure. In class discussions, whatever they've read, generational protocols require they insist they read only because it was required by a teacher.) "Victor Frankenstein creates this monster, and then he repudiates him. But the monster keeps saying stuff like 'I'm yours. You made me. How can you repudiate me? You have to recognize me as your creation.' That's what Shylock is saying. I'm not your reverse. I'm not your opposite. I'm only your reflection."

Is Shylock right? It's an argument the Venetians can't deny, but does the play corroborate it anyway? After all, we don't see any slaves, do we?

Jacqueline: "But we see that the Christians are really hateful."

Duke: "Like, absolutely. I feel, like, totally no respect for any Venetian."

Jacqueline: "They abuse Shylock, all the time. And they boast about it. They do treat people like animals, just like he says they do."

Miss Haag: "And it's a world that's all about buying and selling. Everything. It's all merchants, and exchange, and money."

Beluga: "Our whole discussion last week, about Portia being the Golden Fleece to carry off. It's the same thing, making people into commodities."

Clyde: "And that's what Shylock says from the start of the play, every chance he gets: you taught me everything I do."

And isn't that why, I chime in, it seems such a mistake, no matter how well intentioned, to play Shylock as "good," or even merely as a victim. We have to see that Shylock does behave inhumanly. That his revenge makes us shudder. But that behavior, that revenge, they are the script's brilliant way of showing us the much worse, and inexcusable villainy, of his masters, his persecutors, his world.

Now I can see, even before he says it, what Willy Voltaire, still thinking about Rotgut, needs to say next. And, good for him, he does.

Willy: "So the play is really about interpellation, then, isn't it, even though they didn't have the word."

Faustina: "Couldn't we just call it scapegoating? Isn't that really the same?"

Willy: "Whatever we call it, the play is really turning the whole process inside out. You have a group, or a community."

Duke: "Whatever."

Willy: "And the group says this outsider is monstrous because the monster reverses everything we believe in. But what the play shows is that the society is really forcing the outsider to embody, or maybe just represent, its worst fears about itself, the self-knowledge it can't stand to contemplate."

So, I ask, have you just answered your earlier question about why the Venetians compel Shylock to become a Christian?

Ardita, who has almost never before spoken in class, begins to puzzle it through. "He says I'm just like you. And he makes them admit that. At least concede that because they don't answer him back. So they have to turn that around. They have to make him just like themselves, as they see themselves, not as he makes them see themselves. By making him into a Christian they make him into the self-image they prefer, not the image of themselves they can't stand to admit."

Why not just kill him?

Duke: "Alive or dead, the guy's an unanswerable witness against them. But converting him, it's like so cool, because it's just like putting him in a witness protection program. They make the guy disappear."

They like where they've arrived. They're proud of themselves and they should be. They are like a team at the end of a rally. They've just pressed hard down the court and now they've scored. Of course, they like what they've done.

Should we try one more thing? Is this the moment to stop, or can I push them still a little further? When we started it was bright, then rosy. Now the light is pale pink and fading fast to gray. A cold wind, it's too strong to be called a breeze, has come up. Sweaters and jackets, discarded when we started class, have long since been taken up and pulled tightly around shoulders and across chests. What if they are too tired to keep up at this level, and we end on a low? I don't want to go into the long break on a low note. They deserve to glow.

But my confidence in them is now as high as their confidence in themselves. I decide to throw out another, the final ball. There is something about the cold up here right now that also makes us and the world seem clear.

So what does all this say about Shakespeare and Italy? Is Venice con-

sonant with the Italy of the earlier plays, another Padua or Verona? Or has something changed?

Betty: "I think Italy has been, like, getting darker all the time, play by play. It was, like, dangerous, almost from the start. Especially for women. Julia gets raped in the woods, and that's, like, in a light comedy. Kate gets trapped and starved and pretty much generally abused. Juliet dies. Hero almost dies. But now it's dangerous for men too because—is this right?—because, like, there are no good guys anywhere."

Judy: "No good smart guys."

Faustina: "No good smart guys with power."

Beluga: "I think what we've got here is what I think is called a cautionary tale. You've been saying from the beginning of the course"—you is me—"that for the English Italy was—how did you say it?"

A Chorus: *The alternative modernity.*

Beluga: "Right. By which I understand you to mean it was the way England could go if it became fully a part of the new, expanding mercantile order."

The first global order. In fact, Venice was on its way down at the end of the sixteenth century, but Shakespeare could not have known that.

Beluga: "Exactly. So I think with all this much ado about money he's showing his English audience, in this Venice he pretty much invents, what happens when you really and fully become a global marketplace."

Clyde: "Where your daughters and your ducats become interchangeable."

Beluga: "You solve the puzzle of the three boxes and you get the greatest heiress of the age. Everything's up for grabs."

Jacqueline: "Everything, including human flesh, can be bought and sold."

Ripley Snell: "Which means that today's Merchant of Venice could be next year's Merchant of London. Could be. So think about it, think hard about it all on your way home from the theater."

Benny: "And do otherwise."

"But remember," I say, and now I know that we were right to push forward but I also know this is it, we have come to the end, "remember Belmont."

Shylock, the Doge and the Senators, they can't ever leave Venice. But the other Italian characters do have an alternative to Venice. They have Portia's villa at Belmont. Where your whole business is keeping valuable things safe, like Portia's and Nerissa's rings, like marriage vows, and honor. And, though this may seem too big a stretch, I suggest they think of Belmont as a name for, as a way of thinking about, Shakespeare's own theater.

Shakespeare's theater is the beauty-seeking, high place from which one can look down and across at the troubled town or the troubling future. A place of music and performance, of role playing, of game playing, of disguise, a place where girls play boys, and boys play girls, patronized and protected by a brilliant and witty Grande Dame, who takes on a man's role easily. We can claim then something like: Belmont is to Venice as Shakespeare's theatre is to London, the preposterous supplement that offers both an anatomy of, and an alternative to, the gruesome life lived on the other side of the waters. From which his audiences can think across the waters to Venice, forewarned. And from which they can return across the Thames water to London, chastened.

But then there is also us. High up in our Fiesolan villa, looking over at the silvered Villa Medici, and down at Firenze in twilight, exactly where Galileo set up his telescope to view the moon, we are as close to being in Belmont as anyone since the Renaissance has been or ever will be. Le Balze: exquisite, enclosed, protected, privileged. Our own alternative to the vaunted and *second* global order. Because on such a night as this we too have withdrawn, so many Portias and Bassanios, Lorenzos and Jessicas, to play a while with words and thought, to weigh the world and its consequences, to dally and to determine what we can, or should, or must not, bring back across the waters.

That's it. Time's up. We close. Cheered.

Alone now in the Loggia, the pinnacle of our exquisite Belmont, I can see at last the answer to the question I asked *gli studenti* at the start of the term: does it matter that we are reading "the Italian plays" while we are living in Italy?

Yes, it does matter, because Italy itself and all these places, Venice, Milan, and the rest, are now real for *gli studenti* in a way they could not be if we were reading the plays in Georgetown. The settings are not just that—settings. They represent a world we know and which, to some extent, we share. And because we share this space, *gli studenti* now grasp a fundamental truth about all literature: how much in every story place, the exact place, matters. This particular world is not any world, or every world, it is, richly, densely, importantly, only *this* world.

Mercy

Kyra returns. She found on Ryan Air, the Irish airline, a roundtrip airfare, London-Pisa, Pisa-London, for only five pounds. It cost her more to take the quick train from Pisa Airport to Florence, little less than an hour, than it did to fly back and forth between Italy and England. Such are the wonders of the new Europe. We spend the day in Volterra, which we passed through on our first day here. It's just two months but it seems a very long time ago.

While we are gone, Marcello has his talk with Rotgut. It turns out not as planned but as Maggie predicted. Though this was the verdict of our meeting, Marcello did not tell Rotgut he had to go home. Instead Marcello told him that if there were any other outbursts, of any kind, in any part of the program, no matter what might constitute the provocation, he would be flown home on the first possible plane, with no chance of appeal.

This is, after all, Italy.

In 1958 my favorite modern poet, W. H. Auden, wrote a remarkable poem about Italy; actually, he wrote several remarkable poems about Italy where he lived on and off for about ten years. This one, which he wrote as he was leaving Italy to live in Austria, he called "Good-Bye to the Mezzogiorno." *Mezzogiorno* is the Italian word not only for midday but also for the south of Italy, the boot below Rome. It is the best single piece of writing in English that I know about the differences between Italy and—well, every place else, at least every place else in northern Europe or, by extension, in places like the USA shaped by northern Europe.

Among those differences Auden distinguishes between northerners who "mean by life a /*Bildungsroman*," a life-long process of education, and Italians (southerners) "to whom living/ Means-to-be-visible now." Between them Auden insists "there yawns a gulf/ Embraces cannot bridge."

Across that yawning gulf I observe my friend Marcello. I think we have to help Rotgut learn from this experience. He thinks we have to help Rotgut, and Le Balze, save face. And I now know that, however much Marcello and I like and admire each other, we will never agree on Rotgut, or indeed on much else.

Worsening Conditions

The torrential rains have returned. But we are in fact much better off than the North. In Piedmont and Lombardy the extensive flooding that started when Thad and Sarah went to Como and (almost) Venice has now brought mudslides and death. The papers are calling these the worst floods since 1994, perhaps since 1987. In Turin it got so bad that Fiat had to shut down its factory. The entire city became inaccessible even from the air. Twelve people have died so far, another fifteen are missing, with as many as 7500 homeless. Worse may still come at the junction of the rivers Po and Ticino south of Milan. The damage is blamed on pervasive soil mismanagement, illegal building, and illegal industrial activity along the river banks.

Rome

Dora calls. She sees her detective almost daily. All of those hunches he's been able to verify. But he's also discovered other details that are truly shocking. Now he's putting together a dossier of evidence. Cip is back on Dora's side, against his father. They are both convinced that Waldo will have to relent. She sets a time and place for us to meet next week when Maggie and I are in Rome. She asks when we are going to move into her friend's apartment. I say we have to see the apartment first, we have to see if Maggie will like it.

I save face; perhaps my difference from Marcello is not that *yawning*.

Assisi

Seeing Assisi is one of the dreams of Judy's life. But usually gentle Maggie turns grinch at even the name Assisi. The last time we went was Good Friday, 1987. The three-hour drive down to Umbria was not so bad. And then we got there. Easter-tourist Assisi was repellent: sublime architecture debased, street after street, with cheap eateries and tawdry souvenir shops—not quite but almost "Authentic Stigmatas Tattooed While You Wait." On that Good Friday, swollen with pilgrims outshouting each other's rival rosaries, it was appalling. Nevertheless, once we'd adjusted to the spectacle, the four of us plus two of that year's students, Magoo and Kip, we all agreed that the few great things of Assisi, mostly by Giotto, redeeemd the ambient vulgarity and excess, even in these conditions. We had a terrific picnic up on the *rocca*, Assisi's high and empty, rock-strewn acropolis with its staggering views of the Umbrian plain. But we found nobody wanted to go back down into the town after the intervallo.

Maggie prudently suggested we should start right back to Fiesole, since we'd face the burgeoning Easter weekend traffic. What had taken three hours coming down would probably take more like five going back. But I insisted, buoyed with false confidence, that instead of going directly back to Florence, we detour by way of Gubbio. (The kind of thing that got me my title of Nazi Tourist.) Gubbio, a small walled town about forty miles northeast of Assisi, is where St. Francis famously removed the thorn from the paw of the murderous wolf. An additional hour and a half drive. Two hours tops. We were already inside Umbria. Why not take advantage of it, and sweeten what was left of Assisi's sourness?

Cecilia, Thaddeus and I actually remember that drive quite fondly (Maggie was doing the driving), because we kept spotting tantalizing posters for a circus called *Moira Degli Elefanti*, Moira of the Elephants, with a close up of Moira in boot-black hair, dazzling spangles, and sizzling cleavage, backed by more trumpeting elephants than Hannibal ever dreamed of. (The first thing my son asked when he arrived this time was "Seen any signs of Moira?") We kept hoping we'd come upon the circus en route. We never dared think we could actually see the elephants in performance, let alone Moira. But just to see the parade passing by would have been enough. Maggie thought it was all, I think I recall her word precisely, dumb.

Gubbio turned out to be well worth the visit, Assisi sans-tourists, Assisi as it might have been when Sts. Francis and Clare were kids. A medieval town tall as it is wide, breath-stoppingly vertical, with stoney streets blocking every turn at angles that can be only slightly less than ninety degrees. And so crowded in on itself that nothing new can have been built there since the late thirteenth century. That particular Good Friday the sun was setting blood orange. The *Gubbisti* moved noiselessly up and down the darkening alleyways in black robes and black, pointy, Spanish Inquisitor hoods, with only slits for eyes. Bonfires burned at every crossing. Something was clearly planned for later on, something you were dying to get to see, but you might have to die in order to see it. It could have been Good Friday 1229.

We set off home all jolly again, until we realized that we were now at sunset a good half day's drive southeast of Florence. Silently, frown incised, Maggie pointed the car northwest, and refused all further chat. "Just tell me what the map says." Which I did. But I misdirected her terribly. To this day she insists I did it on purpose. On to more and more degraded roads we drove, no sign of life anywhere, until cutting across a pathless meadow, which I insisted was marked on the map as a major highway, we just managed, alerted by Cecilia screaming, not to plunge into a canal, mysteriously and without a hint of warning, yawning before us. We did get home, in the early hours of Easter Saturday. But it took the full force of Easter's renewal to get us all behaving just civilly to one another.

So on this trip back to Assisi with Judy and Kyra, Maggie is once again silent. Remembering. Ominous. Except when she takes delight in pointing to the pale mist that becomes thick fog as we cross between the tunnels that separate Tuscany from Umbria. "We won't be able to see anything," she says, "if it keeps up like this."

She doesn't add: And I'm glad. She doesn't have to.

Assisi, up under its *rocca*, is, indeed, invisible. We take what we think are roads but find they are merely driveways. There's lots of backing out followed by sudden swerving to avoid barreling tour-buses going the other way—away from Assisi, where, obviously, no one wants to linger.

After a very long and silent search we find we are beginning to climb, though what we are climbing, and where it's taking us, we have no idea. It's more like flying than driving, cloud banks pressing every window. Unexpectedly, what may indeed be a turn off suddenly looms. We skid into it, and then keep on climbing, suddenly discovering ourselves in—of all things—a parking lot. The fog has entirely disappeared. Everywhere around us the October light is glorious. Our spirits lift. Kyra is relieved, Judy is thrilled. Maggie becomes glad because they are glad.

But when I reach for my wallet, so that I can pay for the toilet I now desperately need, I discover that my Visa card is gone. Deliberately calm, and saying nothing to the others, I work through all my pockets, and then every place else where the card might have fallen, including the space where the car seats fold down. We live on plastic here. Without it even the most ordinary aspects of life will clamp shut. And of course if the card is lost, it is stolen, which means all the squandered time of stopping it, applying for a new one. Finally I have to explain to the others what I am doing.

"Don't worry," Kyra says.

"I have plenty of cash on me," Judy says.

"It's probably back at the villa,' says Maggie.

Kyra and Judy speak what they think. Maggie does not.

"Thorough Dope."

I resolve that I will not let this spoil our visit to Assisi. But of course it does. I find pleasure in nothing we see, and indeed Assisi seems not sordid but a sad place now, the signs everywhere of the great earthquake of 1997.

We go first to the basilica of Santa Chiara, which covers the mausoleum of the founder of the female Franciscans, known by Catholics as the Poor Clares. There's not a single frescoed surface left in the upper church. It looks like it could have been completed last month, which, in effect, it was. Down below, the crypt chapels have been completely refaced in brand-new marble veneer in the colors of Italian honey-nougat candy, almond, dove-gray, puce. It could be an upscale subway stop. We can't wait to get away.

Through surprisingly empty streets we make our way to the great basilica of San Francesco. Despite the earthquake, the fabled frescoes on the side walls of the upper church are unharmed. The major damage was sustained by the high vaults over the central crossing. You'd have to look up and deliberately search before you notice they are gone. But with so much richness on the walls, their loss doesn't intrude, or wouldn't intrude if I could get myself to care. But all I care about is that damned piece of missing plastic.

Maggie performs prodigies of kindness, drawing my attention to the beautiful inlays on the choir stalls, talking about how one never noticed these secondary beauties before the earthquake. I try hard to concentrate, but it's just not possible, not with an electronically amplified Franciscan barking out at regular and rapid intervals *Silenzio Silenzio*. We could be in a penitentiary.

We descend to the lower church. We have come armed with small flashlights so that we can see the marvelous frescoes in the many dark, unlighted corners of this dim and looming space. Some of the greatest painting from the end of the Middle Ages is down here, all but invisible in the heavy gloom. We withdraw into a side chapel, and unobtrusively begin to pick out one by one the superb, monumental figures hidden high above our heads. And then another officious little Franciscan friar bursts in, — in Italy most priests and all nuns are tiny; there's clearly a rigidly enforced height maximum. This one is right at our elbow, ordering us in venomous Italian to put away the flashlights or we will be ejected. "This is a church," he says, "not a museum." I want to answer back, 'Oh Yeah, then why do you think the international art community is coughing up all this dough to pay for your restorations. It's not because they believe in indulgences.' But I say nothing, and we move on.

I now hate this friar. Both friars, actually. In the upper church and in the lower. I hate the pilgrims, who are chanting rival rosaries to untuned guitars in national and regional clumps. I find I actually loathe all Catholics, despite the fact that I am one, my wife is one, my children are two. I hate, deeply and lastingly, Assisi, and swear to myself I will never come back here, no matter what the provocation.

We climb back into the upper church. I let the three women move on ahead, trying to spare them the dampening effect of my sopping wet blanket. I dawdle near an exhibit of recent photographs. Churchmen of all sorts praying here. The Dalai Lama. The Archbishop of Canterbury. The Pope, of course. It is the official European Center for Peace in the World. I suddenly feel excrementitious. I have spent half a morning in one of the holiest places on earth, hallowed by almost a thousand years of fervent prayer, and I've squandered all my time worrying about a piece of plastic the loss of which is causing me no harm, and which can be replaced easily with slightly more than a hour of phoning.

I go back into the nave and kneel down. I apologize to God and to St. Francis for being, as usual, such a dope. I pray for everybody else in my life I can recall at the moment who needs or may soon need prayers. I try to say thank you for letting me be here. For letting this basilica remain standing. For Giotto. And I also acknowledge that I am a miserable sinner whose weakness would certainly be helped if I could find my Visa card waiting at home.

I know I shoud leave and join the others, but I find I can't.

I stay sitting quietly.

I ponder my twin paraoblas: Ivo and loss, Maggie and reovery.

Why haven't I, until this moment, seen that there does not have to be only one principal story at a time? It's because I spend my time at home teaching people how to write plots, and plots always have a through-line, one through-line. Of course, there are sub-plots, but those are the plots that are happening at the same time to other people. And there are parallel plots, supremely the double plots of *Anna Karenina*, most sublime of novels: Anna's death-drawn story and simultaneously Levin's quite different story of love and renewal. But the tyrannical through-line, connecting begining, middle and end in a single trjaectrory, demands that for each principal there be only one story.

Life, I now acknowledge, doesn't work that way. Life is indeed parabolic, *crisis, mystery, moving on,* but life also sustains multiple simultaneous plots, going in different directions, generating entirely different sorts of experience. I don't have to choose between them. In fact, I can't choose between them. Both arcs are real.

Now restored to something like calm, if not genuine serenity, I rejoin Maggie and Kyra and Judy, and we go off to find lunch. In the unvisited back streets we discover a little place that promises good things, only to find it mobbed with Germans. It's Italy, but in here they're serving *bratwurst* and Rhine wines. I deserve this, I know. This is my punishment for spoiling everyone's morning. I refuse to let myself get glum. I reach into my pocket to exchange my sunglasses with my reading glasses so I can torture myself with the repellent details of the ersatz menu. I find my Visa card. I have poked around in that pocket half a dozen times at least since we arrived.

Ah, St. Francis, first the *Celle*, now this.

I get it.

WEEK NINE
October 29- 31

Sant'Antimo

Actually this isn't week 9, it's 8 ½. We're only here till Tuesday morning. Le Balze has already embarked on Fall Break, scheduled to overlap the Italian national holiday *Ogni Santi*, All Saints, November 1. (Halloween is growing here but it's not yet anywhere near as important as it is in the States.) Everything shut down inside the villa on Thursday evening after the final class. We don't start up again until Monday, November 6. Maggie and I could have left for Rome after my class when classes ended but we wanted to stay on for a bit to host Kyra and Judy.

I am tickled by this coincidence. Fellini's *8½* is my favorite film. In the film his alter-ego/protagonist Guido (Marcello Mastroianni) is stuck. Like Fellini, he's a film-maker, now with eight films behind him, who can't figure out where to go with his ninth. He's got about half a film done—hence the title. It's seems to be some sort of science fiction flick, centering on an enormous space rocket. The rocket's been built on set, but Guido has no idea now what to do with it. While he dithers, hounded by his increasingly frustrated producer and cast, he flirts with all sorts of other stories, some autobiographical, some fantastical. He begins to think he can actually turn out a movie about his memories, going so far as trying to cast actors who look like the significant others in his life, parents, wife, mistress. In one of the film's indelibly magical moments, we even get to watch one set of actors watch a second set of actors screen-testing to play the roles which we've seen the first set playing since the film began. Finally, the much-hounded Guido realizes he can't connect the dots and settles for a magical, symphonic sort of chaos as the only possible finish.

Although it's been my favorite film since it first appeared in 1963, never before have I so clearly seen myself in its feckless, vacillating hero. Of course, I am no Fellini. I'm not even Marcello Mastroianni. (Given the choice, which would be preferable? Easy. Look like Mastroianni, think like Fellini.) But just like Guido I seem to be in several different stories at once. This could, and maybe should, paralyze me as it does Guido for much of the film. *Vicolo cieco*—the Italian for dead end. Literally: a blind street. Instead, I take this *8½* as an augury—in Italian, *auguri* is the word for best wishes, good luck—and trust that the ending delivered to me when the ending arrives will be, just as it is for Guido, and for Fellini, unerringly right.

And as though to encourage that course of action, today we discover Sant'Antimo.

Despite another Sunday of less than promising weather, we drive back into the sublime Crete to find Sant'Antimo, a few miles south of the dread Montalcino. I've read ravishing accounts of Sant'Antimo, a church, all that's left of what was once the greatest abbey in Tuscany. It is thought to have been founded by Charlemagne. The present building dates from about 1118. From what the guidebooks say, there is nothing like it anywhere in Tuscany. There may be nothing like it anywhere in the world. We decide to take a chance on it since it is in the sublime Crete which I very much want to revisit.

Standing isolated at the center of its own valley, the abbey church appears first below us and off to the right, in an improbably green and gold plain. We are stunned into silence, until the Kansan in Judy murmurs, simply and accurately, "Geezy-Peezy." Exactly. It's not that it's big. Or grand. It's just that it's perfect.

The mesmerizing thing about Sant'Antimo is that in any light it seems to glow. From far off, as we descend, it's a lemon-gold. Later, on the plain, it's closer to cream. And then, after we've parked the car, and are walking toward it, it seems more honey-colored. But it always glows. It is made of stone. There are only a few narrow windows. Most of the arches are blind. The sun is behind, not inside it, and yet the light seems to be coming out of, not into or against, the walls.

Later I learn this is because the walls are actually combed with large pieces of translucent alabaster. (Alabaster is the chief product of Volterra, not far away.) But why this happens doesn't matter. Sant'Antimo erases any need to think, any desire to analyze. The only other building in Tuscany that has this effect on me is San Biagio at Montepulciano, though they are styles and worlds apart.

But each seems to sit simply and unsupported in its setting, making no claim with arcades or staircases or supporting wings, saying simply: *here I am, unique, here I have been, I can be no other than what I am.*

We spend a long time inside, outside, inside again. A community of three monks lives in a restored barn nearby. They chant the Gregorian hours at regular intervals. They do not sing well. But they do sing beautifully, because they sing their love and care for this space, and for the Lord that prompted the makers of this space.

We can't bear to leave. We go outside again. Then one by one each of us says I have to go back inside for just a few minutes more. Because the alabaster renders large sections of wall almost transparent, the light inside the building changes from moment to moment, but in ways that are far more subtle than anything that might be managed by even the most nuanced of rheostats. Just as at San Biagio, we circuit it inside, and then go outside and just as slowly encircle it. Again and again. We move back to the car but no one gets in. How can you let something like this go, when you know you can never find its equal?

Finally we force ourselves to go saying that we will drive up the opposing hill and get the view we haven't yet had of its south façade, closed off by the walls of the monks' barn. Maggie admonishes me that as driver I have no right to look. Nevertheless, I keep craning round to get a last glimpse as the abbey recedes from view. Which is not a good idea since we are driving at the edge of a cliff.

And then we have left behind the cliff but we are no longer on a road. Somehow we've gotten onto a dirt track. I know I didn't make a turn. Maggie insists I must have turned while I was trying to see the church. Judy and Kyra are ominously silent. They are not going to venture into this marital squabble, but it's clear whose side they'd take if they did. The track tells us after a while that it is taking us to something called Sant'Angelo in Colle. Holy Angel on the Hill. Maggie insists it is taking us nowhere. With injured pride, I explain that, wherever it is going, there is now no turning back. Deep hedgerows push against us on either side. The car is thick with dust. I have to use the windshield wipers. I hear the bushes scraping the car doors. How will I explain to the Villa what has happened to their car?

We climb and climb and then without warning we are there. Sant'Angelo in Colle. Everything Sant'Antimo is not, and yet everything we need right now. It's such a teeny tiny town, Volpaia is a metropolis by comparison. You can see it all inside of ten minutes, just a postage stamp piazza, one circular street going round the ramparts, and the stone houses crammed within the walls. Off the piazza a comparably tiny, insignificant church. And a wine bar, with glorious local wine, served by of all people a Scotswoman. We sit outside the wine bar on the piazza facing the church. The proprietress arranges four glasses. These may be the most beautiful glasses any of us has ever seen. Each has an enormous bowl. The bowls are not perfectly round. Just where your index finger would make an indentation, if the glass were malleable, someone's index finger has done just that. Which makes the glass easier to hold though the indentation is actually designed to release the wine's bouquet.

We sip the gloriously robust wine made from the café owner's own vineyard. It is bright in the piazza. A wind comes up; it becomes chilly. We can see Mount Amiata, the highest mountain in Tuscany. We can see valleys fingering out on every side below us. We drink the perfect wine in the beautiful glasses, sniffing the clear cold air.

We agree we want to live here, all four of us. We don't ever want to go away. We want to spend our mornings down at Sant'Antimo, looking and listening, and our afternoons up at Sant'Angelo, sipping wine and talking. We know we can't. In fact, I know that I had better start driving back soon since I have no idea how to get home from here. But I am confident I will.

I pray: *Holy angel on this hill, bring me back here again, please, soon, and often.*

Away

Very early this morning Kyra left for London via Pisa. Now we go over last minute instructions with Judy who will baby sit the villino. She professes to be delighted to be left entirely on her own to explore the art of Florence at her own pace. Maggie and I will take the good fast train, the Eurostar. It should get us to Rome inside two hours. We will stay there for the remainder of this week. We've booked a hotel near the Spanish Steps, on Via Margutta, the same street where Fellini kept his apartment.

Maggie is humming as she finishes packing. An excellent sign. Maggie is a horrible hummer. She takes one phrase. The first line of "Getting to Know You" or "America the Beautiful" or (her favorite) The Supremes' "Baby Love." And then she repeats it, just that phrase, over and over again. When she's on, and happy, she can do this for hours. It drives me crazy. But this morning I couldn't like anything more. This morning it's her whole spirit that's humming, not just her voice, like a top on point, like a toddler delighted by its toes. I remember that this is the way she used to be.

I am convinced now that she and I are on—not quite parallel, that's not right—on interconnected, intersecting, similar but not identical paths. Each journey has to do with survival and recovery. But Maggie's experience, as the one with the disease, and mine as the partner, are essentially different. It's just not the same thing for her to think *I might die of this* and for me to think *she could die of this*. But, though they are neither the same nor equal, it's also not an inconsequential thing to think *she could die of this*. Maggie, typically, as well as clearly and boldly and smartly and bravely, started on her work of recuperation almost from the day of she arrived here. I am beginning to realize I have to do something similar. I can't share her path but I have to follow her example. I am also, in a sense, a survivor. I have to make myself become well.

The first step along my path is this: to admit frankly that I arrived here needy and damaged. The second step is to see everything that's happened to me since, including the confusions, and misjudgments, and pyramiding errors in tactic, as rooted in that damage. I didn't discover, I invented what I found.

Suddenly, it's our cab that skids into the steep turn on Via Vecchia. We pile in the luggage and then ourselves. As the driver pulls away from Le Balze, we watch Judy start up the hill in the opposite direction, to get the bus, while Alessandro and Ruggiero push their hand-made barrow through the gardens, taking out the bedding plants, quieting it all down to start the winter's long rest.

Rome

The time in Rome was tourist time; it doesn't belong in this book. What does belong is what I heard there from Dora. I spent the better part of one day with her, without Maggie. She made no fuss when I told her I was staying on at Le Balze. The only thing that mattered to her was that I agree to write Ivo's story.

Dora's Account of the Detective's Discoveries

When Ivo left his parents' apartment on that hot, muggy morning of Friday, September 1, it was true, as he told them, that he was planning to take his new car to the beach. But he did not tell them that he was planning to meet someone at the beach, someone he knew very well, someone, in fact, they also knew very well. She was, literally, the girl next door. Her parents owned a business very much like that of the Capolagos. The two families had worked with or beside or in competition with each other for decades, entertaining each other regularly, in town and in the country. In fact, Dora Capolago was this girl's godmother, had held her at the font when she was baptized, and when she was fourteen years old had given her a pearl necklace that remained the costliest item of jewelry she owned. Or would have been if the girl had not pawned it several months before. Something she kept hidden for her parents by saying that pearls were dowdy on a girl her age.

The girl addressed Waldo and Dora as *Sio* and *Sia*, uncle and aunt. Ivo and Cip did the same to her parents. She was the youngest child of five, the only girl. The two Capolago boys and her four brothers had known each other at school, competed against each other at sports, and for girls, and would have stayed close friends if the Capolago boys had not gone to college in America, a choice all the others in their set rated a mistake but a choice on which Dora was adamant. Cip's success, head and shoulders beyond all the sons of their friends, proved to her the canniness of her decision. A point she was careful not to make with the other women with whom she regularly lunched. In that world, a world very small and highly notched, every detail was noted, and rated. It was not good to appear to be out of step.

Which is why the girl told Ivo that she would meet him at the beach, but he was not to tell his family they were meeting. Nor would she tell hers. She didn't want them, she explained, ground down by the conversational mill into which was fed everything that everyone in those families did. Ivo scoffed at her fears but, scenting a promise he found unexpected and titillating—this is the detective's supposition of course—he agreed to say nothing, even to Cip. A point she particularly stressed. She had left for the beach an hour or so after Ivo, with a group of friends. At a pre-set time, she complained of a headache. She told her friends she would make her own way home. She then met Ivo at a spot she had specified. They drove a couple of miles further down the coast, to a place her friends never frequented. They bought some food from vendors, and spent the rest of the afternoon in the water and tanning. As the day began to wane she suggested that he take her to the Capola- gos' villa in the Alban hills. He was of course delighted, hoping but never quite believing this might be the outcome of the afternoon. She was a very desirable young woman. He had always admired her but from childhood she had treated him only in a friendly way, as a cousin, indeed as a younger cousin. She had not gone to uni- versity and was thought by the ladies with whom Dora lunched to have fallen into a very fast set.

It was almost dark by the time they got to the villa. Ivo un- locked the door, ushering her inside. She said she wanted to shower away the remains of the beach. He showed her into one of the bath- rooms, hoping she would suggest they could shower together. But she suddenly realized she had left her purse in his car. It had her comb and her make-up. He offered to retrieve it. He left the house and was walking toward the parked car when he was seized from behind, blindfolded, gagged and manhandled back into the house.

Of course it was a setup, though he was not to know that until shortly before his death.

The girl had sold him to the kidnappers.

For years she had supported a drug habit that was serious but manageable. Her generous family allowance could be stretched to cover her requirements. But early in the preceding spring she had started sleeping with a fellow several years older than herself, as glamorous as he was penniless, and a serious addict. She began to cover his needs as well as her own. That's when she started doing things like pawning the pearls. When she had nothing left to pawn, the boyfriend, very discreetly, started to pimp her among wealthy tourists. She hated that but she was besotted with the guy. At the start of the summer he moved to Brazil. He didn't offer to take her. But he did leave behind a significant debt to their dealers, a debt which they insisted the girl pay. They offered her what they termed a choice. Pay up in full or they'd feed her to the paparazzi. When she explained that she didn't have access to a sum of that kind, she was told to arrange a small abduction.

For several years criminals in all the major Italian cities have relied on the small abduction. These are entirely unlike headline-grabbing kidnappings, in which million-dollar ransoms are required, with victims held for long periods of time, often mutilated during that time, and sometimes even abandoned. The small abduction is precise, rapid and a sure thing. A target is selected from a well-to-do but not famously rich family. Research ensures the family can easily produce the not insignificant ransom without resorting to an extensive financial transaction. From start to finish the abduction is planned to last no more than forty-eight hours, generally less. The family gets the ransom demand, due within a very brief window in time. The cash is turned over without fuss. The victim returns to the family, unscathed. That last is crucial. Families in the Capolago class know the deal, a quick, not inexpensive but relatively painless quid pro quo. It is all about liquidity, a way for organized crime to replenish its ordinary cash flow.

The small abduction depends on the widespread Italian contempt for taxation. Virtually every Italian conceals the real extent of his or her wealth. Shockingly large sums—shocking at least to an American—are concealed in places to which individuals have easy access. As a result families can usually respond to these relatively large ransom demands without a paper trail. This urge to conceal is elemental. Dora shared with me every detail of her son's death, no matter how painful, but she never mentioned the amount of the proposed ransom, a sum which her detective must have passed on.

Told to supply a victim, the girl picked Ivo. He and his family fitted the requirements exactly. Rich enough to provide the ransom without difficulty. Devoted to the boy. Whom the girl could easily entrap. She was assured nothing bad would come of it. Ivo would not be harmed. He would be back with his family within two days. And the amount, though large, would not burden the Capolagos.

What went wrong?

In a word: according to the thugs, Ivo was a *cowboy*. He had spent most of the previous four years in America, at MIT during the school year, interning in New York in the summers. He hadn't internalized the rules that a typical young man in his world could be relied on to follow without question. One of the girl's brothers, for example, would have understood from the start what was happening, and accepted it. He would have known that cooperating with the thugs ensured his swift release. But Ivo had been formed by a radically alternative culture, one that insisted a real man fight back, that a real man never give in or up. Real men don't merely make the best of the world, they master it. As the thugs said, a cowboy.

Dora saw this quite clearly. Her insistence on their American education had made Cip such a success but it was, she admitted, what ultimately had killed Ivo.

Once the thugs, who were masked, got Ivo into his room and tied him down, they presented him with pen and paper and dictated the ransom note. He refused. They threatened but he kept demanding to see the girl, to know what had happened to her, to be certain she wasn't hurt. Finally, the thugs tied her up and brought her in. She tried to calm him, assured him they hadn't touched her, and urged him to comply. All they wanted was the money, it was simple. His parents would want him to cooperate. This happened to their friends all the time. It would be a story to tell. The important thing was for the two of them to get free as soon as possible.

When he continued to baulk, the thugs tried a new tack. Alright, they said, in effect, we get either the money or the girl. Write the note or we rape her, and you watch.

Of course, that did it. They untied his arms. He wrote the note. They tied him to his bed and left him for the night.

A while later, he called them, told them he needed to use the bathroom. When they released him, he tried to jump them. A cowboy. His youth was nothing to their experience, and bulk. This time instead of tying him to the bed, they hustled him out to a small building at the end of the garden, where the gardener kept extra pots and soil. They made sure there was nothing in there he could turn into a weapon, then left him joking that if he still needed to piss he'd have plenty of pots to choose from.

They went back to the house. Just before dawn on Saturday, one of them left to bring the note down to the city. And then the unforeseeable happened. Earlier in the week Dora had called their gardener. Ordinarily, he did not come to the villa on the weekend, but she was afraid of the harm the dry hot spell was doing to the gardens. She asked him to come over the weekend to see if anything needed tending. Before the remaining thug or the girl realized it, he was already in the garden, watering.

Actually, Ivo saw him first and called out to him from the shed. That call alerted the thug. But the gardener, of course knowing nothing of what was going on, just called back a greeting and kept on examining his flowers. Before Ivo could make clear what was at stake, the girl was in the garden. Wrapped only in a towel she explained to the gardener that she and Ivo had come up for the weekend and it would be better if he went away and told no one anything about it. She promised they'd water whatever needed tending. She told him he could hear how angry Ivo already was from the tone of his voice.

The gardener, embarrassed, feeling like the intruder, made his apologies and hastily left. Ivo saw the encounter. He couldn't overhear the words but he saw the crucial thing, the girl was sending the gardener away. Finally, he got it, and he went crazy. He started tearing the shed to pieces, yelling every sort of threat to revenge himself not only on the thugs but on the girl and her entire family. At that point, of course, he sealed his doom.

The thug overpowered him, then gave him a shot that knocked him out. He called his boss and his boss constructed the new ending. Another call to the partner, on his way into the city, turned him around before the note had been delivered. When he got back to the villa, they stripped the unconscious boy and slipped the noose over his neck. Once he was in position, they kicked away the chair. Even while the murder was taking place, their boss was arranging the cover up with the police. Just at the end they had the girl go through the house to make sure that everything was at it should have been. A nice touch since she noticed the kinds of detail that would have completely passed this pair by. And then they left, dropping the girl near her house, which of course was also next door to where Dora was now trying to alarm her husband and son.

No one knew about the gardener. Now Dora is sure he's the key. The girl is gone. By the time Dora returned to Rome from Brazil the girl had left for the UK, where she is supposed to be taking a course to improve her English. That's one of the first things Dora was told when she started seeing people after she came back. The family made a point of explaining why she was unable to come in person to offer her condolences. But Dora is confident they can use the gardener's story to bring pressure on the police to bring the girl back to Italy, and once they get the girl to cooperate, they can find the thugs.

But no one, not even the detective, has been able to locate the gardener.

NOVEMBER

WEEK TEN
November 5-11

Reversals

Rome was superb. We relied on the little guidebook put out by the American Academy there, a compendium of mostly hidden treasures stretching from exemplary coffee shops to exquisite cloisters. We managed to see almost everything there is by Borromini (aka Enrico Schnauzer), for me what Palladio is for Thad. And on Via Lazio Maggie literally fell into a shop called Albanese—she thought the door was locked—bespoke shoemakers who at this moment are hand-crafting for her a nonpareil pair of pumps in black lizard and red leather. Everything is better in Rome, and a lot of it is best, especially when, returning from Rome, you approach Florence by night and by train. You can see then, what the daylight disguises, the Florence tourists never see and travelers ignore, a quite small and provincial place, faded, cramped, and ordinary.

Rome was summery but it's chilly when we leave Santa Maria Novella, the Florence train station. We're feeling the first sharp edge of Shelley's wild West Wind, which he called the "breath of Autumn's being." (He wrote the famous ode in Florence and he must have written it on a night just like this one.) Certainly, the Le Balze we return to is not the villa we left. Shrouded in scaffolding, the flower beds denuded of color and leaf, the gardens now all put to bed, it seems, glimpsed between bursts of rain, irredeemably shabby, rundown, well past its prime.

But not to Judy who tells us she made herself completely at home while we were away. Independent, self-reliant, she enjoys the enviable gift of living well alone. Each morning she made her way up the Via Vecchia to Piazza Mino to catch the bus down to Florence. At first, the climb seemed overwhelming. (It's a challenge for me and I've got long legs; I regularly arrive at the top breathless.) But then, ever resourceful, she figured out that if she tacked while climbing she could manage it. And so she patiently first zigged and then zagged from side to side until she arrived at the summit, all the while dodging madcap motorcyclists hurtling down the other way. It took her a chunk of time but she always got to the crest.

At the end of the afternoon, she took the bus back up to the Piazza and did her shopping, just like an ordinary Italian housewife, the *supermercato* for staples, then the baker for bread, the wineshop, Maggie's *Frutta*, sometimes the florist and other times Mastro Ciliegia at the top of the Via Vecchia to browse for just the right ceramics to bring back to DC.

Going down the hill, of course, was much easier than up, and made lovely at the moment by the blooming persimmon trees, the glory of the Italian autumn, their clusters of thick red-orange globes dipping over every garden wall. The Italian word for them is *cachi*, pronounced exactly like khaki, if you are a Brit, but in every other way khaki's reverse. It is in fact an Italian adoption of the Japanese word for persimmon, *kaki*. The trees were an exotic import from the Far East in the nineteenth century. They are ubiquitous in Italy because Mussolini required every family farm to plant at least one. He believed they would nourish soldiers.

In the evening, Judy put a fire in the villino fireplace (something I never managed to accomplish), turned the radio to the classical music station (something I never managed to find), and had her supper enjoying the raucous shouts from the soccer stadium far below. The Florence stadium is miles away from Fiesole but when Italians cheer soccer distance dissipates.

Clearly, our presence would have been superfluous.

But inside the villa there's quite a different story.

The master bedroom is now gone, the only interior to survive intact from Strong's day. Apparently, earlier in the autumn an undetected leak opened high within the rafters. Throughout all these weeks of record-breaking rains, water has been secretly seeping in. (The room was kept for guests during the term.) Friday night finally brought down the entire bedroom ceiling, still beautifully painted in the original trompe l'oeil. The weight of the sodden plaster in turn flattened the heavy, mahogany four-poster bed, with its damask hangings, disintegrating the mattress, and blistering the surfaces of an antique chest, called in Italian *cassone*, the best piece of furniture in the house, part of the room since the villa was opened. Nothing of the room or in the room can be saved. Even the tiled floor will have to be pulled out and stored to dry, before it can be relaid. It's likely to be January at the earliest before the room can be used again.

Worst of all: our wonderfully named architect, Rudy Rooms, investigating the collapse, discovered that we must now replace the entire roof if we want to avoid even more extensive damage in future autumns. Not only will this cost a fortune, but the entire second (the bedroom) floor of the villa will have to remain empty for at least three months during the repairs. In effect, this means closing the villa for a semester, a financial disaster.

Mid-day: I learn from Ripley Snell that I misunderstood Rotgut's sentence. Yes, it's true he can remain here for the rest of the semester, but he's been forbidden to return for the spring term. So much for mercy.

This has almost broken Rotgut's strange and wayward spirit. Nevertheless, Ripley says Rotgut believes he can behave so well during the remaining month of this term that his sentence will at the last moment be commuted, and he will be able to come back. So he refuses to pre-register for spring courses back at Georgetown, or to look into housing there.

Later I run into Rotgut in the denuded orange garden and see the change for myself. He is like a little child, one who, having misbehaved, sees a promised treat retreating, and now quivers with his intensely concentrated effort to be, and to be seen as, good. If he knelt on the ground with a cup at his feet and a mangy dog at his side, he could not be more miserably and affectingly mendicant. *Please, please, like me enough that they won't send me away.*

For the next three weeks everyone here, *studenti* and faculty and administrators, will be, willing or not, his judge.

If any one of us reports the least sign of dissatisfaction with him, he knows any hope of reprieve will vanish.

Finally: This day of dark reversals culminates in a call from Dora. Her detective's vamoosed.

This morning he suddenly appeared in her apartment. She doesn't know how he got in. He never rang the bell; he didn't come through the foyer. She was out on the terrace after Mass with coffee and the papers. (While it's been storming up here, Rome remains not just warm but sulty.) She heard a slight noise, and there he was in the living room. Staring at her.

He wouldn't come outside; she had to come inside, out of the light. It's because she's continuously spied on now, he says. He came to tell her he's through, and he's leaving Italy. He wanted money, whatever she had in the apartment; he can't wait for what she owes him.

Dora was stunned. They'd been together just the day before. He had assured her things were going even better than expected. He was almost there. He only had to locate the gardener who has disappeared.

He won't tell her what has changed. He hasn't even told his family he's going. He'll find a way to contact them after he finds someplace to settle. Anybody connected to Ivo's death, he claims, is in danger. He pushed her to stop now too, if only for her family's sake. She'll never get the proof she wants. If she sticks with it, she should at least get Cip out of Italy for a while.

Dora couldn't stop him; actually, she didn't even try. She says it was clear he had made up his mind and nothing she could say would change it.

Did she think he might have been bought off? Was it possible he'd been paid to scare her?

No, she feels that he was truly spooked. All the swagger was gone. He was a man on the edge of panic.

So she heard him out and when she got over her intial surprise she handed him all the money she had in the house. It wasn't enough. He said he needed a lot more to secure his getaway. She offered to give him some of her jewelry. But when she got back from her room, he was gone.

The maid was in the apartment the whole time but says she didn't hear or see a trace of his presence.

I thought she'd be distraught. After all, now she's back where she started. Worse, maybe: the only person she could find to help her has quit. But that's not the way she sees it. She insists she never liked this guy. Not only was he obviously corrupt, he was also vulgar and, she thinks, a coward. She was disgusted when he was around her, and on her guard. Now she claims she's relieved to see the last of him. What matters now, the only thing that matters now for her is our book, my book. That will tell the truth and set the record straight.

I urge her to take his warning seriously. This is a guy who has lived with conspiracy and corruption all his adult life. Even Cip thought he was big and tough. If he's been terrified into flight, she should give up now too. She knows what happened to Ivo. Isn't that enough?

I should have known better. This is an Italian mother. Nothing is going to deflect her from the vindication of her son.

Now she will find the gardener. Tomorrow she's moving up to the Alban hills. I urge her not to go alone, at least to get Cip to go with her. She brushes that aside. The gardener has worked for the family for decades. She can trust him. And he will trust her. After I hang up, I think about how hard she worked to frighten me about staying in Fiesole when she wanted us to move to Rome. But now, when she risks much more by going on alone, she dismisses any notion that she could be in trouble.

I call Cip. No answer. I start to leave a message but then cut it off. What if the phones are bugged? Will I be making things more dangerous?

I think about that slow leak in the villa ceiling. How under the surface ruin steadily accumulates.

Race Matters
The weather, having now gone from cool to cold, and the light, dimming early, have together driven class out of the ilex grove and back into the library. But it's a lot more accommodating in here now than it was at the start of the term. In September the room was glaring, airless. Now it's cozy. We start with the lamps already on; we need them to read by. Students who can't find chairs loll comfortably on the carpets. I'd like to have a fire, but I am told the hearth is lighted only for Thanksgiving dinner.

The change in Rotgut's situation is immediately obvious. He doesn't sit, as he used to, off by himself to the side. People offer to make room for him. And even Beluga, with whom he came to blows, seems guardedly cordial. Nobody wants to be the one who accidentally provokes him into doing that one untoward thing that will confirm his exile. We're all being drawn into the conspiracy to secure his reprieve.

And the script we are about to start, *Othello*, offers us no Belmont, no easy out, no out at all.

Unsurprisingly, since everyone knows this is one of Shakespeare's greatest tragedies, right up there with *Hamlet* and *Lear*, a number of the orts center on Othello's tragic flaw, assumed by most to be jealousy. None of these orts do I intend to use.

High school students are taught that tragedy is precipitated by what Aristotle famously called in *The Poetics* (@335 BC) the protagonist's tragic flaw. This flaw, a moral weakness like pride or anger, causes him to fall from an exalted station at the start to a debased condition at the end. Unfortunately, this widely-endorsed account both misreads Aristotle and disserves tragedy.

In Greek the term translated as flaw, *hamartia,* comes from the lexicon of archery. It actually means to miss the target, to misfire. It refers not to a character flaw, but to an error in judgment, a mistake you make at a crucial moment that leads to the most undesirable of consequences. And you make such a mistake, not because you are flawed, but because the circumstances at the moment make it difficult if not impossible to choose accurately. That's what makes the situation tragic.

Take the Titanic, perhaps the iconic tragedy of the twentieth century, sadly trivialized recently by a blockbuster film that reduced the sinking to sentimental romance. (Completely unlike the remarkable British Titanic film of the 1958, *A Night to Remember.*) Treated as tragedy the story centers on Captain E.J. Smith's catastrophic choice to do nothing on that Sunday evening but post the ice messages he had started to receive as the night closed in. This was no flawed careless skipper, but the commodore of the White Star Line on his final voyage, one of the most experienced officers on the North Atlantic. And what he did was completely correct. In hindsight it was the most grievous error, but he made his choice, a choice among countless others in his busy day, in the moment, by his best light. And that's what makes him a tragic figure, not that he was a flawed individual but that he wasn't. That is hamartia: the wrong choice that at the time seems exactly the right choice.

Why does this matter? It matters because of how much the tragic flaw theory costs us. It costs us tragedy itself, tragedy as a way of understanding the human situation we all share. Tragedy does not belong only to a special class of remarkably flawed individuals. Tragedy can overtake anyone, at any moment, irrespective of individual character. Every choice, no matter how well considered, no matter how carefully made, has within it the potential of a tragic outcome. That's why Aristotle insisted that the emotions prompted by tragedy are fear and pity. We pity in the tragic character what we instinctively fear for and about ourselves. There is nothing more human than tragedy. All of us live always at its edge, and that edge is easily crossed unaware. The ancient Athenians insisted on that, as did Renaissance Londoners. But we don't want tragedy, we want blame, because blame insists bad outcomes are always someone's fault.

When Maggie was so ill, well-meaning people used to say: "You don't deserve this." It drove me crazy. Who does deserve cancer, I wanted to shout. Hitler? Life is never about getting or losing what you deserve. But without tragedy we can delude ourselves that life is for the most part fair.

So why not teach hamartia now? Because *gli studenti* are too young and it is a lesson you have to figure out for yourself. If you are twenty, no aging professor can make it seem either relevant or convincing.

Instead I use June's ort, on a problem no less serious. She notes a key, and appalling, passage at the end of the play, after Desdemona's murder's been made known. Emilia is taunting Othello: "What should such a fool/ Do with so good a wife" (V:2, 240-241). Othello, Emilia insists, was unworthy Desdemona: "the more angel she/ And you the blacker devil" (134-135). He's unworthy, she seems to be saying, because he's black. Since Emilia rightly reviles the murderer of this innocent and trusting young woman, June asks, does the play want us to conclude that Desdemona was indeed wrong to elope with the *black* man against her father's wishes.

A tricky silence follows. One of our young women is black; no one wants to talk race.

I try to expand on what June's asked. If Desdemona marries across racial lines, the play seems to say, what else should she expect but a violent death. That's as far as I get before Duke interrupts. By claiming the toxin I inoculate everyone else. *He said it first.*

"I don't get what's going on here. I mean, you never said anything like this when we began *Merchant of Venice*. If you don't bring this kind of issue up with Shylock but you start off this way with Othello, isn't that being racist?"

"No," says Faustina. "It's not the same thing."

"Don't get me wrong," Duke hastily adds. "I don't think Professor Glavin is really racist."

I thank him.

Over and over again, Faustina explains, *Merchant* makes you feel how much, and how unfairly, Shylock suffers. "It makes anti-Semitism an issue, but in *Othello* racial stereotyping seems like it could be the basic assumption."

"But what," Willy Voltaire objects, "what privileges Emilia as a reliable let alone the best reader of the play?" He points out that she stole Desdemona's handkerchief in the first place. And when she could have revealed all and saved her mistress, she didn't. That makes her complicit in all of Iago's evil.

"And Iago says she is really Othello's mistress," Jacqueline remembers.

"So," Willy cleverly concludes, "why should we trust her?"

But now June, bless her, gets us up to the boil. What bothers her, she explains, is that the crisis passes so quickly. She's studied *Macbeth* in another course, and talks well about how the protagonist moves back and forth, attracted by the witches' promises but repelled by the horrific things he does to fulfill those promises. Even at the end, when he is up to his eyes in blood, he can still go on and on about how he wishes none of this were happening. But that doesn't happen here. Only in the final minutes of the play, when it is obvious to everyone that Desdemona was framed, does Othello come close to a second thought.

One by one *gli studenti* contribute supporting instances of complexity from other courses they've had. Gloria talks about how the Fool keeps making Lear—and the play—face the folly his vanity has brought on his world. No matter how hard Lear tries to avoid admitting his own complicity, the Fool won't let up on him. Faustina brings up Antony and Cleopatra who twist back and forth and forth and back, struggling with the un-resolvable tension between their imperious passions and their imperial destinies.

"And Hamlet," Betty adds, triumphant, "is like a byword for postponement because he is always rethinking everything."

"That's what I don't get about Othello," Beluga adds. "He's this famous, tough general. So why doesn't he just say to Iago that first time something like: *Look, you lying, little sonovabitch, that's the woman I just married. I'm nuts about her. To me she's perfect. And you can just get your double-dealing ass off this island before sunset, and be glad I don't kill you for what you've just done.* But instead he makes it so easy. All Iago has to do is introduce the topic and Othello is bagged."

Which seems to make Othello, I explain, his culture's stereotypical dark-skinned man, violent, passionate, easily duped and unswervingly vicious, the ugly typing that, of course, in all its horror remains with us still. That's the profiling we know that Shakespeare's audience expected. The only non-comic stereotype in his entire career Shakespeare seems uncritically to deploy. We are stopped dead. Which is good. We would certainly not have done this sort of grappling if we had spent the time talking about jealousy as Othello's tragic flaw. (Of course he is jealous, not as a habit or flaw in his character but as a result of his bad judgment in believing the one entirely evil person in the story. There's his hamartia.)

We can build on this. I ask them each to select a passage of about twenty lines, anywhere in the play, irrespective of the characters' gender, to prepare for performance next time round.

Though he contributed nothing to the discussion, at everything anybody else said, no matter the content, Rotgut vigorously nodded encouraging assent. For weeks before this all we were shown was either a sardonic smile or a scowl: that is, when he wasn't staring off into the distance.

I know which I prefer.

Paradise
Last night another apocalyptic lashing from the skies, and then the power failed

Suddenly, just after dinner in the villino, Judy, Maggie and I found ourselves plunged into darkness. Surviving several near tumbles down the steep villino stairs I managed to make my way over to the villa to borrow candles. Inside, Le Balze was half haunted house, half enchanted castle. Ironically, having lost its power the building had managed to rediscover its dignity. With all the scars of tough use and recent indignity obscured, you had a rare chance to feel the claim, and charm, of its original austerities.

Dispensing candles Heidi explains that it's not just us. It's literally a communal failure, a failure affecting the entire *commune*. All our side of Fiesole is powerless, and the power may be out for quite a while. Perhaps days. The old equipment can't be repaired, it has to be replaced.

One thing is in our favor. Fiesole is no longer a stronghold of the (no-longer-in- existence) *Partito Comunista Italiano*, the Italian Communist Party. In 1987, when the PCI dominated the *comune*, every request to the local bureaucracy from our little American enclave was haughtily dismissed. Especially hostile was the elderly postmistress. She would sell you stamps only in the lowest possible denomination. This was back before email when we all actually wrote and relied on letters. To send off even the simplest card you had literally to cover every bit of surface with stamps except for the narrowest possible window showing the address. If you were lucky. Sometimes there were more stamps than space. I remember the bewildered Thad and Cericlia asking: *But why does that lady hate us so much?*

That year there was a very long postal strike. Entirely cut off from home, we were thrilled to read in the papers that the strike was about to be settled. Then Stefano explained that during the strike all mail coming into the country was being stored. But with the strike settled it would be taken out and burned, because delivery would be too onerous for the mailcarriers.

And that is exactly what happened.

It's good to remind myself that some things here have indeed changed for the better.

By daylight the power loss is not so limiting. Still, it seems smart to treat today as a holiday. So we pack Judy into the car and go down the 222 to take lunch at Pietra Fitta. Judy is delighted to go. The non-stop rain had pretty much trapped her in the villino since we got back from Rome. And tomorrow she returns to the States.

Having just come from Rome, I see Tuscany anew. Rome, of course, is a world historical city, the capital of a nation and of an international church, with a past that stretches to the beginning of recorded time and turned into monuments of staggering man-made beauty. In contrast, Tuscany is about consumption, consuming good things, notably leather goods, but supremely consuming food. Essentially, Tourist Tuscany is for eating meals and/or buying food and wine to eat at other meals later. (Traveler Tuscany was, of course, about The Higher Things. Food was a concern for the staff.) And this is strange because—the truth that cannot be loudly said—Tuscan cuisine is really the poor cousin of the truly great Italian cuisines, farther north, east and south of here. A revelation, of course, compared to American fast food. But beyond the tourist-driven hype, the unvarnished fact is this: in Tuscany you can eat neither very badly nor extraordinarily well. And after even a single week here there's nothing on any menu you haven't seen before.

What you can get, as every Tourist brochure proclaims, is a chance to eat up close to your source. From one of Pietra Fitta's two small dining rooms you can peer easily into the kitchen. From the other you can hear the kitchen's from-time-to-time vociferous proceedings. No chefs in there, just two or three women in ordinary house dresses, exactly what they would wear at home. The owner's wife, perhaps, or his mother. Her mother. Their aunt. The owner himself, the *padrone,* welcomes you in cords and a checked wool shirt, very much what I am wearing. And the two young waitresses, with their careful, correct English, are no doubt daughters of the house. Everything is cleverly arranged to assure you this is not a professional restaurant. This place is authentic, honest, natural. Here you'll get, as food magazines, tourists guides, and cookbooks all aggressively affirm, *cucina all casa.* Home cooking. Of course it is home cooking at its best.

Cucina all casa relies on ingredients that are not only easily, but cheaply, available. Except for the black and white truffles. But they do grow abundantly here in autumn, no matter how exotic they may seem to Americans. For the rest, it's a matter of filberts (*nocciole*) and chestnuts (*castagne*), and above all mushrooms (*funghi*) in staggering profusion: *porcini, pinaroli, ovoli, finferli, chiodini, columbine, sanguinelli, gambesecche, trombette, cardoncelli,* and *mazze di tamburo.* And those are just the edible sorts. Pasta and olive oil and wine, of course. But not generic, store-bought, mass-produced pasta and olive oil and wine. From the restaurant's rough stone terrace you see the olive trees that produced your olive oil. Through the open door you gaze benevolently down on the vineyards that produced your wine. In the distance meander sheep and cows, a little closer up the odd pig, whose cousins you are at the moment consuming. But at Pietra Fitta, and in all the other and usually lesser Tuscan trattorie, and locande, and albergi, the nastier aspects of husbandry and slaughter have been scrubbed out of sight. Only the acceptable side of nature remains.

What you get, then, is nature harmonized to human use, a revelation to those of us for whom America the Beautiful and America the Bountiful no longer overlap.

Tourist Tuscany is a sort of anti-tragedy. It reassures us that somewhere easily accessed we can still live harmoniously not only with but within nature. The Tuscan landscape just waits to deliver its abundance easily and fully to our untroubled consumption. Which is actually why, I am convinced, Tuscan food is almost always only good. If food here were great, we'd be in France. (Of course, if the food were not good, we'd know we were in Germany.) In France, where art trumps heart, ingenuity transforms nature. But in Tuscany, if you took notice of the talent of the chef, if you were to ask, *what in the world can this be made of*, or even more damning if you were to concede, *well, we'd never be able to make this ourselves*, Tuscany would at that very moment fail. Sour. Evaporate. You'd lose that which makes Tuscany Tuscan.

South of Tuscany in Umbria (site of the no longer dreaded Assisi), you find the same intensive and ancient cultivation. But except for the sudden spring of a hill town, the land is flat and unvarying, glib and monotonous. To our north, Emilia swells up into the Apennines, awesome, but also steep, harsh, imposing. But in Tuscany for three thousand years, in relatively tiny plots on undulating hillsides, men have softened and detailed the earth with exacting care. Those soft turf and stone terraces, were they shaped by wind and rain, or by man and donkey? Who now can know? Sure, the olive trees must have been planted. Ditto the vineyards. But what about the cypresses and the pines? Did that stone-clad creek always flow down in just that gentle curve, or was it shaped to bring water where cattle could come to drink? You can't trace a difference between what nature gave and what men made.

We have of course a very ancient name for this sort of landscape, in which we are at once in and with and of nature.

From time immemorial we've called it Paradise.

And most of the time Tuscany manages to disguise for us time's recurring claim: that all paradises are paradise lost.

Othello Reclaimed

Recharged by our Tuscan lunch, and finding the power miraculously restored, I plunged into my files last night and discovered—perhaps re-discovered is more accurate—Emily Bartels's "Making More of the Moor." I think it points the way, at least a way, to follow up on June's ort.

Somehow, when I first read it last summer, its originality escaped me. But reviewing it last night, I saw what I've missed all along: the crucial difference between Shylock's and Othello's relation to Venice. It's embarrassing to admit this, so obvious does the difference seem when Professor Bartels points it out. So first thing tomorrow I will xerox the chapter, leave copies for all *gli studenti*, and ask them to use it in preparing the next class.

Here's what the article has helped me grasp.

The Venetians consider Shylock the ultimate outsider, a monster who can be redeemed only by complete conversion. But they treat Othello the Moor from the start as their hero, the only man to save the Republic in the crisis of the Turkish invasion. He's universally admired, relied upon, trusted. Even the Doge says to Brabantio that Othello's telling of his life story "would win [his] daughter too" (I:3, 173), just as it won Brabantio's daughter, Desdemona. Shylock may be the monster, but Othello is The Man.

Sure, the play, especially at the start, brims with ugly racial epithets and slurs. Othello is called "the thick lips" (I:1, 68), "an old black ram" (I:1, 90), a "barbary horse" (I:1, 114), "a lascivious Moor" (I:1, 129). Sex with him is described as making "the beast with two backs" (I:1, 119). Brabantio cannot believe his daughter would desire "the sooty bosom/ Of such a thing as thou" (I:2, 71-72). But, surprisingly, those few passages, plus what Emilia says at the end, the passage June referred to, account for just about all the racial barbs, besides, of course, the continual use of the non-pejorative term, Moor. And here's what's really striking: aside from Emilia's final insult: all of the other derogatory references come from just the first two scenes of the play, and all of them, except for one by the crazed dad Brabantio, come from the villain and his dupe, Iago and Roderigo.

In the third act Othello refers several times in close succession to his own blackness. When he first thinks Desdemona has been unfaithful, he lists what might be her reasons, beginning with "Haply, for I am black" (III:3, 279). Cuckolded, he fears his name is "now begrimed and black/ As mine own face" (III:3, 402-403). And, a few moments later, resolving to destroy those who have betrayed him, he calls out "Arise, black vengeance, from the hollow hell!" (462). But the second and the third do not add up to much more than conventional description and rhetoric. And the first, the most telling, only starts a list of drawbacks, like his lack of polish and his age, which quickly leaves racial difference behind. Othello clearly believes Desdemona has fallen for Cassio because, unlike her husband, he's young and handsome and from her own class and milieu, not simply because he's white and her husband isn't.

Shakespeare's playmaking skills show to unsurpassed advantage here. He starts off pounding these slurs in our heads. Okay, we think, we get it: race-defined protagonist in a race-obsessed world. But then, when the Act One trial scene opens, all those preconceptions get upended. (Do we hear Shakespeare smirking: Been there—*Merchant, Act Four*—Done That.) In this trial Othello is superb, grave, temperate, poised—and admired. The Venetians, including the Doge, treat him with the respect that he deserves. Ugly Iago is muted, and foiled. The play appears to have engaged the racial stereotype only to refute it.

The perfect Act One Othello for our time? Obviously, Colin Powell.

As the script continues, we will be wrong about that, sure, but the point we have to remember in everything that follows is this: Othello and others are aware that he is black, but only the villains or their connections make a significant point of race. For everyone else Othello is the general, the leader, the hero. Thus, when Ludovico sees him behave badly in public to Desdemona, he is staggered. Nothing in Othello's previous behavior or known character prepares for this ugly outburst. Aside from the frustrated patriarch, Brabantio, the other Venetians are up until the very end, and to a man, eager for his company, eager to have him lead them. Outsider he may be by birth, but he is the consummate insider in everything else.

I do find it worrisome that Othello falls so easily into Iago's trap. But so do the impeccably white Roderigo and Cassio. Race doesn't make the difference in this matter: everyone falls before Iago. So what was for me a problem of content and meaning—the black man as easy dupe—now becomes (much less fraught) a problem of form—the ease with which the villain hoodwinks the entire company. That doesn't make the play any easier to read, but it does make the play, for me, for the first time, remarkable. "Speak of me as I am," Othello begs, just before he stabs himself. "[N]othing extenuate,/ Nor aught set down in malice" (V:2, 352-353). No simple task, but a task, I now feel, we can face.

I anticipate eagerly how the students will perform their speeches, with Bartels's article under their collective belt.

And then on my way to class I hear the news of the stalemated Presidential Election and I am staggered. Silenced.

The Election

I am so struck by the bizarre irresolution of the presidential election that for the first time this term I am unable to take notes during class or to recollect after class anything that happened.

What is going on back home? Is it still the same place we left ten weeks ago?

I was a senior in college, at Georgetown, on November 22, 1963 when John Kennedy was shot. The news came through just after lunch, a very warm day, we were all still wearing shorts. We crowded into the chapel to pray for his safety. (It is a Catholic school). But there were so many people in the chapel that we were told to move to the couryard outside where Mass would be said.

A portable altar had been set up and in a few minutes the priest, the indelibly named Father Devine, came out in red vestments because November 22 is the feast of Saint Cecilia, a martyr. He was only a few moments into the Mass when someone came up and whispered in his ear. Shockingly, he left the altar. A moment or two later he reappeared. This time in black vestments, in those days used only for funerals. And then all of the bells in Washington began slowly to toll. And we knew.

That day has always been for me what my parents told me December 7, 1941 was for them, the day that marked the great divide between life-before and life-after. After that divide it is not just that life-before seems no longer possible but that after the divide you wander how you could ever have been so naive, so trusting, so sure of things. Your world, everything in your world, has changed, as Yeats says, changed utterly.

I have something of that feeling today.

Is Tuesday, November 7, 2000 going to be one of those days of epochal divide?

Ventuno

The weather has turned crisp and dry, but *Corriere della Sera* discourages optimism. This is already the wettest autumn in European recorded history. England is one damp ruin. In Italy the rains have cost four lives. Places to the northwest like San Remo are in imminent danger of becoming completely cut off. Worse still, this weather pattern will continue for the foreseeable future. Whether from global warming or not, Italy is getting rainier in autumn and winter, hotter in summer. Italian beaches, the story goes on to say, hitherto reliable refuges from torrid cities, will in future years become infernos. And the skiing industry stands on the brink of ruin as rain replaces snow in the mountains.

Closer to home, the horizon has lowered. An even poise between landscape and skyscape has given way to a view that offers far more sky than land. Florence has shrunk into itself, huddling before a gray scrim of enclosing hills, a view more Dutch than Italian. Everything that in late October seemed reliably blue and bright is now opaque, and stilled, except for thick and pouchy clouds that scrum mightily from west to east, dusky and ominous.

Lit Crit used to teach something called *the pathetic fallacy*: the belief that the nature reflects our moods and needs. Pathetic, maybe, but fallacy? I'm no longer sure. The view here oddly and ironically does line itself up with the news both here and at home.

What a week. What a world.

This colder weather also means it's time to take the lemon and orange trees out of the garden and into their winter shelter, the *limonaia*. Watching this process, I feel I glimpse something immemorial, rooted in those three thousand years of Tuscan history. Before there was an Italy, before there was a Rome, the Etruscans, the primordial Tuscans, must have carried out each November a ritual exactly like this.

The *limonaia* occupies the ground floor of the villino, a series of glass-fronted, unheated bays facing south into the first garden. During the warm weather these bays store extra garden and building equipment. Now they've been emptied and sprayed against fungus so that, one by one, the trees in their terra cotta pots can be ferried inside.

It takes all three of our powerfully built gardeners, Ruggiero, Andrea (a man's name here) and their chief Alessandro, working together, to hustle each heavily-weighted pot through the narrow boxwood alleys. Once free of the alleys the pots are hauled up on to a wheeled aluminum platform. After that, transfer into the limonaia is relatively effortless. But once inside new challenges emerge. The trees grow each year; the *limonaia* does not. And it's crucial that the dozens of trees not crowd each other.

Alessandro in command is fascinating to watch. In the garden he seems to be choosing the order of movement completely at random. But once inside it becomes clear he is carrying around in his head a carefully segmented map of the limonaia exactly matched to the space each tree requires. The last tree to enter precisely matches the last space available. No adjustments required, no second thoughts. And this is how they will remain, unmoved, from start of winter to early spring.

Until recently, the wheeled mover would have been made from wood not aluminum, but the shape itself seems ancient. Nothing else about the process is new. Three strong men. A moving device. Terra cotta pots. Fruit bearing trees. November in. April out. Year in. Year out. The garden empties, Life stays full.

Alessandro invites me to join them a few weeks from now when they pick the olives from our trees, to start the process which produces the olive oil the villa will use throughout the year. "*Ventuno.*" He tells me. "Twenty-one." November twenty-one.

Not a day before. Not a day after.

Not pathetic. Not fallacious.

Verona
Marcello has invited me to join a student trip he is leading north

to Verona. Since two of my scripts are set in Verona, he thinks I must have something to say about the place. Of course, he is wrong. I go along for the ride but I have to explain that the Verona of *Romeo and Juliet* has nothing to do with any real Verona. It's just a name Shakespeare took from his source for the play, a novel by Luigi da Porto. The so-called *casa di Giulietta* is a back-formation, the upshot of English visitors needing to verify the vision of their national poet. What tourists now take to be the Capulet house was actually an inn, called *il cappello*, the hat, that had nothing to do with the Cappelletti family of the novel, Juliet's Capulets. The male *studenti* are therefore deeply dismayed to learn that I wouldn't be guiding them to the house. They've read about the tourist ritual of rubbing for good luck the breast of Juliet's statue. They had plans for the lunch break.

But once in Verona I find unexpected verification for Shakespeare's vision of Italy. Marcello masterfully guides us around the della Scala family tombs near the *Piazza dei Signori.* The most distinguished member of the family, Cangrande della Scala, was Dante's great patron. What does it say not only about a family but about a culture that calls its patriarch Cangrande della Scala, Big Dog of the Steps, and no one laughs? In fact all of the della Scala preferred to be called by dog names. One of them, Mastino, is even buried in a tomb topped with statues of mastiffs, the word for which in Italian is, no surprise here, *mastino.*

Shakespeare didn't know the actual Verona but he did grasp something enduring about a far side of the Tuscan paradise: a liking to be led by those who perform as fierce and powerful dogs.

After *pranzo*, we head toward the great Romanesque church of San Zeno Maggiore. Rotgut joins me. He now constantly seeks me out. I think he senses that I am one of those against his staying on here. Actually, I'm probably the only one left who still thinks he should not return in the spring. *Gli studenti* seem to sense this. As if to reassure me of his normalcy, Jacqueline has confided that *he's now going out to the bars,* as though to say, 'what more could you want.' And a day or so ago Ripley took me aside to say, "I respect him." It was completely sincere. Suffering this grave *gli studenti* almost never encounter first hand, and certainly never with Rotgut's sort of sustained, uncomplaining exposure, day in and out, class, and meals, and leisure. Like all suffering bravely sustained it—and he—awes.

So now he is trying also to change my mind, and heart.

He tells me that he also went to Rome for the break. As we compare itineraries, we are moving along the banks of the river Adige, rushing past, battleship gray, swollen by rain up to the roadbed of its bridges. Marcello warns there is some fear of flooding even this far downstream. We may need to leave for Fiesole earlier than planned. Rotgut drops that he is not going back to Fiesole with us.

He's made an appointment for nine tomorrow morning to see all on his own Padua's Arena Chapel. (Padua is about an hour away from Verona.) Also called the Scrovegni Chapel and finished in 1305, this set-apart church ranks as one of the iconic art historical monuments of the early Renaissance. It was designed by Giotto, the Picasso of his day, and with scores of assistants he covered virtually every wall and the ceiling with fresco. It was and remains overwhelming, one of the greatest works of art in Europe. Rotgut insists he must see it, he cannot leave Italy without having seen it.

Since he couldn't manage to reserve a room for the night in Padua, he plans to go on up to Venice for the night, and then early in the morning backtrack to Padua, less than an hour away.

Alarms go off in every corner of my mind. I tell him I think that plan's too grueling. He needs to rethink it now. He certainly shouldn't be going off to a strange city on his own. I remember Orvieto.

He concedes he already feels exhausted. He hasn't slept very well, he says, for quite a while. But he is adamant about seeing the Arena. He has read everything in the Le Balze library about Giotto, who like Dante has become a hero for him. Rotgut may not like my Shakespeare, but he's hooked on the Italian late Middle Ages that he's found in his overlapping history, art history and Dante courses. In every way, but the one crucial way, he's the ideal student for the Villa, the person for whom the program was devised and targeted. But how much is missing in that one crucial way.

He thanks me for my concern but insists he can ignore his exhaustion and press on solo by train.

We find our bus driver is parked outside San Zeno, edgy about the drive home because of the threat of flood. He'd like us to leave now but Marcello insists we have to see the great Mantegna altarpiece, the glory of Verona. So we rush inside and stare briefly at a work that would reward hours of careful observation. By four we have been herded back into the bus by the disgruntled driver. Out have come the *telefonini,* Everyone's planning Friday night with friends still back in town. *Ciao, Bello. Ciao Bella.* Everybody, except for Rotgut and Duke.

Duke is taking an overnight train for Paris, where, he told me earlier in the day, he is planning just to chill. I don't think he has reconciled himself yet to the failure of his Masked Ball proposition.

And as we drive away I spot Rotgut trudging alone along unfamiliar streets, map in hand, searching for the train station, clearly lost already. We call out to him, offering a lift, but he insists he can find his own way.

We don't see Duke walking. Well, you wouldn't really, would you?

Return
Early this morning, a call from Dora.

She saw the gardener.

He never got to the villa that weekend. His little boy was sick. There could have been a girl. Ivo could have been trapped in the shed. But he knows nothing about it. He hasn't been in hiding, he's been taking care of his boy at his wife's mother's in the Abruzzi. He asked a friend to look after the villa. No one told him the Capolagos were trying to get in touch. He didn't even know that Ivo had died. He is so sorry he cannot help *la signora.* He is so sorry for her terrible loss.

Dora pushed back as hard as she could. He wouldn't budge.

"Did he seem frightened?"

"No."

"Was he lying?"

"Of course."

I don't ask why she doesn't believe the gardener but trusts the detective, why she relies on a guy she loathes rather than someone who's been working for her family for years. The reason is too obvious.

If the gardener is telling the truth, then Ivo is a suicide. Perhaps involuntary but still the cause of his own death.

That is the one thing she will never believe.

She's decided to hire another detective, a more legitimate one this time, to find out more about the gardener. It's only been ten weeks. It should be easy to prove whether the little boy was in fact sick that week, and to prove or disprove the story about the Abruzzi. And what about the friend who never seems to have showed up to take the gardener's place?

I don't point out that even if the little boy was sick, that doesn't mean the father could not have nipped over to the Capolagos' place to have a look at his plants. That's not something I need to tell Dora.

Later, on my way into the villa, I encounter Rogut in the scullery brewing tea. It's just about the time he should have been lost in admiration at the Arena Giottos. Here's what he says happened.

When he gets to the room in Venice, being alone starts to overwhelm him. The previous week in Rome he had spoken to no one but ticket takers and waiters. Now in Venice he's alone again. No one to talk to, nothing to do, no distractions, for the next fourteen hours. In this very cheap room there are only a bed, a chair, and a basin. Nothing else but white walls. White, he repeats. *White. White. White. White.* He can't stop shouting the word.

Suddenly he fled the room, and Venice. Mercifully, he managed to find a late train to Florence and was back at Le Balze by eleven last night. Only an hour or so after the much-delayed bus dropped us off.

Of course, he should be sent home. Now. At once. Each well-meant gesture of mitigation is only postponing catastrophe. These postponements must make the inevitable final collapse more terrible and perhaps more dangerous.

I feel as helpless with Rotgut as I do with Dora. But Ivo's destruction was at our edges. Rotgut's won't be.

WEEK ELEVEN
November 12-18

Purgatorio

This Sunday even the allure of the Crete can't get me out of the villino. It's not just the ongoing deluge. It's also the incomprehensible election at home, Dora, Rotgut. Especially the election. Perhaps if we were at home, with magazines and newspapers and radio, with the chance to hash this out with friends, and not-friends, it would not be so bewildering. But we're so isolated here. I'm like a steerage passenger kept down in the bowels of the Titanic. I can tell that something bad, very bad, has happened, but I can't access anyone or anything that can explain what it is.

Maggie seems impervious to this. Once she decided to put the office behind her, she has rigorously refused all talk of politics. And she seems just as happy to stay inside now to draw and to sew. I try to follow her example; that is, I try to read, since I don't know how to sew and can only draw stick figures. And even those I draw badly. But utterly lacking her iron disciple and inner compass, I soon give up and trudge out to the news stand in Piazza Mino. I've been haunting it since Election Day. Unfortunately, the kiosk offers only Italian papers. We'd have to get down to Florence for something in English. And for the Italians this election is not big news. They treat it with just the same irony they use for the recurring collapse of their cabinets. *What else do you expect from politicians?* Nevertheless, I buy up anything and everything I can that might explain what feels from over here to be the complete implosion of our national life.

Lagniappe

These frustrating visits to the kiosk have produced an unexpected lagniappe. It does nothing to resolve the puzzle of the election but it does show me a side of Tuscany I've otherwise overlooked.

I was about to splash my way back down the Via Vecchia to Le Balze when I spotted on a rack, encased in cellophane, a thick and glossy magazine with the bizarre title, *CASE & COUNTRY*. Despite what look like English words, it turned out to be a genuine Italian magazine. *CASE* isn't our case, as in Sherlock Holmes is on the case. This is *case*, the plural of the Italian word for house, *casa*. And *COUNTRY*, not an Italian word, has recently been annexed as a new and key Italian concept. Ditto the issue's subtitle: *CLASS*.

Intrigued, I bought it and paged through while huddling near the kiosk, umbrella askew, rain soaking my shoulders. And even within the first few pages I could see that all my ruminations had missed something vital about today's Tuscany. I thought that Travelers' Tuscany had died out with people like the Strongs, to be replaced by the Tourist Tuscany with which we are surrounded. I could not have been more wrong. The Travelers are with us in force, as *CASE & COUNTRY* makes dazzlingly, and indeed somewhat comically, clear.

As the glossy cover indicates, these new Travelers come to Tuscany for *class*, i.e. the chance to own a *country house (case country)*, in which to enjoy what the British have been calling for almost two hundred years now, *country life*. Or, as the magazine's other subtitle puts it: they buy property here in order to get *Il piacere di vivere e viaggiare la campagna*, the pleasure of living and traveling in the countryside.

Here's the cover. I am not making this up. It actually reads *SPORT DI MODA TUTTI A CAVALLO! LA CACCIA ALLA VOLPE VIRTUALE CONQUISTA GLI ITALIANI. Fashionable Sport. Everyone to Horse! Fox Hunting Has Virtually Conquered the Italians.* And sure enough there he is, right on the cover, a mounted, pink-coated huntsman, furiously blowing his horn, as panting hounds lop toward us from the ambient woods, in this case from woods somewhere just outside Milan. And there are additional phone numbers furnished inside to help you contact foxhunters in the outskirts of Rome, Friuli, Bologna, Turin and Brescia.

The word on that cover that says it all is *Virtuale*. Tuscany, the virtual England.

Hard to believe? Just browse the pages that follow.

Why not try a hotel in Puglia, described as a *Hotel di Charme* because it has *"atmosfera liberty,"* as in the London shop Liberty's, the one that still stocks Victorian chintz. The Liberty piece leads into another called, not in translation, but actually called, "Old England in Piedmont," recounting *La casa, le passioni, gli amici di Luciano Bar-*

bera, gentleman di Biella. Gentleman is another English word that's become Italian. Barbera, a tweed-clad textile manufacturer, invites you into his country place, Biellese, *"intima come un cottage."* And so it goes. You can get decorating tips for your Tuscan country place from *Nel Nome dei Tudor,* a bed and breakfast in Wales. Or pick up your own *style liberty* stuff shopping the itinerary outlined in a driving tour across *"La Terra Delle Due Rose,"* the Land of the Two Roses, as in the War thereof, that is: Herefordshire. There's also a piece on the Tuscan Maremma, where, we are assured, *Gli inglese continuano ad arrivare"* (the English continue to arrive), silently and discreetly, the article continues, restoring farmhouses and farmlands. And of course there's the big cover story on fox hunting.

France surfaces in two of the stories. One covers the now very smart cuisine of the French Southwest. The other tours a beauty spa in the Dordogne, itself the site of an earlier British incursion. But no one, it seems, actually wants to live in France. That is: no one reading this magazine. France is where Travelers go when they want to play Tourist.

So here's the skinny: though Tourists come to Tuscany for Tuscany, lured largely by Travelers' memoirs of paradise, the Travelers themselves, including English Travelers, come to Italy to get—not Tuscany but England. Who'd have thought it!

Traveler houses now dot the Tuscan countryside. You can tell they're not Italian houses because Travelers live in farmhouses without farmyards. No heavy equipment. No working sheds or barns. And no animals even when the shutters are down. That's the surest sign. If, as you approach, no person appears, and nothing unseen moos, lows, barks, brays, or quacks, you know that the owners are perhaps Germans, more likely Americans, and most probably Brits. The Francis Scott Keys over for the autumn from Houston. Miriam, between pictures, in from the Coast. Ted the painter back in his studio above Borgo San Lorenzo, after summering at his studio on Nantucket. Travelers like these live part time in Tuscany. Part time is the crucial part. Because Italy, oddly, isn't essentially what they've come for. Italy is merely the way, the means, to get what they really want—England.

Even the English themselves, it would seem, now come to Italy for English country life. They tend to be those who can't have it, or can't have it easily, at home. Authentic country life in England is hard, expensive, and iffy. And that's English country life at its best. Try driving back into London from the west on a Sunday evening. A misery. And the cottage you left behind is just that: a cottage, cramped, drafty, dark, and demanding constant repair at those staggering English prices. The highest in Europe. And even if you got there easily, with a few pounds left in your pocket, it probably rained all weekend, while the people in the big place on the hill pretended they had never seen you before.

But with just a little bit of planning ahead you can fly here from England inexpensively, and certainly more comfortably than you can drive to a comparable place in the UK. Kyra's Ryan Airfare Five Pound round trip is a rarity. But there are lots of only slighter higher fares for inter-country travel within the newly connected Europe. As for houses here, you can get a substantial country place in Tuscany at far less than what you'd pay for that leaky cottage in the deluged dales. Right now there's a place for sale in the hills south of Siena, a beautiful old stone complex, completely modernized, staggering views in every direction, and its own olive grove, for $600,000. In England there's not a house you'd want to live in that's available for a comparable sum. Not to mention the fact that, blessedly, the weather here is almost always benign, at least for nine months of the year. And at its worst, it never descends to English staples like drifting sleet.

That's the British picture. Of course, the pond makes things a bit different for those Stateside.

Far fewer North Americans yearn to own in Tuscany. Those who do tend to be somewhat older and significantly wealthier than their British counterparts. Some are academics or artists. But mostly they are the retired, or the semi-retired, since you can't fly over to Tuscany from the States on the spur of the moment unless you are very rich indeed. To make Tuscany habitable you need to plan on spending several weeks at a time here, if not for an entire season, then at least for significant chunks of the summer or the fall or the spring. For the most part, then, US Travelers sublet for relatively brief periods from English Travelers who live here off and on all the year round.

But why don't folks from the US buy in the UK? If you want country life, why not go for the real thing rather than the virtual?

It's not just that English snobbism is tough on all new money, or that English weather is torture to everyone. It's really that Tuscany now does a better England than England itself can provide. And that's not true only for UK bargain hunters, or for the US new leisure class, it's true for Italians as well. For country life, England remains the preferred model, but Tuscany has become the standard issue. Italy has become, even for Italians, the new, the improved, and the available England.

At the turn into the twentieth century wealthy Americans like our Charles Strong and British men and women like his neighbor Lady Sybil Cutting (herself living off income from a sizeable American railway fortune) came to Italy for Italy. They anglicized it of course, all those un-Italian flower beds. But the idea that drove them, and kept them, here, even as the Fascists took control, even as the Nazis invaded, was that in Italy you could live a life profoundly different from, because significantly larger than, the life you left behind. Indeed, Sybil's husband, Bayard Cutting, on his death bed, asked her to raise their daughter Iris some place where she would never feel at home. Hence the villa in Fiesole. But now that is entirely reversed.

So for me, after all these weeks trying to see what Henry James would call the *figure in the carpet*, Tuscany takes clear form.

There are actually not two but three Tuscanies. There's the Travelers' Tuscany of CASE & COUNTRY. We live in the vestiges of its first formulation, the Tuscany of the Strongs and their coterie. And all around us this autumn there's been Tourist Tuscany, the Tuscany of *gli studenti* and our house guests. The perfect lunch at Pietra Fitta. The David, the Uffizi, San Gimignano. Italy the incomparably sublime. But enclosing those two Tuscanies there is Italy itself, the Italy to which Dora has opened my eyes. And here is the surprise, Dora's Italy is also Shakespeare's. Violent Verona. Patriarchal Padua. Venice borrowing and morally bankrupt. All the Princes either perfidious or powerless. The Italy in which everything is forbidden and everything permitted, in which Ivo Capolago is killed, and no one except his family seems to care. The Italy in which Death always lurks, and not always at the edges.

If you leave the beach and enter the hinterland, the Italy which tourists never see and travelers turn aside from, four-hundred year-old Shakespeare is your most reliable guide.

I'd be teaching an entirely altered course, same scripts, completely different approach, if I started the term tomorrow.

The Bright at their Best

Today *gli studenti* do wonders with *Othello*. Easily connecting character to setting, they set about cleverly repositioning the script within its particular, Venetian context. The class dynamic has completely changed. Even as I now see Shakespeare mapping our present, they've been won over to reading the scripts rooted in history.

This is what you teach for, the moment when you can stop instructing and leave things in the students' skillful hands. Content, I sit back, and let them dazzle.

A month ago Betty was insisting that she couldn't relate to a text that didn't echo something in her own life. Period. Now she volunteers as soon as the class starts that *Othello* seems to her to be built on the same contrast we found in many of the other Shakespeare texts: between two different places that support two different ways of life. With *Merchant* it was Venice v. Belmont. In this case the contrast is between Venice and Cyprus.

It's harder to appreciate this, she says, because once we get to Cyprus in Act Two, we stay there. We don't move back and forth between Cyprus and Venice as we do between Belmont and Venice. Nevertheless, she insists, we've got to keep this contrast in mind because the play is shaped by the differences between the metropole and its colony.

She does actually use metropole, and knows what it means. A lagniappe you get teaching at Georgetown where everyone sooner or later picks up Foreign Service Speak.

She explains the difference between the two places. In Venice, when Iago early in the play disturbs the night, his plans are swiftly and smoothly foiled. The Venetian Senate and the Doge provide a quick and fair re-imposition of order. Othello explains to them his wooing of Desdemona. Desdemona confirms his story. And then, despite her father Brabantio's standing as one of themselves, the Venetian grandees side with the Moor, awarding him both the generalship against the Turks and the bride he's sought. Order disturbed gives way at once to order restored. The Venice of Act One couldn't be crisper or cleaner.

But when in Act Two we get to Cyprus, Venice's colony, we find Venetians again but Venetians operating without Venice's legal machinery. And shockingly we find ourselves in a completely different world, a garrison frontier like the American Wild West, ongoing and apparently uncontrollable riot. It's corrupt, with no adequate legal authority. In fact, the appropriate authorities, who have been sent out to impose order, almost immediately themselves become the malefactors, first Cassio in a drunken rage, and then, altogether more seriously, Othello in his literally murderous rage.

Gloria sums it up neatly. On Cyprus we get Venetian life without Venetian law, in other words: catastrophe.

Ardita adds that she's read in a commentary that Venetian rashness was commonly attributed to epicureanism, their notorious devotion to sensuous pleasure and luxurious living, for which they had a reputation that stretched beyond Europe to the Ottomans. And, clearly, to England.

Rotgut—yes, Rotgut, back and somehow, at least momentarily, in old form—reformulates that charge in usefully Freudian terminology. Pointing out the preposterous speed of this play, how rapidly the Venetians are inflamed, engrossed, engulfed, turned on a dime toward a stranger or against a loved one, he characterizes Venice as a world which has never internalized repression. (Therapy has its uses, even applied only to texts.) What Venetians hear they believe. What they think they say. Whatever they feel, they do. In Venice itself a strong legal system, its established superego, effectively constrains these passions. But on Cyprus, without those external controls, characteristic Venetian intemperance at once takes hold, and swiftly consumes them all.

Willy Voltaire follows by showing how, in counterpoint, the first things we learn about Venetian life all have to do with rank and position, with generals, their lieutenants, their ensigns, masters and their followers, with great ones, patriarchal senators like Brabantio, and the Doge, here called the Duke. This is a different Venice from that of *Merchant*. *Merchant's* Venice was all about money, making it, lending it, marrying it. *Othello's* Venice, however, is all about place and power, reverence, and hierarchy, and order. Furious at being disturbed, Brabantio can bellow: "What tell'st thou me of robbing? This is Venice; / My house is not a grange" (I:1,108-109). His point is this: in that pearl of a place, unseemly disruptions simply do not occur. But the play's point is just the reverse: given the typical excess of Venetian character, disruptions occur here all the time. That's why they need a strong Doge and Senate. (Verona's parallel Mastino and Cangrande come to my mind.) Venice is a world where everyone, or rather every man, strives to be Master, and no one wants to follow. The state has no option except to police severely.

Willy continues. Clearly our closest and subtlest reader, he points to the language of the first act, rightly making much of the moment when Roderigo calls Othello "an extravagant and wheeling stranger/ Of here and everywhere" (I:1, 139-140). How can Othello be a *stranger*, Willy asks, if he's not only of everywhere but also of *here*? Can a *stranger* be *of here*? If that's true, then whatever *stranger* means here, clearly Othello's menace—or glamour—is more subtle than Shylock's entire, absolute difference. Yes, Othello is the Moor. But isn't he also the Venetian Generalissimo? In looks, and presumably in dress, he's Arab, not European. But he's also like the Venetians a Christian, not, like their enemies, a Muslim. On the one hand he's the Venetians' reverse; on the other hand, he's their commanding idea, ideal. That's Othello's paradox, right? He can be of *everywhere*, and he can be of *here*, but he can't ever be of *anywhere*. This "here and everywhere" Othello subverts the oppressive Venetian hierarchy, even as he supports it. In a world shaped as a pyramid, no wonder Roderigo calls him a *wheel*.

On a roll, Willy continues, while this *wheeling* repels Iago and Roderigo, it seems to be exactly what attracts Desdemona. Locked away in her father's house, hard pressed even to overhear Othello's conversation, she finds in his "strange… passing strange" (I:3, 162) and extravagant accounts of a life here and everywhere, a release from her father's Mastery. She calls her father "the lord of duty" (I:3, 186). To him, she claims, she owes "obedience" (182). But in and with Othello she thinks she's found exactly what Iago claims Venice must fear in him, an equalizer.

Betty, excited, chimes back in: But of course they're both wrong. When, on Cyprus, Iago figures out how completely Othello identifies himself with Mastery, he knows the Moor is finished. Iago understands everything about how to play on, and play with, that sort of narcissism, since it's also his own. With one huge difference.

Iago and Othello are both narcissists but Othello is compellingly forthright and Iago is appallingly dishonest. In any contest of two such narcissisms duplicity will always trump candor.

And a few scenes later, Claudia Hipp throws in, Desdemona makes that same deflating discovery about her "lord." But she then knows that means she's finished too. Claudia rereads the romance for us from this viewpoint. Assuming she and her "lord" are partners, Desdemona thought she could ask Othello to change his mind to please her, and he would. But, she swiftly learns, he won't. Othello is just as concerned with Mastery, with ownership and obedience, as her father or any other Venetian signor. "O curse of marriage," he laments, "That we can call these delicate creatures ours/ And not their appetites." (III:3, 284-286).

Miss Haag now offers a gem. The corollary to this insistence on Mastery is the supremacy of the private in Venice. Brabantio cannot stand the idea that his private domain has been violated, even though his daughter has gone off with a man Brabantio himself has been assiduously courting. As soon as the private becomes in any way public, it is immediately and only trash. And Othello feels precisely the same way about Desdemona, when he "learns" she has chosen another. In the middle of the play the husband repeats what the father did at the start. For both men, when they find out there's the possibility of another in their private space, they immediately render the woman they have loved worthless, a whore, nothing. The mere assertion of movement outside the man's control so deeply sullies a woman that she must be stripped of every value, including of course life itself. In one of the great ironies of this bitterly ironic play, her husband does to Desdemona at the end almost precisely what her father did to her at the start.

At this point it's the hitherto silent Consuela who connects our reading of the two Venetian plays. Shakespeare seems to be doing with Othello what he earlier did with Shylock. In this play also, the figure set up as the apparently marginal Other actually turns out to mirror the central and dominant class, and mirrors them in a way that is "extravagantly" enlarged. Of course, Shylock is the monstrous outsider whose claims to similarity the Venetians cannot bear to concede. Othello, however, the outsider-become-insider, is a kind of corporate ego ideal. That's why, Consuela suggests, an exclusive emphasis on the ugly racist language of the first two scenes can actually misread the play. If you only see the ways in which Othello differs in look or voice from the white Venetians you miss the more crucial point of his perfect introjection of their distinguishing ways and means. He is not just like them. He represents their own self-justifying Mastery writ large. His defects echo theirs. His collapse predicts their own.

Which must be why at the end of the play, adds Judy, the Venetian emissaries find it so hard to condemn Othello. Even after they have the proof of the murder. It is Iago, the Venetian ambassador insists, who is responsible, as though he had been the one who did the smothering. "Look on the tragic loading of this bed. / This is thy work" (V:2, 374-375). At the same time the ambassador does everything possible to keep the blame off Othello, to see and present him somehow as merely one of the victims, simply "this rash and unfortunate man" (291). But that *rash* says it all. This rashness is not traced by race. This is the *rash* that Roderigo shows in following Iago's every command. As *rash* as Brabantio in abandoning his daughter. *Rash* as Desdemona, first in fleeing with the Moor, and finally in refusing any outlet from or palliation of her doom. *Rash* as any one of the Venetians' own.

We are almost to the end of the class. But just before we close the always reliable Faustina summarizes intriguingly key coordinations between Othello and Cyprus, and between *Othello* and *Merchant*. Cyprus and Othello, she says, represent Venetian *supplements*. She smiles at me. The rest of the class laughs. These are your words and your ways, she is saying, but since you insist, I will play by them. And notice how well I do it. But, at the same time, if she hadn't thought about it, she couldn't do it this well. So the gentle mock also carries a distinct boast.

Cyprus is Venice's colony, Othello is Venice's ally. They are supplements because they are not the "real thing." Cyprus is not Venice, Othello is not a Venetian. Nevertheless, the "real thing" depends on them. They are vital not just to the security but to the continuity of the Republic, which cannot, the Doge says in Act One, continue without them. But in this supplemental pair—and here is where Faustina clearly earns her right to show off—colony and ally exactly reverse that other pair of Venetian supplements we saw in *Merchant*, outpost Belmont and its mistress, Portia.

How are they supplements, someone asks. They seem like alternatives, not supplements.

Faustina stops short, and goes silent. It's a continuous and curious feature of our undergraduates that they choke when they hear challenges from fellow students. Some peer-enforced protocol drives them to back away from anything in class that might sound like confrontation. To answer would be showing off, trying to impress the teacher at another student's expense. One student can question another and even disagree. This is about sincerity, about sticking up for your own opinion. But then the student questioned has to back off, back down, back away, murmuring something like: 'Sure. You could be right. This is just the way I see it.'

I can see that this retreat is just about to happen here when, happily, supremely self-assured Beluga explains Faustina on Faustina's behalf. The whole first part of *Merchant*, he says, centers on that wimp Bassanio. Beluga has never gotten over his ort about the fortunate fortune-hunter who goes out to Belmont to win the heiress with all the money. That's supplement number one: the wealth of Belmont supplements the destructive extravagance of Venice. Then, in the second half of the play, Portia has to come back from Belmont to Venice because these Venetian losers are once again about to cash it in. And she shows them how to beat their adversary and spare Antonio's pecs. That's supplement number two. In both cases Belmont supplements Venice. Belmont is the different thing, outside of and apart from the real thing that the real thing needs to survive.

Exactly, say Faustina. And now, supplemented herself, she can continue. How fascinating undergraduates are, and how, after all these years in the classroom, mysterious they remain to me.

We talked, Faustina goes on, about how Portia represents a kind of Classical revival. She's got a famous Roman name. She's compared to the Golden Fleece. At Belmont people talk easily about classical figures, like Troilus and Cressida, or Dido and Aeneas. It's very peaceful and harmonious. All kinds of foreigners, the suitors in the early acts, are made welcome, even when Portia actually can't stand them. So Jessica, even though she's Jewish, easily fits in. But Venice itself is all about competition and rivalry. Economic competition. Religious rivalry. And it's all about right now, this bond, this sale. So it's a whole different set of values, that are never actually found inside Venice, that Portia brings to the Venetians who seek her out, or into Venice itself. Without what Belmont stands for and offers, Venice can't make it on its own.

Jacqueline sums this up: "if it weren't for Portia, what she does and what she means, *Merchant of Venice* would be a tragedy. It would be horrible. The Venetian scenes, most of them, *are* horrible. But what Portia does to the play is: her vision and her values turn it into a comedy."

Faustina nods, and continues. In *Othello* the Venetian state appoints Othello officially to be what Portia has to disguise herself to become, Venice and the Venetians' savior. That's the starting point of *Othello*, but it's the climax of *Merchant*. Like Portia, Othello then leads the Venetians to a night world, Cyprus. But where nighttime on Belmont is a dream, night on Cyprus is a nightmare.

I think I can see what Faustina wants to say, but I also sense she can't quite say it. I intervene. "So you want to suggest that Cyprus is a kind of negative supplement. Belmont recuperates Venice. But Cyprus—... "

"Cyprus" she completes my sentence, "Cyprus lets Venice out of the bag. All of the stuff that Venice manages to suppress while the Doge is in charge gets released in the colony, where there's no Doge, only his representative. So Cyprus subverts Venice. Othello can't carry off what the Doge can manage. He winds up subverting the secure Venetian world of the beginning of the play, showing all its ugliness. But in a funny way Portia does the same thing. She—deliberately—shows the Venetians exactly what they have in a world that can rely on law but cannot also produce mercy. And Othello—not deliberately at all, but still—shows the other side of the equation: what it's like to live in a world of power.

"Of Mastery," Willy reminds us.

"Of Mastery," Faustina concludes, "without law."

She is finished, and so are we. We are stunned, and so is she.

Three things emerge clearly for me as we file out of the library into the now dark long corridor of the villa.

One: what an extraordinary play *Othello* is. It's a revelation for me.

Two: that revelation would not have happened were if not for the extremely talented group of young people who make up *gli studenti*.

Three: the unexpected contours of this term have completely renewed my love of the classroom. I am not only ready now but eager to go back, and to work, and to keep on working.

Marcello's Star Turn

Today my old adversary, Muldoon, long vanished from the Shakespeare class, announces that *gli studenti* propose to strike. I've got a hunch this move emerges in reaction to Rotgut's new role. As Rotgut has increasingly magnetized villa interest, Muldoon has become somewhat isolated. Standing alliances, formed through the first two months, have radically shifted. Muldoon, hitherto a social center for at least a significant segment among *gli studenti*, now sees his accustomed preeminence threatened. And so, Lenin-like, he is determined to rally his followers round by fomenting revolution.

Muldoon has called for a formal meeting with Marcello as the Director. All *gli studenti* take his required course in medieval history. They take *pranzo* with him every week day in the dining room. He is both admired and popular. But this is a confrontation, and it demands a formal setting. Genially, Marcello agrees to see them in the library after lunch. Marcello is constitutionally genial. I tag along to observe.

The meeting is impeccably civilized. Italian students, Muldoon says, are famous for going on strike. So *gli studenti* feel they should now go on strike also, in order to enjoy, before the term ends, the full experience of being in Italy. It would, Muldoon claims, be "so fun." He doesn't seem to think there's much difference between a strike and a costume ball. So, if Marcello doesn't mind, the strike will take place next day. However, mysteriously, they intend to exempt my course and the course in Italian Government taught by Bruno Wanrooij. They will strike only the Italian language courses and Marcello's own history course, that is: only courses taught by Italians. Presumably, non-Italian faculty don't play convincingly as powers that be. Or perhaps we play that role all too convincingly.

After Muldoon's self-pleasing and insouciant introduction, a number of *gli studenti* exit, voting, they say, with their feet. This includes most of the alpha males, like Duke, Beluga and Ripley. But a surprising number remain, including almost all of the women, and Rotgut, loyal to anything that seems to constitute the group, determined to play nice. It is hard to tell why the others stay, since the meeting is almost entirely structured as a dialogue between Muldoon and Marcello. Is it just curiosity, or real interest in the proposal? Perhaps only a desire to watch Marcello perform, in what turns out to be both a star turn and a real treat.

But of course, he begins by assuring them, they should have a full Italian experience while they are in Italy. That is only right and fair. But a strike, a real strike, cannot be held like this, without any preparation. And of course it must not be held with the consent of those struck against. He has himself been involved with strikes before, as a schoolboy. He and his friends took over their school and held it for days, sleeping there, lest the police seize them and the building. In the end, he was expelled from the school. It was very hard on him and very painful for his family. And yes, that is also something they must remember. There can be no strike unless it costs the strikers something. A strike must be difficult, it must be hard. You are not on strike if being on strike does not hurt.

And also there is something else, he has remembered to add. "To have a strike you have to have something you are striking for."

Curiously, this seems to come as a revelation to Muldoon. Hard to tell about the others, since he remains the only one who speaks.

Marcello's a bantam boxer, a Rossini tenor. Light, incredibly light on his toes, full of energy and spring and bounce. He's having fun, and he's fun to watch. You never know where to have him, or where he'll have you. Rarely if ever do you get a performance like his in the American academy any more. You do get people, especially younger guys, who do a version of Stand Up, relentlessly deflating, obscene, outrageous, knowing. Students eat it up. But self-righteous and sincere or angry and heavy handed, that's the range for almost every academic voice I know, including my own. There are remarkable exceptions. In my world the incomparable Jim Kincaid or the lustrous Gina Barreca at Connecticut. But they are sparse on the ground. When I started out in this work, I remember trying to achieve an effect something like a shot of straight, good gin. Tart, quick, and right to the brain. But over the years, like an opera singer's, my voice grew darker, and now I sermonize in class with the rest and best of them.

Marcello continues with exquisite courtesy. "You must have a list of demands. You must have a meeting with the administrators. You must present your demands formally. You will then be given a set of counter-demands by the administration. These you must bring back to your friends. Then you must discuss all this, discuss it in full, for a long time, several days at least. Then you must come back and meet again with the administrators.

"Perhaps this will happen several times. It may involve not only days but probably weeks.

"And then, if your demands are not satisfactorily met, only then, you go on strike.

"So," he concludes, "I will leave you now and you will be able to begin to formulate your demands, and when you have them formulated we will arrange our meeting. Our first meeting. The first of our many meetings. And then you will have the full experience."

Of course, at this point there is something less than three weeks left to the semester, but Marcello does not point that out. He could not in fact be more obliging, more open, more welcoming. "Oh but you must have the experience you desire, in full, of course."

What a delight to watch Marcello perform. But I'm astounded when, leaving, Muldoon assures me, sincerely, "he"—Marcello— "really wants us to do this. I can tell."

An act is only as good as its audience, I guess.

Becoming Othellos

With their new and rich understanding of *Othello's* complex text, the students' Wednesday performances of monologues are remarkable. Except for Rotgut who takes me aside before we start to tell me that, though he has tried, he has not been able to memorize any of the speeches. He looks as though he has not slept for several days. He admits that he has stayed up the last two nights trying to commit twenty lines to memory. They go out of his head as soon as he thinks he's learned them.

Of course he can't memorize another role. His mind is too busy grappling with the role he's been assigned by the Villa. For the past week or two, he's been like an unsure actor at early rehearsals with a cast he's thinks beyond him. Careful, watching, intent, trying to get the rhythm of this piece, its style, its lilt, so that when called on he can creditably do his bit. But miscast from the start, knowing it and knowing we know it, wondering whether it will come through, and he will be let go. And now to play Othello or Iago on top of that.

Of course I let him off the hook. My hook. If only it were within my power to ease his burden entirely.

All of the other *studenti* are good. But the best performances come from Duke, Clyde, Willy Voltaire and, entirely surprising, Judy. To some extent this is because they take up some of the most remarkable poetry in the play, Othello's speeches in the harrowing final scene.

Judy goes first and is, in that word much overworked by students, amazing, but it is the only word for what she does. She performs the beginning of the scene, the actual murder. She insists Duke play her Desdemona. She makes him lie down on the coffee table. He hates this. He feels weak, vulnerable, girly. Just what Judy wants. She even takes away the scarf he always wears, now that it has gotten colder, and wraps it around herself as a belt. Does it take a woman to make us see the power at stake here, the deep play of gender beneath the dark performance of personality. She delivers the speech carefully, accurately, and then—-shocking—she smothers him, taking a pillow from the couch. He's absolutely still, and for a moment we do believe he's dead.

It's terrific and they are both embarrassed as if we had all seen them doing something lewd together. Which in a way we have.

The three men do the later parts of the scene. They find it easy to read themselves into the heartbreak and shamed narcissism of the ruined hero. Duke gets his own back as a self-defending broken boaster. Clyde plays eloquently Othello's too late awareness of what he lost in Desdemona. Willy concludes. He has been a quiet controlled performer throughout the course. Tonight he reveals an unexpected power as he delivers Othello's last speech.

He first turns off all the lamps until there is only one dim light left. The room is now full of shadows. As he starts to speak he shows that he has taken an ugly, long knife from the scullery. It's a surprise and an anxiety. We see he loves this *sword*. It's all that remains of his power, his manhood. The sword is his friend, the last one he loves that loves him. And then aware of the others' attempt to stop him, Willy begins to wield it as a threat. We all shrink back when he swings it in a wide semicircle, though none of us is really in danger. And then we do become frightened. Really frightened.

This is a kid, a student, not an actor, but the performance is transforming him. Rather it's releasing something in him his ordinary life never shows. I should stop him from handling this knife. He's twenty-one, responsible for himself, the most serious guy in the group. But now he is entirely at one with the passion, the speech, the role. I grow convinced that he will stab himself at the finish, perhaps only to draw a little blood. He really seems like Othello now, no longer in control.

I am literally on the edge of my seat. I'll grab him if he goes too far. "I took by the throat," he starts. The knife point is now against his own throat. "[T]he circumcised dog/And smote him" —I'm out of my seat—"thus." The knife blade sinks into his throat, without cutting. It's impossible to know how he came so close, and drew no blood. I am speechless. He is in tears. *Gli studenti* are mesmerized.

Afterwards, meditating on this pair of wonderful classes, I wonder at what these amateur, convinced, and convincing performances have made me feel. Throughout his career, Shakespeare loved and loathed Mastery, in all its splendid, arrogant formulations. Mastery swells throughout the Italian plays. But nowhere did he trace its attractions and its evils as effectively as in *Othello*. In this play his writing is so powerfully dramatic, so commanding that, attentively internalized, it can release performances of great authority even from the unpracticed.

And finally I think how odd it is that by the end of his career everything Shakespeare feared his England might become can be summed up in that enchanting/alarming word, *Italy*.

Waldo

Cip calls. Everything has collapsed.

Dora had to go to Waldo to replace the money she gave her detective. Of course, that meant telling him everything else she's done behind his back. Cip was not there but he says that, from both parents' account, it was the worst moment of their marriage, in some ways even worse that finding Ivo's body. Maybe even the last moment in their marriage.

Waldo now doesn't speak to Dora. They communicate only through Cip. Waldo will probably move out of the apartment, perhaps to the villa, at least for a while. Dora is on the verge of a breakdown. Cip wants her to see a therapist. So far she refuses to see anyone.

But why does Waldo believe the detective rather than the gardener? I don't get it. Why not use the gardener to prove that the detective has been lying from the start?

No, Waldo *does* believe the gardener wasn't at the villa that morning. What he doesn't believe is the tale of a small abduction gone amiss. All along, he believes, the plan was to murder Ivo, as retribution for Waldo holding out against the takeover of his businesses. The kidnapping story was just a ruse. When the detective pushed too hard against it, he got a glimpse of the real story, and fled.

Waldo told Dora she should light candles every day in every church in Rome, praying that Ivo's killers don't find the ex-cop. If they do, who knows what he'll invent about the Capolagos to mollify his tormentors. With men like that you tell them what you think they want to hear, not to escape death but to bring an end to the torture. After that, the Capolagos couldn't stay in Italy. Indeed, they'd be lucky to escape with their lives.

Waldo is by nature sober and laconic. Business has taught him to suppress any sign of strong feeling. This kind of language, hyperbolic from anyone else, can be from him only cold and sober fact.

Among other restrictions Waldo has forbidden Dora to have anything more to do with me. Despite her and Cip's explanations of my marginal role, Waldo is convinced I was the one egging her on because I want material for this book. Of the many ironies in this story that is probably the least important. If it helps mitigate Waldo's fury, what harm does it do me? I don't expect to see any of them again.

Cip is holding his breath until November 21 is past, next Tuesday. Ivo's birthday. If they can get past that day without a crisis, then he'll get them to leave Italy for an extended holiday, perhaps back to South America, or maybe even to the States.

We say goodbye awkwardly. There are apologies on both sides but at this stage they are pretty meaningless. It's not until he hangs up that I recall why the twenty-first seemed to ring a bell. *Vent-uno*— the day the gardeners have set for the olive pressing.

The Slaves

As though to follow up on Cip's bleak message, Italy decides to show that it contains even other Tuscanies. There is also, hitherto invisible, Slave Tuscany.

We see it on Friday afternoon. It's a handsome day, not quite the bright light of October, but soft and gold and beckoning. And not raining. Maggie and I rush down to renew ourselves in the joys of Sant'Antimo and Sant'Angelo. Late in the day, coming back north, we use a road I haven't driven before, the 223, a major artery connecting Grosseto to Siena, and then to points north and east. There is a steady stream of traffic, more trucks than cars, as dusk and the weekend come on.

We are coming down a long, slow curve, heavily treed on both sides. Making her way toward us, picking a path at the side of the road, where there is no path, walks a striking, exceptionally tall, black woman in a purple pants suit with a matching head scarf. She is striking because she is so lovely, and also because she is so out place. There is a significant African diaspora settled in Florence, centered in Piazza Santa Maria Novella. And Rome is now a major African city. But you rarely seen a black man or woman in the countryside, and certainly never someone so smartly dressed in so forlorn a situation, alone in the dusk, getting apparently nowhere.

Inside the car we speculate. Perhaps she is an au pair or a nanny, coming back from her afternoon off, to employers too mean spirited or stingy to pick her up or lend her the car. As we speculate we pass another black woman, this time stationary, standing by herself up a small byway off the main road. Dark stockings, denim hot pants, a bright halter. She makes no attempt to engage the passing cars. You might almost think she was lost, or stranded. Perhaps her car has broken down nearby, except that the uniform is unmistakable. She is statuesque, immobile, frozen.

After that, every couple of minutes along the road, we find her variously dressed doubles. Of course we recognize who they are and what they do. But it is also mystifying. How did these women get to this lonely stretch of road? Who are their customers? Once they've been hired, where do they go? The only building we see in two hours of driving is a gas station.

Their intended customers, we later learn, are the truck drivers who begin driving this road as dark comes on, timing their trips to make deliveries in the north before or just at dawn. They will find women like these all along the way, not only on the 223 but also on the 78, which crosses the 223 at Siena, branching eastward to climb the Apennines, and wind up on the Adriatic coast between Ancona and Rimini.

I live in a city. I am used to the invitations, the self-advertisement of urban prostitutes. Of both genders. But to find these women, in droves, in what is not just a rural, but a genuinely pastoral, setting, I am not prepared for that. And yet they are not out of place. They look like, they are, lambs led to slaughter, herded, driven, to fill human needs, to satisfy demands for pleasure not their own. It's heartbreaking in its way that they make no effort to attract, to solicit. They simply stand, to be seen, to be taken, to be used.

And they are truly slaves. From the Italians at the Villa I learn that they are taken from Africa to Italy, lied to, betrayed, sometimes just brutally kidnapped. Once here, they are forced into sex work. Their pimps drive them to these remote locations. After the women leave the cars, they must stay out on the roads until the end of the night when the pimps come back at dawn to collect them. The sex happens in the trucks. If the customer drives one of them too far away from her starting point she must somehow find her way back, alone, to the starting point. At sunrise they are driven away again, held captive until the night returns.

I knew a Florentine lady of great elegance who once told me with absolutely assured authority: "Italy ends in Rome. Below that it is Africa." As if.

Cecilia Returns
Cecilia is returning today from Boston to join us for Thanksgiving, and she will bring her friend, Douglas Gordon. Doug's an

especially appropriate Thanksgiving guest since three of his four grandparents descend from the marriage of John and Priscilla Alden, the first marriage among the Pilgrims. His parents even have a piece of Plymouth rock under glass in their house, but Doug, despite constant pressure from us, has not been persuaded to bring it over to authenticate our celebration. Cecilia says that she will try to get him to wear a pilgrim hat on the day. But she has her doubts. Hats are not Doug's sort of thing.

Cecilia and Doug are actually crucial to Le Balze's Thanksgiving. They are bringing with them, at the cooks' instructions, bags of fresh cranberries, cans of pumpkin puree, and sacks of pecans, all essential to an authentic version of the feast. None of these can be had in Italy. Apparently Italy does not produce the cranberry. There are plenty of pumpkins at this time of year, but they turn out to be a different sort of squash than ours, sweeter and pulpier. No one seems to be able to explain why we can't get pecans here. But the Italians don't even have a word for pecan. The Italian cook, Sandra, can only call them "those little nuts you Americans like in *dolce*." You can tell she can't understand why. But big-hearted and determined, she is going to do her best to give us what we want on our big day.

Cecilia and Douglas are scheduled to arrive around 11 this morning, having left Boston on Alitalia around six last night, with a brief early morning stopover in Milan. But sometime around two in the morning we got a call from Thad in Chicago. His sister and Doug got to Logan Airport only to find themselves bumped from their oversold flight. Alitalia is putting them on a later flight and now they will arrive in Florence at five Saturday evening. It sounds horrible, twenty hours in transit, especially since Doug only got into Boston on Friday afternoon after spending most of the week shuttling on business between Seattle, Los Angeles and Las Vegas.

Midmorning Saturday Cecilia calls from Milan. They have tried to get from the airport to the train station, since the train from Milan to Florence only takes a couple of hours, and their connecting flight won't leave till 4:30, but Alitalia refuses to release their luggage. The bags can only go on the 4:30 flight, and only if Doug and Cecilia go with them. Sorry, but no, there are no other planes from Milan to Florence this day. We assure Cecilia we will be at the airport when they arrive ready to waft them up to Fiesole.

Of course their plane is late. Nor can we see them when it does land, because the Florence arrivals terminal closes off the luggage area with frosted doors that open only from within. We wait. And we wait. Everyone off the Milan plane has clearly left the luggage area. The doors remain firmly shut. There is no one in the terminal whom we can ask. Everyone is on the other side of the frosted, impenetrable portal.

Finally, I grab an attendant on his way out for a cigartette and explain that *mia figlia, arrivanda da Milano, è perduta*. My daughter, arriving from Milan, is lost. Except that *perduta* is more like very very lost as in kidnapped. I do not explain that my daughter is twenty-five years old, and a member of the Massachusetts bar, or that she is accompanied by an exceptionally fit specimen of American manhood capable of meeting any threat to her person or property. *Figlia... perduta*. In Italy an open sesame.

I discover Cecilia and Doug at the far end of the terminal, at the lost luggage desk. The single attendant, busy at her computer terminal, will not speak to them, or even look up. Cecilia seems to be at wit's and energy's end. Doug looks like a Lazarus who'd prefer to return to the tomb, swiftly. My appearance at least gets the attendant to look up. This is clearly worth nipping in the bud, she seems to say.

Cecilia explains to me what she has already explained to the attendant. In return the attendant gives her a lost luggage form. Something which for some reason she has hitehrto withheld. It may be days, she explains. As she drones on I see there behind her, plainly visible, Cecila's distinctive black and purple luggage. (Most of it filled, Cecilia later tells me, with the requested food items.) I point out that those are their bags. The attendant explains that this could not be even a possibility. We must fill out the forms. We must submit the forms. We will have to wait to be notified after the forms have been processed. No, we cannot go behind the counter to examine the luggage.

We submit the forms. Luggage-less, we start toward the lobby, where Maggie has remained.

"Glavin, oh is the name Glavin?" The attendant has glanced at the forms. "*Mi dispiace*. I'm so sorry. I did not hear the name correctly. But I have had luggage for Glavin here all day." The luggage did indeed come down on the flight for which they were originally booked. Cecilia and Doug have been waiting in Milan all day for no reason at all. I think Doug will weep except that there is no moisture left anywhere near his eyes.

I ponder the stupidity of this entirely wasted day, of the careless, arrogant systems that enforced it.

I think of the sex slaves on the highway.

I think of the Capolagos hungering for justice and now in fear for their lives.

Shakespeare got it just right.

WEEK TWELVE
November 19-25

Closing In
Wiped out by that gruesome journey, Doug sits for hours on the villino sofa, in T-shirt and jeans, barefoot, absolutely still. He looks like someone delivered over to the power of the Inquisition. From time to time Cecilia tries to persuade him to attempt just a short trip down into Florence. He only stares back, sometimes in blank incomprehension, other times in horror.

The student strike is over. Actually, it never got off the ground. Enthusiasm tended to wither once *gli studenti*, or at least the strike-mongering cohort among them, realized that a strike does not equal a Hollywood day in bed. Nevertheless, dissatisfaction seems to have become general, the unanimity and good cheer of the last few weeks all but gone. Even those who blithely refused to discuss the strike now murmur in unrest. We've crossed a sort of a dateline. And the name of that dateline is End-of-Term.

We have only have two more weeks, this one of class, and the next one of exams, and then Le Balze shuts down and *gli studenti* vacate so that the place can be readied for the short winter break program. As a result, all those too long postponed major assignments must be tackled in the next few days, and—somehow—finished. And at the same time exam prep has to start.

Complaints swirl. They are being worked too hard. They are made to take too many credits. (There they have a point. At Le Balze they average 17 credits; at home it's 15.) The teachers demand too much. They're also starved for Internet access; the Villa supplies only email. They even complain that they never get the chance to see Florence (as though the program mandated those weekend jaunts to Munich and Prague). To top it all, the menus for *cena* have taken on a dispiriting sameness. Villa food was a much touted highlight of the first months. Now they grouse about endless iterations in the evening of cold pizza and quiche.

Happily for me, most of the unrest is directed at, and deflected by, Marcello. But I don't escape entirely.

Next week, in lieu of both a final paper and a final exam, my *studenti* will stage a reading of the second half of that strange, rarely performed, somewhat repellent play, *All's Well That Ends Well*. It's not an Italian script in the sense we've used that term this semester. The major characters are French. But in the first half, they find France doesn't work for them. So, in the second half, they go off to the Italian wars. Once in Florence they learn surprising, significant things about themselves, about their associates, and about the way of the world. And that's why it's relevant to us. *All's Well* is the first, perhaps indeed the last, great script about Study Abroad in Italy.

There's lots of muttering about how rehearsing this script is a much heavier burden than writing a paper *and* taking an exam. If they had started rehearsing a month ago, as I suggested, they might not find it so burdensome. I doubt it would help for me to point this out.

Clyde is directing. He has politely suggested I leave everything to him. He's even asked me to keep out of the villa's public rooms where, I gather, something like a set is being devised. They want to surprise me, he says. I am happy to be surprised. But I notice that his hands are covered with ink-scribbled to-do's. I ask if by performance time the writing will get as far as his face. The living text. Clyde tells me that yesterday he had writing up to his right elbow. He seems grim.

Late in the day Duke drops by the villino. He winsomely confesses he has not read *The Tempest,* this week's script, nor has he written the paper due on it tomorrow, or rewritten the paper on *Othello* he was supposed to complete by the beginning of this week. He has been in Rome. Recently he's taken to alternating his Thursday to Mondays between Rome and Paris. Yesterday he snagged a last minute invitation to dine with, among others, the daughter of a formerly famous film director and a German prince whose family once gave its name to a sauce for lasagna.

I tell him I think them a sad substitute for *The Tempest*.

He is deeply hurt.

When I come across him later in the evening I realize he has stopped talking to me. When I push, he murmurs he is not well. As proof he sinks into the nearest sofa and wearily closes his eyes. Then covers them with the scarf that now rarely leaves his neck.

What a Ferdinand he would make, if we were staging *The Tempest*. He's the perfect picture of a shipwrecked aristo. He even has the right clothes. Duke's the one whose father advised him never to go anywhere without bringing along black tie. Indeed, more and more, he does seem Shakespeare's idea of a Prince. Which is not, of course, an entirely good thing.

It's also not a good thing that I have to double up on Monday: one class before *cena* and another afterwards. The Villa celebrates Thanksgiving on Wednesday, not Thursday, to accommodate some students' families who come over to tour while their kids are still abroad. With siblings out of school and offices closed, it's an easy time to arrange a family get away. But that means everybody doubles up on Monday and Tuesday—non-stop class on both days. I didn't protest the arrangement when Marcello introduced it in September. But in September I didn't realize that by this point in the term *gli studenti* would be, mostly, zombies. Maybe earlier in the term they could sustain four hours of class. It's sadly obvious they're not up to it now.

So I am steeling myself for catastrophe, especially since it'll be our last class of the term, with no chance for recuperation.

Should I join Duke on the sofa? Perhaps he'd share the scarf.

Better, perhaps, the villino sofa, with Doug.

Last Classes

To pace our marathon session I propose to *gli studenti* that I lecture before *cena*, putting *The Tempest* into context, and then after *cena* we can move to discussion. No objections. It's already late afternoon and they're clearly too benumbed to counter. I know this is a dubious strategy. Lectures are fine for large classes in large rooms, but they seldom work in settings as intimate as the villa library and with classes as small as this. But I don't see much choice here. *Gli studenti* are certainly not up to four hours of discussion, even with pizza at half time.

The Tempest comes at the end of Shakespeare's long career, 1610-1611, and some folks think it may have been his last work for the stage. The plot traces the revenge of a distempered wizard Prospero, formerly the Duke of Milan, but now exiled with his daughter Miranda to a remote and barren island. He uses his magic to shipwreck his usurper brother and his brother's crony, the equally corrupt King of Naples. But this revenge plot is countered by the romance that emerges between the beauteous Miranda and the King's son, Ferdinand. In the end Prospero relents, the villains repent, the Italians leave for home, and harmony is everywhere restored.

For all kinds of reasons it is a good choice for us to end with, particularly since it is probably also Shakespeare's shortest major script.

Its reception history has been varied. It was frequently staged in the eighteenth and nineteenth centuries, largely because it offered, and still offers, so much opportunity for spectacle. Quite recently Sir John Gielgud starred in an all-nude film version, "Prospero's Books," directed by the great Peter Greenaway, actually not quite all nude, Sir John was clothed. About which he complained bitterly.

But it gradually came to be taken seriously as Shakespeare's "farewell to the stage," treating Prospero's great speech abdicating his "art"—"this rough magic/ I here abjure" (V:1, 50-51)—as Shakespeare's own retirement speech. Approached in this way, Prospero's island of magical sounds and preternatural creatures becomes itself a stage, and the play in turn became a kind of model of the theater-going experience. Just like the shipwrecked Italians a theater audience is transported to a literally preposterous and manifestly artificial supplement: the theater in which the play is staged parallels the island staged within the theater. There the characters and the audience discern patterns that assist them in making sense of their experience. And from that encounter both groups can return to real life, (ideally) chastened and transformed.

After which Shakespeare like Prospero calls it quits and goes home to Stratford.

Reading *The Tempest* in this way was especially congenial to the so-called New Criticism (ca. 1920-1970). New Critics insisted on a simultaneous connect/ disconnect between art and life. Art is not the same as life—it has form, shape, clarity—in order that art can comment on life. Art, then, at least great art, can become life's magisterial guide, a respectable, and easily accessed, substitute for the rapidly fading lighthouse of religion. This idea dominated English departments and English classes for five decades, and in that half century the short and oddly truncated *Tempest* rose in critical esteem to equal Shakespeare's greatest works.

The decades since 1970, however, have seen a radical rethinking of "literature" and inevitably a radical re-reading of this script. During the island = theater era, scholars merely footnoted connections between the script's shipwreck and contemporary travel accounts, like Richard Eden's 1577 *History of Travel* or Richard Rich's 1610 *News from Virginia*. One catastrophe was particularly suggestive, given the script's explicit reference to the Bermudas (I:2, 230): the 1609 wreck off Bermuda of the ship Sea Venture, described in Sylvester Jourdain's *A Discovery of the Bermudas, Otherwise Called the Isle of the Devils* and William Strachey's *A True History of the Wreck and Redemption... from the Islands of the Bermudas*. But to earlier critics these references merely added topicality to a script timelessly concentrated on art and life. Gossip for groundlings. A frisson for the merchant class.

Over the past twenty-five years, however, those allusions have emerged as clues to a timelier, and very provocative, pattern. Now critics argue that what Prospero calls "the direful spectacle of the wreck" (I:1, 26) mattered urgently to his audiences. They lived in, and in large measure depended on, a great port city in an age of increasing global exploration: the era in which England began to contest Spain as an Atlantic power. *The Tempest*, once about Creativity, for these critics began to be about an entirely different sort of capital C, Colonization.

This shift also transferred primacy from Prospero to Caliban, the aboriginal inhabitant of the island.

For many readers now Caliban has come to be accepted as what he claims to be in the script, the indigenous inhabitant, disenfranchised and enslaved by the island's colonizer:

> This island's mine, by Sycorax my mother,
> Which thou taks'st from me....
> *For I am all the subjects that you have*
> *Which first was mine own king* (I:2, 334-345, 344-345)

The inescapable wordplay between Caliban and Cannibal and Caribe seems to anchor this suggestion. And so, Prospero for decades the hero of the New Critics (who liked to see in him an image of themselves) swiftly declined into the villain of the New Historicists (who see in him the figure of the detested oppressor, using his superior knowledge and skills to expropriate and repress). (*Not* themselves.) And Caliban, neglected for years, or marginalized as a merely comic monster, emerged as the script's moral voice. A role curiously prefigured in Robert Browning's great nineteenth-century poem *Caliban upon Setebos*.

But this shift has done more to unsettle than to settle this tantalizing script. Within the broadly historicist consensus, new and vexing questions continue to emerge. If *The Tempest* is_about colonization, with whom does it side: colonized or colonizer? And *which* colonization does it figure?

Does the script line up behind Caliban's protests against the intruders? Is it part of the contra-colonialist movement that we know circulated in Shakespeare's world? To support this contention scholars point to particularly resonant connections between the text and Montaigne's anti-colonial "Of the Cannibals" (1603). Montaigne persuasively reversed the pro-European master-slave dialectic, insisting that it was the violent, exploitative Westerners who were the real barbarians, and the so-called cannibals who were genuinely admirable, living in harmony with nature and one another. A powerfully suggestive argument, since we know in other places how deeply Montaigne influenced Shakespeare.

Or, despite the echoes of Montaigne, is *The Tempest* actually complicit with the colonial enterprise? Is Shakespeare in effect endorsing those toxic colonial stereotypes, Prospero as white master-hero, Caliban as absurd and appropriately debased slave? Does the text function as a defense of the colonial land grab?

More recently, the Irish critic, Dymphna Callaghan, has reoriented *The Tempest* from the far to the near Atlantic, to England's first and oldest colony, Ireland. John Bull's *other* island, she writes, "provides the richest historical analog for the play's colonial theme." It was in Ireland that England first learned, she argues (quoting an earlier critic, Jimmie Durham), the "violent xenophobia," the "disgust at the idea of inter-marriage," the "mind-boggling self-righteousness" that mark all subsequent British culture, and—of course—this script. In this light it is interesting to recall that the great actor Richard Burton claimed that the part he wanted most to play was Caliban—and this in the 1950s. It makes perfect sense when we remember that Burton came from Wales, the first in England's long series of colonial expropriations.

The text also rotates 180 degrees as re-read by Jerry Brotton, a British cultural materialist. (Which means something like being a Marxist without expecting or even much wanting a revolution.) Brotton returns the central focus to Prospero. But he insists we locate Prospero's island, not in the Atlantic, but somewhere between Italy and North Africa. Sycorax arrived on the island from Algiers (I:2, 269). The wrecked ship is returning to Naples from a wedding in Carthage, present day Libya. That certainly does seem to spot it in the Mediterranean. But why the Med?

Because the Mediterranean, Brotton reminds us, was the other great, indeed competing, site of England's naval energies. In fact, the Mediterranean probably loomed larger in British consciousness at this point than the Atlantic. It was in the Mediterranean that England was engaged in a crucial *mercantile* adventure, opening relations with the Ottoman Empire to offset rival Catholic powers on the European continent. Particularly to rival Venice. A reading that nicely brings us back to key issues driving *Merchant* and *Othello*.

I finish the first half of the Monday marathon with two quotations, neither from the script, but from two texts I'm reading on my own.

The first comes from Michael Frayn's recent prizewinning play *Copenhagen* (1998), about the nuclear physicists Niels Bohr and Werner Heisenberg, the author of the famed Heisenberg Uncertainty Principle. In his last speech in this extraordinary work of theater, Frayn's Bohr insists: "When there's no more uncertainty… there's no more knowledge."

The second comes from this week's *New Yorker*, a profile of the film-maker Jean-Luc Godard. Its author Richard Brody quotes Godard as dismissing current cinema because it lacks a capacity for *doubt*. "With digital," Godard insists, "doubt no longer exists."

Uncertainty. Doubt.

What is *The Tempest* doing?

Silence. Prolonged silence.

"Let's eat."

Even before we resume, I realize I have made a giant strategic blunder, the worst of my long string of mistakes this term. With these different readings I didn't open multiple points of entry for *gli studenti*, I built a stockade which makes them feel closed out. I have yanked the course out of their hands, just when they were about to call it and make it their own.

I try to get them engaged by those ideas of doubt and uncertainty. But after a few desultory attempts to gin up discussion, I am ready to concede. This night is not salvageable. And then just as I am prepared to start to pack it all in, Rotgut commandeers the evening. And thereby saves the evening, and the course.

He asks if he can talk about how deeply he dislikes the script's ending. Remembering his earlier "this guy believes in nothing" spiel, the first sign of his collapse, I am reluctant to let him continue. But anything anyone says, in this Trappist-like silence, will be an improvement.

I expect him to stand up for Caliban, his prototype, the excluded monster. But he says, surprisingly, that he can't stand the ending because it emphasizes forgiveness. (Begging forgiveness has absorbed all his own energies now for weeks.) Of course, the all-encompassing mercy of the conclusion was exactly what the New Critics celebrated in this text, the generous breadth of its culminating vision. Despite everything that has been done to destroy him and his daughter, after the bitter exile to the barren island, Prospero ends by reuniting with his perfidious brother and his disloyal associates.

Rotgut insists that Prospero is wrong to do so. Not only wrong, but despicable. Prospero, he argues, has been deeply betrayed by all these people. Twelve years later, they're still corrupt. As soon as they get back to Italy they will also be back to conspiracy and murder. Sure they repent.—Because Prospero pinches them. He scares them. He taunts them. Then they say they're sorry. What proof is that, he demands, that they are really changed? Prospero's just a fool for thinking they've changed. And he's an even bigger fool for wanting to forgive them. What they deserve, every last one of them, is punishment, really severe, lasting punishment. *The Tempest* is completely unacceptable in its weak-kneed refusal to invent and apply that punishment.

So Rotgut never identified with the monsters at all. Talk about fool: how blind I've been. All along he's seen himself as one with the royal duke. The entitled ruler. The smartest guy. The real paradigm. Of course! The monster's story is always from the monster's point of view the tale of a misused prince.

But Rotgut has struck a chord. For the first time this term, he's a spokesman. He has fans. Heads are nodding all round the room. This is another of those endings *gli studenti* resent and reject, like the endings to *Much Ado* and *Merchant*. The narratives they habitually consume insist the protagonist can and must make his world to suit himself. All the forces that demand he change, that would reward change, should be ignored or toughed aside. They are interested in justice, not mercy.

I try countering with an argument from *genre*. Doesn't the ending in comedy always depend on someone who doesn't have to, but is nonetheless willing to, *give*? To give big: to give *up*, to give *in*, to give *away*, to *for*give. In a world of warring self-interests comedy insists that you can achieve harmony and stability only if someone who has power does not use it. This is why *The Tempest* is a comedy, and Prospero a hero. Because he gives, and in turn, accepts. Accepts a situation not of his making. Not of his preferring. And certainly not perfect. But one in which he chooses to find the elements for a reasonable contentment.

"That's fine, for Prospero," Clyde immediately chimes in. "He's got power back, and he's a magician. But what about Caliban? Here's his final line: "I'll be wise hereafter/ And seek for grace" (V:1, 298-299). What does that mean? Why does Caliban have to be forgiven, if that is what "seek for grace" means? After all, he's the one who got cheated of the island by the colonizers. And where's he going to find that grace he seeks, abandoned all by himself on the island? He can't even make it on stage into the final tableau, where all the other characters gather together. Let alone get back to Italy, where he might learn something about what grace means."

"And what does it mean," Beluga adds, "that Caliban insists he has learned nothing from Prospero's and Miranda's instruction, except—as they admit—how to curse? Only after his exposure to the drunken thieves, Stephano and Trinculo, does he seem to learn about grace. Something Prospero never had the art, or the heart, to model."

I point out that Keith Johnstone, who virtually invented improv comedy, argues that on stage the character the audience admires most is always the one who *over accepts*. That's the character, good or bad, who does not merely put up with, but who actively engages what he or she would prefer not to face.

"That may be true in the theater," Duke says. "I wouldn't know. I'm not into theater," he sniffs. Still on the sofa. Still in the scarf. "But it is not true in life. Not in our lives. We identify with and root for the person who fights for what's owed him, for what he wants, and who gets it."

Rotgut blunts this. He isn't interested in all this talk being deflected to Caliban. He wants to use Prospero to get beyond this script. He needs to denounce something larger and more obnoxious that he finds going on throughout Shakespeare's work.

"It's exactly this constant emphasis on forgiveness running through all the plays," he says, "that sickens me." His long suppressed rage now bubbles to the surface. Suddenly I spot what somehow I've missed. He's cut his long, distinctive hair, the flaunted badge of his difference. He must have done it this afternoon, just before class. Close-cropped at ears and neck, he looks now just like every other guy in the room. Just as he has been trying for weeks to sound like their echo. But, curiously, looking just like them, this anti-Samson now reclaims the outsider status he's so long had to mask.

And will he also now, like Caliban, teach us that we have only given him the language in which to curse us?

No, because what he says, the class clearly echoes. When Rotgut insists that Prospero's final full forgiveness is just a cop out, he's voicing the majority view. As he realizes this new role, rage disappears. In its place he's elated. He's dead center now. Where he's always wanted to be. Where he expected to be. And he's thrilled.

I understand why the others sense Rotgut now speaks on their behalf. This is their last opportunity to voice their bewilderment, their resentment, at what is hardest for them to take in Shakespeare. In script after script, comedies as well as tragedies, they have come across it. For the most part without being able to name it. So I name it for them now. It's the end of the term. They've earned their right to know the name.

What disturbs them, mystifies and finally appalls them is Shakespeare's massive *pessimism*. The obdurate pessimism of what we mis-name the Renaissance. The pessimism that insists on the tyranny of what Shakespeare's great contemporary Edmund Spenser called the Titan Mutabilitie. Nothing stays the same. Nothing can be grasped, and held. All love alters. And all beauty is evanescent. *Lilies that fester smell far worse than weeds*, the Sonnets insist. And fester they shall. Nothing natural or human is permanent, except mutability itself.

Even at its brightest the Shakespearean sky is dark. In the comedies a little light opens toward the west, pink and promising, but only on the edge. Over and over again this is what the texts say, whether tragedies like *Romeo and Juliet* or comedies like *Merchant* or *Tempest*: mostly life is loss. When there is gain it has to be paid for by loss, someone's loss, someone's surrender, sometimes the loss of someone's all.

Any American raised in the Depression would recognize without hesitation this tough, exigent vision of life. Every contemporary immigrant knows it. So does every soldier. But it has virtually disappeared from our common culture, vanishing just at the point when Main Street and Easy Street morphed into one.

That's why for *gli studenti*, despite their new respect for Shakespeare's richness and complexities, these scripts are indeed *preposterous*. But not at all in the sense we've employed that word this term.

So I concede their ground for dissatisfaction, and we disperse, as Rotgut disappears happily into the bunch that crowds toward the door.

The course is over.

Did it end well? No, more like a draw.

The final verdict? Not the failure that seemed inevitable two hours back, but just as clearly not entirely a success. Uncertainty. Doubt.

All's Well will tell.

Ventuno è arrivato

Ventuno brings with it no invitation to join the gardeners at the olive press.

Instead, we get more and worse of the usual: fierce, driving rain. Glum, drenched, Ruggiero, Alessandro and Andrea pack trays of the just picked olives into the back of the Villa car. I watch them from the villino windows. Weather is not permitted to interrupt the meticulous observance of this annual rite. But the set of their shoulders and their stony silence show this is not the moment for the eager amateur to make himself an additional burden. They just want to get it over with. Finally, the last of the trays properly stowed, they drive off to the press. At least the remainder of this ritual can take place indoors.

And I think of the three Capolagos on this day, down in Rome. Have they found for themselves a ritual that can make this blighted day somehow bearable? Or do they sit silently staring at the missing place? Perhaps even sharing the space is too much. Is each is in his own room or hers? Contemplating the difference between what this day has meant to them in the past, and what it must mean for them inevitably in the future.

Thanksgiving, Try the First

Thanksgiving, the essential American celebration, is my favorite holiday. You don't have to feel good. That's for New Year's Eve. Or do good. That's Christmas. Or be good. Easter. You merely have to eat well. I've been looking forward to it all term, especially since we can share it with Cecilia. But can we manage to celebrate it properly in Italy? Where the cranberry does not grow. And the pecan is unknown. Even with Cecilia's and Doug's supplies, will it still feel like Thanksgiving?

Well, we are going to try. Twice. The first time, tonight, in the villa. The second, tomorrow, just the four of us, in Tuscany, at Pietra Fitta, where we made the reservation after our first visit weeks ago.

Le Balze has a tradition of inviting for the Thanksgiving feast not only *gli studenti* and the teaching staff and their families, but also the students' friends and families who may be visiting over the holiday. Several boyfriends and girlfriends are expected. Three pairs of parents. One set of two parents and two siblings. Another consisting of only one parent but three siblings. All in all we expect to seat and feed seventy people. Now that should be a real Thanksgiving.

Maggie and I invite Marcello for cocktails in the villino before the general festivities commence. His wife can't make it. Flu has hit Florence. Because of that he says the guest list is probably going to be closer to sixty than seventy. We review with him our plan for lunch in the countryside tomorrow. We should make sure, he says, to see the restored abbey at Coltibuono. And then there's another little place, Meleto. Meleto, he assures us, we will find *bellina*.

Despite the flu, the villa is mobbed, especially in the library where everyone crowds to the single bar. Most people, students and families alike, try to be quite sophisticated. Cecilia is extraordinary. The three months since we've seen her have been transformative. Most obviously, now that she is a wage-earner, her clothes are fantastic, of the moment, flattering. You can see the appraising and admiring glances she gets from every side. And there's also a new ease and self-confidence. She left us a student; she's come back a professional woman, making her own way on her own terms in a demanding, competitive world. But for me, it still has a feel of back to school night. Several conversations barely manage to avoid clichés of the parent teacher conference.

The villa tonight has been restored to something like Travelers' elegance. In the library next to the generous bar there's a buffet, and the fire roars. Along the main corridor a single long table extends across the entire first floor. Immaculate linen napery and table cloths. Candelabra alternating with vases of late autumn flowers. The house silver set out, and gleaming.

But though they try hard, neither Cecilia nor Doug is sufficiently rested from their ordeal to throw themselves into the gala spirit. Everyone they meet is a stranger to them, while the best of friends to everyone else. This kind of promiscuity can be extremely tiring to the uninitiated. Maggie has learned from decades of practice at semi-social academic occasions that the thing to do is to hold back, spare yourself and try to find one interesting person as soon as possible and then stick to him or her like a limpet. Doug and Cecilia attempt, however, a general civility, and wind up looking merely beleaguered. Happily, we succeed in sitting in something of a family clump.

The cooks Sandra and Sana have surpassed themselves. Food for sixty, as fresh and hot as though it had been cooked for six. And authentic. And everyone is suitably grateful for the haulage Cecilia and Doug provided that produced the key ingredients.

But Thanksgiving is really about friends and family gathering together. We are swamped in a mob of mostly strangers. Friendly and charming strangers. But strangers nonetheless. We all try. We eat and we talk and we laugh but for our two guests the long shadow of their miserable Saturday with Alitalia still looms large.

We are glad to have come to the feast, but equally glad to leave it. We know, after all, we will have another chance tomorrow to nail Thanksgiving. With another night of rest for the visitors we are sure to make it work on the day. Think of all those clichés about dress rehearsals.

Thanksgiving, Try the Second

This time it even looks like Thanksgiving Day. We drive, through bright light, crisp air, down into Chianti. Our reservations at Pietra Fitta are for 1:30. That gives us plenty of time to show our Chianti highlights to Cecilia and Doug as well us dropping in on the places Marcello suggested. We plan on going first to Volpaia and then to Coltibuono, finishing at Meleto just before lunch. At some point Maggie also wants us to stop to purchase the new olive oil.

Olive oil in the States, even very good olive oil, doesn't come close to the newly pressed kind you get here in the late fall. Somehow the new oil manages at the same time to be both strong and light. It tastes a bit like olive oil cut with lemon juice, if you could erase entirely the tang of citrus, with underneath a faint, but distinct and very pleasurable hint of pepper. Even if it didn't taste so strangely wonderful, it would be worth buying because of its color. Not olive at all, but a kind of clouded chartreuse.

We head off merrily. Shortly after Greve we see a *venditta diretta* sign, five kilometers to our left. *Venditta diretta* means sold by the maker. We spin off the 222 to find a rough farm track, winding, and after all the recent rain, puddled. Thick trees on both sides. Nothing else. After what feels like a very long time with no sign of human habitation, suddenly a car is mysteriously close behind us, virtually bumper to bumper. Cecilia makes nervous jokes about kidnapping. I join in, though the memory of Ivo leaves me feeling this is far from funny.

We take turns unraveling a scenario. Unexpectedly, a second car will soon appear ahead. Sandwiched, we will be forced to stop. Then, within seconds, at least one of us, bound and gagged, will be hauled away. Later the others will receive a severed finger. Still later an ear. It may be Thanksgiving but this remains Italy.

We decide it will be Doug they want. At breakfast he explained that his family spends Thanksgiving with relatives at Plymouth. There they are eligible to walk in The Pilgrims' Progress, a march through town by the Pilgrims' descendants. Recently, however, Native American groups have protested the Progress. So, given the time difference, if the Native Americans' agents kidnap Doug this morning, his mutilated form could be videoed to the States by early afternoon in the best Mafioso manner. Just as most American families are sitting down to their holiday bird, they'll find a networked Doug, now minus an ear, a digit, or both. With a threat of further eliminations if the Progress back in Plymouth does not halt.

Perhaps this is what Freud called the apotropaic, where you raise the very thing you fear in order to defang it.

Certainly, the laughter from our visitors in the backseat sounds hollow. We have gone far further than five kilometers, and that car remains on our bumper.

Suddenly an impressive house and outbuildings sweep into view. Elated, we park. The follower parks behind us. An old guy in overalls emerges. He politely bids us *Buon Giorno* and disappears into the olive groves.

We tramp around, we peer into windows, we try doors, we ring bells and buzzers. No one. Nothing.

And then, just as we are about to drive off, a friendly fellow emerges from the woods, no doubt alerted by our follower, and unlocks the cantina where the olive oil is sold. Proudly, he produces a bottle. Last year's. Oh no, he smiles, it is too early for their new oil. They are still harvesting. However, if we will proceed only another seven kilometers up the track we will find their neighbors. Their harvest is completed.

We assure him nothing could suit us more. He returns to the woods. We then U-turn and speed back to the 222. Maggie is disappointed, but not discouraged.

Just before Panzano a very large place appears, the *venditta di-*

retta sign in place. We decide to take a chance. After all this is the only other *venditta diretta* sign we have seen in over an hour of driving. This time Doug and I stay outside amusing a fetching guard dog who couldn't care less about the rights of private property. Maggie and Cecilia go in for the buy. Minutes later they return, empty handed. These people also are not finished with the harvest.

I assure Maggie we will return with oil. Maggie is not convinced. Somehow this is becoming my fault. But then we do find it at Volpaia, the ultimate source of all consolations. Where we thought we'd find only coffee.

Even as we clamber out of the car, we can sense we've arrived at our goal. The little town seems to float in a delicate bouquet of rendered olive. From every one of the little buildings that ring the town—the stillness of which so mystified us on earlier visits—we hear a steady alteration of chug and swish. And when we get a chance to peek into one, we see the wall-to-wall low press, swirling the olives in a steady and delicate crush. I get it now: it's olives that sustain Volpaia, a sort of economic Brigadoon that comes alive for one week a year, only in late November.

While Maggie and Cecilia make their selections, Doug and I celebrate with *Fernet Branca* and cigars. (*Fernet Branca* is what the Italians call a *digestivo*. It looks like sludge, and smells worse, and is divine. Once one acquires the taste. Many, I must admit, don't.)

Then, heartened, and very slightly high, we drive off to the Badia at Coltibuono which Marcello urged us not to miss. But the minute we pull into its drive it decides it's the real Brigadoon and disappears into blankets of thick fog. What does it matter, we assure each other. Still warm from the many consolations of Volpaia, we agree to bag Meleto, and show up early for lunch at Pietra Fitta. We know Pietra Fitta. We can even anticipate them knowing us.

Pietra Fitta is bolted firmly, and shuttered. I manage, after lots of hammering and banging, to rouse a charming young woman. She explains that the *comune* insisted the restaurant switch its closing day from Wednesday to Thursday. I reply that I had a reservation, have had for months. She brings out the book and shows me that I am correct. This gives her great pleasure. Clearly, she would be embarrassed if I proved myself wrong. But, alas, I gave them no phone number. They had no way to warn me of the change. Of course, she will try to assist us in getting a reservation elsewhere.

She tries several numbers. Many numbers. Finally she reaches someplace willing to take us.

No, she has not been there herself, but she has heard very good things.

We drive off.

The new restaurant is entirely empty. From whom could she have heard all these good things? But the waiter could not be more welcoming. We have our choice of tables.

Before we can scan the menu, the chef himself appears to advise us. He's one of those thick, fit, Tuscans of indeterminable middle age, as good at sixty as he was at thirty. The baker in Fiesole is another of the same sort. He wears a high white chef's toque and smokes a cigar. Meat, he insists, is what we must eat here. All the pasta is *fatta alla casa*, homemade, of course. But the point is meat.

We don't seem persuaded. His disappears. He reappears with an enormous cut of beef. This beef he explains was raised right across the road. The farm once belonged to the chef's own grandfather. He has known this cow since it was born. Like a fond uncle he has followed every stage of its life. There is no worry about *vacca pazza* here (mad cow). They never cook an animal they haven't known well. This is true of lambs. It is even true of pigs, though he says that in a way that makes it seem that knowing pigs is not as easily accomplished as knowing other forms of farm stock.

Doug and Maggie have beef, Cecilia pork, I choose ham.

This may be the best meat any of us has ever touched. Ah, what a difference it makes, dining on old friends. When he returns for our praise, we tell him this is a special day for Americans. Beaming, he says he knows. He has prepared a turkey for a party of Americans coming later. He dispatches the waiter to the kitchen for the turkey. This turkey too, he confides, he has known since birth.

The bird appears. It is the size of a young bear.

Julia Child, Martha Stewart, neither of them could ever have surpassed this turkey. I cannot resist. A slice, just to taste?

Of course, he cuts slices for Doug and for me. The turkey becomes another course. And it is perfect, larded throughout with mixed Tuscan herbs and crushed pistachio. For a sauce, the new oil simmered with garlic. Other ideas of stuffing and all brown gravies at that moment depart from my future Thanksgivings forever.

We settle back. We feel compensated, replete, at home. We begin to think of coffee, agreeing dessert is out of the question. Just then a lost blonde woman appears, looking for directions. Nothing will do but that the solitary waiter must leave and show her the way himself. Leaving his apron to the chef, he guides her away. We are left alone. Times passes. The light begins to fade.

It starts to rain.

The waiter does not return. The temperature in the room has plummeted. We put on our coats

I venture into the kitchen. The chef and his assistant are enjoying fresh cigars. Could we have our check? Clearly this is a wrong move. He is not a waiter. He is a chef. The waiter will return soon. I am dismissed.

We wait. We can't skip the bill; they have been too kind. An hour and a half later the waiter returns. He looks satisfied. The lost motorist, we speculate, has been grateful.

A check? Surely we want dessert first, coffee. Coffee and a check, then, if that is what we want. The second half of our stay has obviously let all sides down.

We ought to be annoyed but the food was too good.

As we drive back to Florence the sky is inky. There is no one else on the road. It's changed from chilly to cold. Maggie and I could be driving back from Thanksgiving dinner with friends anywhere between Maine and North Carolina. From the Severs near Albany. The Fratelli on Hoban Road. The Budenhagens outside Raleigh. It would feel and look just like this.

Doug and Cecilia are asleep in the back seat. In front, Maggie and I review our time here. What we expected. What we didn't expect. The uncertainties. The doubts. The one ways. The mysteries. The realizations. We came for a kind of retreat, but found ourselves forced into a quest. This afternoon Pietra Fitta was a kind of mirror of the successive disappointments that have shaped our stay. But then we remind each other of the unanticipated discoveries: the *Celle*, the 222, Volpaia, Sant'Antimo, Sant'Angelo, the soft lunar loveliness of the Crete. I think of driving back with Thad from Montepulciano, of St. Francis retrieving my credit card in Assisi. There are other memories I don't share with Maggie: *Gli studenti* reading *Merchant*, performing *Othello*. Six weeks of incomparable classes. We've got almost two more weeks, we tell each other. Perhaps it's still too soon to see the thing whole. We plan what we will do when we resume, soon, our old life in Washington. The empty silence makes the night magical. All things seem possible.

I know what this is. No, I know what this is the beginning of. I am ready to start saying my own Good-Bye—not to the Mezzogiorno, the South, but to the Centro, to Tuscany, and to my own past.

And then, turning off the 222 to enter Florence, I lose my way, a way I thought I could now navigate blindfolded. We become progressively more lost in the city's outskirts. We drive through Bagno a Ripoli. Several times. Now we are in Ponte a Ema. And then in places with no names, no lights, no signs at all. I U-turn through closed gas stations. I circle around the empty parking lots of dubious hotels. I dead end and reverse. Finally, hours later, we find our way back up into Fiesole.

Even a few weeks back this would have set me into a rage. And now it does not matter. I have made my peace, and I seem to hear once again, as we unlock the door, our friend Stefano reminding me, though by now I shouldn't need to be reminded, "But, Gian, this is Italy."

An unexpected call
Now that he is his real self again, I want to make sure Doug gets to see my two favorite things in Florence: the Pontormos in Santa Felicita and the church of San Miniato. The Pontormo "Deposition," the taking down of Jesus from the Cross, is not only the most beautifully colored painting in the world (azure, tangerine, pink and celadon in swirling clouds of drapery) but it is also probably the least visited great work of art in Italy. No one seem to know about it and that means you can stand in the tiny chutrch of Sant Felicità, next to the Pitti Palace, and gaze at it for as long as you want—which is for me always. San Miniato, properly San Miniato al Monte, further up on that side of the Arno, is an exquisite early church, eleventh and twelfth century, with the most remarkable facade in Florence, all white and green marble placage, thin thin plaques arranged in elaborate patterns to suggest columns and arches like the cover of an illuminated mansucript. It's a style you find everywhere in Tuscany but at miniature San Miniato it reached perfection.

But just as we are leaving for Piazza Mino, I get an entirely unexpected call from Cip Capolago.

It is urgent that I come to Rome. Can I come tomorrow?

I explain that I can't because Cecilia and Doug are with us. Can I come next week?

Yes. The last of our house guests, Maggie's sister, Mary Jo, will be visting from her home in Australia, but I can probably at some point free myself for a one-day trip. I can't set the day until after she arrives.

Cip urges me to come as early in the week as I can manage.

I ask about the twenty-first, the birthday. How did it go?

He tells me that this is what they want to describe to me. But Dora insists she needs to tell me in person.

And Waldo? Does he know I am coming?

Yes, and he wants to see me. I must be sure to call them the day before so that he can arrange to be home for *pranzo*.

What happened? What could have produced such a complete about face?

Cip will not say.

Too late

Knowledgeable people avoid the autumn crowds and come to Florence at the end of November. The rains have finally stopped. Tuscany is well past its incomparable prime, though the golden leaves of denuded grapevine still cover Chianti's hills with row upon row of gleaming shields. But the city itself has become mild, with highs in the mid-fifties, never anywhere near freezing. There's a clear, soft morning light. It's kinder than any artificial illumination, flattering interior glories like the Brancaci Chapel and Michelangelo's New Sacristy. You realize why museologists insist great art should always be seen in the light that approximates the light in which it was created.

Later, in the afternoon, the hazy sun turns everything a misty, languorous pink, through which the Duomo shimmers as though beneath an opaque sea. The streets of the *centro* are not quite empty even now. But they, like the shops, are uncrowded. And at night every street and even the smallest alleys begin to be draped with

Christmas lights and garlands. *Buone Feste* and *Auguri*, they wish us, glittering like angelic trapeze high above our heads.

This makes it very hard to say that Good-Bye.

WEEK THIRTEEN
November 26 - December 2

The Sense of an Ending

Cecilia and Doug flew back this morning to Boston. Of course it was sad to see them go, but not as sad as saying goodbye to Sarah and Thad. We will spend Christmas with Cecilia in Washington in less than a month. And to console us Maggie's sister Mary Jo Pirola, our final houseguest, has arrived all the way from Australia to share this last week.

As our time at Le Balze heads toward what the movie business calls the wrap, I keep thinking back on how we concluded our first stay here, fourteen years ago: the most extraordinary weekend of my life.

On the final Saturday we all went up to Milan, where our friend Pietro Marani was overseeing the last stages of the restoration of Da Vinci's *Last Supper* in the convent of Santa Maria delle Grazie. As the train from the Mezzogiorno pulled into the Florence station we could see it was already mobbed. Maggie and I decided to split. I would start at one end with Thad, she at the other with Cecilia. If she found seats for four she should seize them and we would ultimately find her. But if Thad and I were successful I would send him to find them. About half way through the train, unexpectedly we met up.

"We can't sit back there," Maggie said.

I explained why we couldn't sit in the other half. It was filled with soldiers on leave,

"Well," countered Maggie, "the other half has goats."

We settled for the soldiers. Who behaved, of course, impeccably. As would the goats also, no doubt.

In Milan, Pietro guided Maggie and me past the guard ropes in front of the painting and up into the scaffolding. (Now, I thought, I know what it's like to be the Prince of Wales. Well almost.) Since you see it so often reproduced and reduced, on encounter the fresco itself is shockingly massive, taking up the entire wall of the very large refectory. The scale is so grand that the figures are easily read from quite a distance away. But it becomes indelibly poignant close up. Each head is a vividly realized individual portrait. These men have just realized they are about to lose forever someone they love and adore.

The platform of the scaffolding now puts you at eye-level with the surface of the table. Standing only inches from the wall, we followed Pietro's expert and intimate explanation of surfaces he had come to know better than his own skin. Details appeared that were invisible even to people a few feet away. He showed us the individual infinitesimal flecks of white paint to suggest the salt spilled by Judas, the source of all bad luck. Pietro was even able to point to places where Leonardo used his own thumbprint to create the impression of skin, according to Pietro a favorite technique.

Face to surface we could see how close the painting had come to total extinction. It was magnificent, it was noble, and it was very sad. Close up you could get a sense of what it once had been but—however skilled the restoration—could never be again.

The next day I took the train down from Florence to Arezzo to lunch with one of my literary idols, the great British novelist Muriel Spark. I had been an admirer of her fiction since I first encountered *The Prime of Miss Jean Brodie* in *The New Yorker* in 1961 while still an undergraduate. Hesitantly, I wrote her a note shortly after we arrived in Italy, knowing she lived nearby in Tuscany, asking if we could meet. I received no answer. As we were wrapping things up, I mentioned to Maggie that the only enduring disappointment of our stay here would be not hearing from Mrs. Spark.

Always to the point and practical, Maggie said: "Why not call her. You have her number, don't you?"

I explained all of the excellent reasons why it would be entirely inappropriate for me to call someone who is already a glowing fixture in the pantheon of literary modernism. A letter yes, which she would be free to ignore. But an uninvited phone call is an imposition. Maggie's response was admirably simple.

"Call her."

I did. And did speak to her. She had been traveling for almost the entire autumn, she explained, and had just opened my letter. Would I be in Italy after Christmas? No, I explained, I am leaving in just about a week. Then she would be happy to see me, on Sunday, for lunch. The Hotel Continentale in Arezzo.

I arrived early enough to spend several hours with the Piero della Francescas that are the glory of that Tuscan city. Since it was Sunday morning, there was no one else looking. I had the frescoes entirely to myself, just like our private view of the Leonardo. In the now familiar pattern, I would gaze, then I'd walk outside and ponder, and then go back inside and look harder, and so it went until it was lunch time. Whatever lunch brought, these two days were already a triumph.

Muriel was accompanied by her warm and encouraging friend, the sculptor Penelope Jardine. Which made it easier. I would have been too awestruck to be with her entirely on my own. But in person she turned out to be even better than her books, miraculous as that might seem. To start I was of course tongue-tied so I told her about the first time I read her work. I was a sophomore at Georgetown, with—like every English major—a subscription to *The New Yorker* (then and now). It used to arrive in our mailboxes on Tuesday mornings. That Tuesday morning I opened it, saw this unusual title, "The Prime of Miss Jean Brodie," and began to read. In those days the magazine didn't have page numbers in its table of contents, so I had no idea that what I thought was a short story was in fact a short novel. I read it through lunch, and then through the afternoon, cutting classes, mesmerized. At 5, finished with the story, I did go to my Latin class: "Classical Rhetoric." I was supposed to have spent the day translating Longinus, not reading Spark. But everyone I knew in the seminar had also been reading the story and could talk of nothing else. And then the instructor came in, Professor Schork, who opened by saying: "I usually don't do this but I have to talk to you about the most extraordinary story I've been reading today in *The New Yorker*."

Happily, Muriel liked my story and the ice was broken.

"What interests you about my work," she asked, as we opened our menus. I told her I had noticed that she seemed never to invent a plot; all her novels adapted existing stories. "Ah, you've seen that, have you? Well, let me tell about the first thing I ever wrote. It was a revision of "The Pied Piper." All the children ended happily."

We talked at length about the ways she is and is not Catholic. She defined Catholicism, memorably, for her as the best norm she knows to depart from. And she spoke in detail of the importance to her of the medieval mystical text, *The Cloud of Unknowing*.

From that luncheon came a warm friendship, as well as the chance to publish critical studies of her work that I am happy to say she encouraged and of which, I think, she did not disapprove.

Now, we are again at the end of our time in Italy. Will this week bring anything like those twin moments of unmatched fulfillment?

All contact with *gli studenti* has vanished. They've disappeared into their closed-shop rehearsals inside the villa. Le Balze feels almost ghost-like. And I dread the trip down to Rome, my final encounter with the Capolagos.

The great literary critic Frank Kermode gave a series of lectures while I was in graduate school, later published as his book *The Sense of an Ending*. Endings, he said, belong to stories. It is one of the ways we distinguish stories from life. Life doesn't offer an ending, only an end. Still, I would like to experience something like the sense of this ending.

In the meantime, we decide to break out of what has begun to feel like a shell to bring Mary Jo down into Florence for a real cocktail in a real bar, the *L'Incontro* bar of the Florence Ritz. Maggie, Mary Jo, and I sit together on a banquette, and discuss the ongoing impasse of the presidential election. Mary Jo left for Australia in 1966 when she married half-Italian, half-British Mark, and she now views the US with a distinctly down-under attitude. In her eyes we're the world's bully, strong-arming everyone else to fit the patterns it pleases us to impose. Domestically, we're notable for consumption and violence, an international by-word for excess and waste. What the election means, she explains, is that Americans will now have to see themselves as others see them and admit the country is not special, but just as flawed as everyplace else.

I demur, suggesting that we're not there yet. She's content to move on with a confident "You'll see."

On the next banquette, as though to prove her point, are other Americans, a couple. He's on his *telefonino*. She sits across from him, fuming. Married daughter, I think. Maggie says trophy wife. Mary Jo is convinced it's a girlfriend. He is angry because a subordinate back in the States has ruined a sale. She is angry because they are sitting here, rather than shopping.

He into the *telefonino*: "And tell Stan that if he isn't back to me before we leave this place, he's through."

She to him: "No! We are not waiting for him to call back. We haven't been to Ferragamo, yet. Or Gucci."

If he has his way, Stan's got maybe a quarter of an hour tops to turn his life around. If she has her way, they will leave, and Stan's career goes down the toilet

If this demands we order another round of Manhattans, so be it. We intend to be in on the kill.

We are not eavesdropping. We are hearing, not overhearing. Perhaps the major movement of our time is the utter evacuation of privacy. He and she don't intend to be private. They're reckless in sharing. Which is why I'm convinced, despite Frank Kermode, fiction is through. Ditto drama. With stuff like this happening all around us, gratis, fiction and drama don't have a prayer.

Like poor Stan, because now they are definitely going to Gucci. So long, Stan.

I Tatti

This time, as his parting gift, Pietro has indeed managed to wangle us the promised tour of I Tatti, the villa our builders, Pinsent and Scott, created for Bernard Berenson, just over the hill in Settignano. Berenson, or Bibi as he was known from his initials, was the intellectual eminence of the world of the Strongs, the Cuttings, and all the other Anglo-American Edwardians in and around Florence. A professional connoisseur, he taught the world to appreciate early Renaissance painting. The property is now part of Harvard, which manages it just as it does the great house, museum and gardens of Dumbarton Oaks, the center for Byzantine Studies, just across Rock Creek from our house in Washington.

I Tatti is to the Tuscan villa what St. Peter's is to the basilica. An unsurpassed instance of the type. Its libraries, and they are in the plural, house a superb research collection in Renaissance History, Art History and Music at least the equal, and mostly the envy, of any major university. The collection serves fifteen postgraduate Fellows a year, each of whom gets an individual study in which to work. The Fellows are assisted by an extensive, entirely professional, clerical and security staff. Over one hundred Medieval and Renaissance pictures hang on the walls, most of museum quality. And beyond the buildings extend fifty walled acres. It's not a tourist destination so it is an extraordinary gift from Pietro that we are made welcome. A mark of his stature in the world of Art History. And of his incomparable personal charm.

Abutting the main house there's a small secret garden, lots of shell and sponge work, like ours, distinctly Pinsent-Scott, with a witty mosaic of two bussing bees, the BB of BiBi. Then surrounding the house several—I counted four—long, formal parterres descend to an ilex grove. Further off you find meadows which in the warmer weather (they tell me) glow with spring bulbs and wisteria. Finally, at the horizon, the fields of the original working farm climb the hill toward the Castle of Vincigliata, where we held the second day of the Educating in Paradise conference, and from which Berenson's property was originally carved. Le Balze is almost a miniature, a kind of folly, seen against this scale.

I Tatti's Director, Walter Kaiser, could joke at the Conference about the risks of educating in Paradise. But if ever there were an earthly paradise, surely I Tatti is it.

We are shown first a large upstairs sitting room. This room we know the picky and prickly novelist Edith Wharton, who also wrote highly regarded books on Italian gardens and interior decoration, not only frequently enjoyed but admired. It's still clear why. Think of the morning room in a country house, not televisual Brideshead, or museum-level Winterthur, or The (ostentatious) Breakers. This room is not aristo- or pluto-cratic, it's understated, comfort-above-all gentry. The family room in the house of a family that's always had enough money but even more taste, and which has relied on a connoisseur of genius to select its pictures. Three wide windows, heavily curtained, look down into the many gardens. The dominant colors in the curtains, and elsewhere in the room, are a very bright, almost orange gold, and a contrastingly dark, juicy green. A distinctively Italian choice. The whole space glows. Inlaid and painted tables. Everywhere porcelain lamps and porcelain vases, the vases filled with fresh flowers. Over the parquet floors Persian rugs, gray or blue. And on each wall pictures, Sienese, Florentine, Northern Italian, mostly small or middle scale, perhaps as many as twenty, and each worth much more scrutiny than our tour can provide.

The other major rooms are remarkably like the first: an L-shaped gallery, a dining room, a large and a small library. Though it is owned by a university it is not a museum. It is a well-used, lived-in house. The half empty Scotch bottles in virtually every room go a long way to making this plain. Warm, inviting, it makes you want to linger, hoping the civilized Fellows will let you mingle for the daily afternoon tea. It's the Frick if the Frick had been lived in by people who preferred things Italian to things French and Spanish, and had a sense of humor.

Two things in these rooms repeatedly catch me by surprise.

I had assumed all the art would be Italian. But everywhere you look you also find Chinese bronzes and other Asian figures in stone. And I had also thought everything would be grand and a masterpiece. But except for a single large Sassetta of my good friend St. Francis (1437-1444), the paintings tend to be small in scale, domestic in tone. One of my touring companions, a New York *dealer*, scoffs that I Tatti hangs the pictures Berenson couldn't get anyone else to take off his hands. Laughing — she has heard this before — our guide shows us two pictures in rebuttal.

The first is endearing and awkward. The Madonna, the Child and the background are each painted in a different style, and to a different scale. The baby's head is at least as large as the mother's. Berenson, she says, bought it because he thought its naiveté funny. The second, nearby, is a Nativity, of which at first Berenson could only locate the right half, a Madonna and Child. Then he found the bottom of the left half, an angel. Having acquired these three quarters, he blithely commissioned a restorer to invent the missing section, a starry sky, seaming it all together in a completely obvious way. He was very proud of this contrivance.

Though he had an unerring eye for work that conveyed deep and intense emotion, Berenson also cultivated the playful, the witty, even the whimsical. Think of those mosaic Bees. And he was eclectic in the sources from which he derived pleasure. Anything you can enjoy is clearly worth cultivating, that is what I Tatti murmurs at every seductive turn.

Once again Pietro had given us a never-to-be-forgotten farewell.

All's Well That Ends Well

For a couple of hours, in a late and misty afternoon, as their final assignment, Clyde directs *gli studenti* in *All's Well That Ends Well*. With staggering ingenuity he somehow manages not only to cast the entire class but to give each of *gli studenti* a significant chance to perform. And in the process he restores magic to Le Balze. Nothing could be further from what Marcello intended when he planned to rent a real theatre downtown. And indeed nothing could be further from the performance I thought would conclude the term. But what *gli studenti* offer makes my plan seem picayune.

First here's a brief synopsis of this little known script. *All's Well* is an ugly story of mastery, difficult to stage, and therefore rarely performed, because its hero is thoroughly repellent and its heroine is thoroughly dull. He's called Bertram, a French nobleman. He's one of three principal characters. The second is middle-class Helena, who loves him. The third is a clever sycophant, Parolles, who does everything he can to help Bertram behave as badly as possible. When Helena cures the king of France of a wasting disease, he forces Bertram to marry her. But Bertram, furious at this déclassé misalliance, chooses instead to go to the Italian wars with the braggart Paroles. Helena follows him, covertly. In Italy there's a lot of trickery about substituting one woman, Helena, whom he loathes, for the woman he wants to seduce, Diana. And in the end, shamed, he is forced to admit the virtues of the woman who has been so faithful to him. Everything that Beluga criticized in Bassanio is realized here in as full and as nasty a way as possible. We wouldn't be dealing with the script in this course were it not set, at least half set, in Italy.

Which makes Clyde's triumph all the more dazzling. He has found a way, literally, to rescue it. Rather than being intimated by it, he has decided to treat it as a play about play, about the joys of playing. And as pure play it is both hilariously giddy and subversively smart.

Despite Marcello's wish to bring in friends of Le Balze as audience, Clyde has insisted on keeping the viewers to a minimum, just the staff, Maggie, and the students in the program not taking my course. This is a pragmatic decision: not only does the production move from space to space but the audience moves with it. He has commandeered almost of the first floor. No wonder it's been off limits for so long. And in the best Shakespearean manner, he has

transformed the place. It has become, not only the students' theater, but their Arden, their unknown island, their magic forest, their
green world. Their preposterous supplement.

We start the action in the court of France: here the seldom-used
music room, candles lighted, curtains drawn, cozily intimate for
perhaps the first, and probably the last, time in its history. Then we
move, actors and audience, on our way to Italy out to the long corridor, with the library garden as background. We see a brief scene
there between the Duke of Florence and two of his lords. Then the
trio *gallops*, kids playing cowboy, off under the arch into the ilex
grove. We settle into the staircase hall for a few scenes. And the first
half finishes in the library.

For the second half we alternate between hall and library. Very
soon all this moving about gets to feel a bit like being at a fair, particularly because the significance of the different rooms floats freely. The court of France which started out as the music room easily
transfers later to the library. Which also became, when necessary,
the castle at Rosillion, Bertram's mother's place. The hall mostly
represents Florence, but first as a bourgeois interior, then as the
city's walls, though pots, pans and spaghetti still remain clearly visible.

Identity also floats freely in this randomly assigned space. To
give everyone equally interesting work, Clyde ingeniously chooses
to assign two different performers to each of the recurring roles.
A second performer succeeds the first at a crucial moment in the
character's internal transformation. A bit of costume and a script
(this is a staged reading) go wordlessly from hand to hand, and the
action resumes. It's not only an effective solution to the problem of
having entirely inexperienced performers tackle roles of significant
complexity, but also an ingenious way to point the audience to the
plot's key moments. Theatrically, it's magic.

And Clyde makes this prudent strategy gloriously wacky by
refusing to let the displaced performers disappear. No one is only
anyone. Performers in major roles transition into minor parts, mi-
nors into majors, with a glorious raspberry at rationality.

After Orchid's timid, dark-haired Helena becomes Judy's bolder and blonder version, Orchid continues popping in as various
lords and soldiers, all of whom seem pretty much indistinguish-

able from her Helena. Beluga, the original Bertram, later becomes
the officious chamberlain, identically dressed but now with an out-
landishly comic French accent. The only French accent in a play
full of French characters. And Miss Haag, once she has turned her
provocatively androgynous Parolles over to a fully restored Duke
(not of France, our own Duke), becomes the Steward Rinaldo, still
curiously androgynous. A transfer all the more curious since Duke
up until this point has been, we thought, the giddy-up Duke of
Florence. The Marx Brothers meet *The Turn of the Screw*.

Nor is it only Miss Haag's Parolles that bends gender. The class
has twice the number of women as men, so girls, easily, and persuasively, play guys, gender shifted with the penciling on of a bold
handlebar moustache. Gloria, hitherto one of the class's quietest
members, does an especially convincing sort of machismo swagger. And Betty is the king of France, or perhaps the queen, since
she sports a Tinkerbell tiara bought from the Florence Disney store,
and pearls, which if real would have made the Duchess of Windsor
weep. Half the cast preserves the text's masculine language, calling
Betty things like Sire. The other half defer to Betty's own gender,
replacing Sire with a very correct Ma'am. That simply makes the
whole thing odder, wittier, and finally smarter.

The great Polish director Jerzy Grotowski claimed that theater
requires either the most skilled professionals or inspired amateurs.
Who knew we'd find the latter here? I've been teaching long enough
to realize that much of what we covered this term will quickly fade
away. A year from now no one is going to remember much about
Shakespeare's Italy, or indeed about Shakespeare. About teaching
the title of Leonard Woolf's autobiography applies: the journey not
the arrival matters.

But two things that matter to me have clearly taken root.

Gli studenti now accept seeing the plays as scripts, texts that can
be read but which are realized in a completely different way in and
through individual performance, no two performances the same.
That has given them the freedom, and the pleasure, to own the afternoon and to make it memorable.

And whether they would theorize it this way or not, they've
shown they also are willing to see the self as a form of script, a text
waiting for performance, not a single coherent identity but a host of

roles pushing toward performance. I hope that too will lead them to freedom, and pleasure.

And I also see something else: this afternoon has been their gift to me. That's why they insisted I stay away from, and out of, their preparations. They have undertaken this elaborate, demanding performance, not grudgingly, or just because it was required. They have done it as the Italians say *con affetto*, with love.

In the play Rotgut was a marvel. He played Lavatch the clown. The other students performed, he alone acted. He made himself into what he is certainly not, a fool, and cunning. He was, as all Shakespeare's clowns must be, graphically and boldly genital. But he had also plumbed the deep sense of every line, and spoke the words as though they were his own. There were long stretches in which I simply forgot who he really was.

Perhaps he has just discovered what his future holds. Certainly he has had the painful history all actors require. And he has that compulsion toward the examined life all strong actors rely on. Sure, it was only just a spark. And in the theater there's no telling if that spark will eventually sustain a flame. But the spark was there. Bright. Arresting. And when, after the performance, I suggest that he try to take some acting courses, he beams.

He has been reprieved, he tells me. Not in those words. He is being allowed to come back. Next term he will live outside the villa, with an Italian family. He's acquired enough Italian this term to manage that, barely. I think he's likely to find outside the community of our *studenti* the associates and associations that will help him thrive. So it does, in balance, seem a good thing that he's coming back. Especially because, as Maggie, Mary Jo and I leave for dinner, we see him walking back from the piazza, eating gelato, accompanied by a very pretty girl.

He disappears with her under a villa archway, still (of course) under scaffold. The work of restoration continues. It will resume after the Christmas break. And probably after that still.

Rome

I take the train down to Rome. On my last visit to Dora I took a cab from the train station. This time the Capolagos send a car and driver to the train. And this time I am greeted at the apartment by both Dora and Waldo. Last time it was Dora not only solo, but furtively solitary. I'm told Cip will join us after *pranzo*. Clearly, this is going to be a very formal occasion. We begin with *crostini* on silver plates. *Aperitivi* in crystal. The maid hovers in anxious attendance.

At first only small talk. How are my children? What a pity they could not come to Rome while they were in Fiesole this time. What do I hear from Joanne? From other mutual relations? Maggie's health? The recovery continues? How wonderful.

We move to the dining table. One by one the maid's specialties follow each other. Roman artichokes. Buttery veal. The only surprise, a distinctly American cake. Not something Italians would offer each other at lunch. A swift exchange of glances between husband and wife suggests there's some significance here. It is explained as a treat the maid thought I would prefer.

We move back to the *salone* for coffee. More very small talk. This could indeed be a diplomatic occasion, between allies who are not quite friends.

Finally, to everyone's relief, not least his own, Waldo excuses himself. He has another engagement. It displeases him deeply that he cannot stay. I must remain in touch. How content he would be to see Thaddeus and Cecilia again. He leaves. I am about to settle back into my chair when Dora indicates we are changing rooms.

I follow her to the back of the apartment into what I see at once was Ivo's room.

The typical room of a well-off young man. Of a well-off European young man. It's better bred that any American equivalent would be. Lots of books, most of them garnered from courses taken. Souvenirs of extensive travel. Closets full of clothes. Some of them still under plastic from the shop. A suitcase and a duffel bag, both unpacked, on the floor. Dora explains the room has been kept exactly as it was the morning Ivo left it for the last time. She will not allow the luggage to be emptied, let alone the rest of the clothing to be given away.

I am in the shrine. The one which kept Joanne awake all night. Packed on each shelf and surface—these I know she has been adding since his death—are pictures of Ivo at every stage of his life from infancy to his college graduation. Pleasant-looking as a boy, he had, I see, become an exceptionally handsome young man. I sit in the only chair. Dora perches at the side of the bed.

Same linen, I wonder, or does the maid make up the bed fresh each day?

The latter, I think.

Same with the small vase of flowers.

It is a winter afternoon. Dora does not light any of the lamps. The curtains are half drawn. We can see each other, barely. She points out the window to the balcony of an apartment across the courtyard.

"That's her room. The girl. See how close she lived to us. Thank God, she never came home again. If I knew she was there—just across from us—we would have to move. I couldn't stand it. That's why I keep the curtains pulled. So I don't have to see their place." She pauses. "How does she live with herself?"

And now she is ready to tell me what she sent for me to hear.

On the twenty-first, the birthday, she was sitting at her desk writing Christmas cards. She always writes out the cards that go to America well in advance to make sure they arrive on time. In each card she includes a long, individual message. Not for Dora the easy vulgarity of the one-size-fits-all family print-out. Toward the end of the afternoon she looked up to see the maid coming into the room, carrying a little tray on which rested a small cake with a single candle. The same kind of cake I've just been served.

"It's his birthday, Signora. This is his favorite *dolce*. The kind we always had for his birthday. Let's sing *Auguri* to Ivo, Signora. And blow out his candle for him."

Dora found herself swept by rage. Without thinking of what she was saying, she started screaming at the woman to get out, to get out of the room, to get out of the house. How could she imagine that Dora would want to mark the birthday? To sing *Auguri*? To blow out candles? Only a cretin, only a monster, could even have conceived of such a thing. And as she screamed she began mechanically to tear at the cards she had written, shredding them into tinier and tinier pieces, snowing them across the room. Until finally, gasping for breath, she sank back in the chair. She has no memory of what followed.

When she came to herself, the room was dark. She stirred because she heard the maid returning. This time she carried a small brandy and a stiff pasteboard napkin to catch drops. Silently, she offered the brandy to Dora who found she couldn't manage to hold it herself. The maid had to help her drink in small sips.

It was the maid who first noticed what was happening to the candle. In her anxious flight from Dora's terrible rage she had set down the tray with the cake on the edge of the desk. It was still there, and the candle was still burning. But now the flame from the tiny festive candle began to pencil, growing higher and higher until it seemed almost to touch the ceiling of the room. And there it stayed, unflickering, a bright, slender column.

Both women crossed themselves, and stared.

Without realizing what she was doing, the maid set down the empty glass and the pasteboard, but as the pasteboard touched the surface of the desk it started moving. Pulling her hand over the desk. Exploring among the scattered bits of card and envelope. Hovering. Pausing. Darting. Dora could see in the woman's startled face, and in the way her hands resisted, that she was not the mover but the moved.

The card floated low over the scattered paper stopping, searching then stopping again.

A long pause. Then the pattern repeated, quicker this time, knowing where it had to go, returning to the same places.

The third time Dora began to watch more carefully the spots where the card stopped. She realized the card was spelling. Ten letters. Three stops. Three words.

Mamma, sono io.

Mama, it's me.

"Ivo?"

Once again, the same movements, now six letters, two stops.

Sono io.

Dora was dumbstruck, her eyes tearing, heart quickening. It was the maid who thought to say: "Signora, talk to him. He wants to talk to you. Talk to him."

"Ivo, where you are, are you safe?"

The card moved. Two letters.

Sì.

"Are you happy?"

The card moved again. The same two letters.

Sì.

At this moment Dora believed. To that point she thought it might be the maid. Not a hoax. Not deception. But the maid, who had always loved Ivo best, desperate to break through to him. But now she knew it had happened the other way round.

"Ivo, have you seen *Gesù?*"

The parchment moved. Two words. Nine letters

Non ancora.

Not yet.

And then the candle returned to normal and they both knew the conversation was over.

"This is why you are here, John" Dora continues in the gathering dusk. "Not just here in the apartment, or in Rome. This is why you are in Italy. This is what you were brought here for. It is no coincidence that as you were leaving for Italy Ivo died. You have been brought back to us to write his story. You came to write a book. Well, this is your book. You write the truth about what was done to my son, and then he can find his final rest. Then he will see Jesus."

I want to explain that I came here to write a very different kind of book. But of course I don't say anything like that.

"Did Ivo tell you that?"

The door opens. It is Cip.

"Yes," Dora says.

Later, in the car, as Cip drives me to the train, I ask if he and his father also believe. Is that why Waldo insisted on being there when I arrived?

His father only cares that this has brought his mother peace of heart and peace of mind. She's restored. The woman who only a week ago seemed on the verge of insanity, ready to smash every bit of their common life in her reckless pursuit of the truth, that woman is gone now. Dora is not just at peace, she is serene.

I sensed that all afternoon. This was not the woman I had been dealing with all these weeks. It wasn't even the Dora we had known fourteen years ago. There's now a depth of calm, a poise and balance, I have never seen in her. The kind of focused peace one used to encounter in long-cloistered nuns. The convent term for it was *recollected.*

And what about Cip? Does he believe?

It takes a while for him to answer. It's Rome's rush hour. The traffic is terrifying. At least to me. Bred to this, Cip seems to find it just a challenge. Nevertheless, he takes his time before answering.

"On the day after Ivo's birthday, the day after this thing with the candle and the cards happened at home, I decided to go up in the plane. Just to think it through on my own, without interruptions. Maybe go up to Milan. Maybe spend the night there. It was a beautiful morning. Perfect flying weather. Ideal for this kind of jaunt.

"About an hour into the flight, I heard a voice. Not a voice. I heard Ivo's voice. As clear as though he were sitting behind me. Not a voice in my head. I even turned round when I heard it. It was that real.

"And he said, just: 'Turn around.'

Cip stops then to begin a series of figure eights across oncoming traffic that I find myself unable to watch.

"And I did. It didn't for a moment occur to me to question that this was really Ivo. I knew his voice, and I could hear he was completely sure about what he was telling me. What I didn't know until I got back to Rome was that just ahead of where I turned there was a freak storm. It came out of nowhere. No one was prepared for it. Devastating. Could I have made it? Maybe. Maybe not. Probably not."

"Well, then, I can see why you believe."

"That's not all."

I am in a Mercedes moving across Rome. I recognize some of the churches and monuments flying past us. But I am also moving into some other kind of other world here, a world I don't live in, a world I don't believe I want to live in, a world that to Dora and Cip and probably Waldo seems now completely the norm. I am being engaged by something that comes from nowhere inside my own experience, turned toward a horizon I can't even outline.

"When I got closer to Rome, I tried to make contact but I realized my radio was dead. I tried the back up. That was dead too. And then all my instruments died. The whole panel—as though struck by lightning—all out. Everything else, as far as I could tell, working perfectly, but now I was flying blind. Everything I needed to rely on—gone. This is it, I thought. And then Ivo said to me. And I could hear the laugh as he said it, the younger brother's revenge: 'Hey, Cip, you've got a phone.'

"I had completely forgotten. The cell phone. I fished it out. I managed to get through to the guys in the tower. They talked me in. It should have been terrifying, you know, but it was just the reverse. It was a lark, something for Ivo and me to share.

"So, yes, Gian, I believe."

Corridoio

And then I get that moment of clarity I was hoping for.

It happens in that wing of the Uffizi called the Vasari Corridor. The Corridor, in Italian *Corridoio*, stretches for about a kilometer connecting the Uffizi Gallery with the Pitti Palace on the other side of the Arno. At one point it actually becomes the top story of the Ponte Vecchio, unbeknownst to the crowds of tourists buying gold below. It is shown only by request, to small groups. We hadn't previously been able to match our schedule to the available reservations. But now, just when we had given up hope, our request comes through.

The Uffizi's late seventeenth- and eighteenth-century pictures hang here, notably the superb *Judith and Holofernes* by Artemisia Gentileschi. There's also a famous collection of painters' self-portraits. But the most moving, indeed harrowing, picture on the walls is one of the mercifully few paintings ruined by the Mafia bombing of the Uffizi in 1993.

On May 27, 1993 the Mafia exploded a powerful car bomb just under that section of the *Corridoio* that connects the gallery to the bridge. The blast killed five people and wounded many others. It impacted twenty-four of the Uffizi's rooms and it took almost two months before the gallery could reopen. Though most of the collection was unharmed, many paintings were damaged. Three were destroyed. Seven years later no signs of the outrage remain, except for this painting described only as by a follower of Caravaggio. But the violence and brutality of the crime give the canvas a stature and power no famous name could enhance.

It hangs alone on the landing of a steep staircase, the landing only slightly wider than its frame. Nothing lights it. It is to every sense a dead thing in a dead space. When you do manage to see it up close, you realize that most of the paint has simply been blown off the canvas. What little remains on the canvas is unreadable. Is that a hand? A wing? Could this be the outline of a shoulder? What were the faces that go with those forms? What did they show? Who now can say?

Little wonder you get to see it only by permission, and that rarely. The wonder is that it is hanging here at all. It stands for everything negative and fearsome Tourist Italy is designed to screen and Travelers Italy to ignore: the innate toughness of Italy, cruel, duplicitous, brutal. Everything the Capolagos have endured. Everything Shakespeare pointed toward. But it also shows me the favor Italy has done me.

As with the painting, Italy has forced me to look at my life as a surface scraped clear of everything that was usually and consolingly legible. If I had spent these three months in the UK or France, I could not see that. Their familiarity would have kept me incased in the same habits of thought and feeling I rely on at home. But Italy's utter difference from the way we live—before and beyond law, regulation, even at times beyond rationality: everything forbidden, everything possible—has led me to confront and then surrender every customary evasion, about myself, my life, and life itself. Italy, my own ort, has forced me back into time.

Veschi G. e Figli

I want to buy a coat. Waiting for me in a closet at home I have the standard middle-aged, mid-level man's black overcoat. (My Italian family always insisted that if you have only one overcoat it has to be black—for funerals.) But I want to go home with an Italian coat, a particular Italian coat, the dark green woolen loden coat that all European men of a certain age and professional status wear through the colder months. It's cut straight from the shoulders, with a military collar, and stops about mid-calf. It flatters everyone. Especially as worn in Italy, a land where the cassock still carries cachet, it is the layman's answer to the vestment.

Stefano explains that to buy such a coat, not a copy but the real thing, the only place to go is Veschi, Veschi G. e Figli, in the center of Florence. That is where the coats I have been envying are bought, and only there.

So, on this our last full day in Fiesole, Maggie and I go down the hill and into the city, to Veschi. It's drizzling and cold, a good day to buy a coat impervious to weather. I usually don't spend a lot of money on my back but I have decided this is my Italian souvenir, and the sky is, almost, the limit.

We stop off first at Rivoire on Piazza della Signoria for coffee. We do this to celebrate Stefano who brought us here for the first time years ago. He thought we were spending too much time isolated up in Fiesole and needed to taste, literally, the glories of Florence. On this chilly December morning the caffe is almost deserted. We can sit in the wide window watching the rain drive the very few tourists across the piazza and into the palazzo across the way.

The coffee is, of course, superb.

Maggie surprises me by asking what I am going to do when I get back to Georgetown.

"The same thing I always do."

I am a tenured full professor in a department where I've worked for more than 30 years. I don't expect much to change.

"Well, I am going to look for a change," Maggie says. "Whoever wins this election, there will be a change of administrations, new people, and I am going to look around. It's time."

"Would you leave the government?"

"We'll see what happens."

I could not be more surprised.

"I'm open," she concludes.

I pay the bill.

"You should think about that, John."

The salesman at Veschi—is this one of the Figli?—knows what I want. It turns out to be Austrian, not Italian, made by a company called Steinboch. He thinks I am exactly right to want it. As he leaves to find a coat to try on—they don't carry many in my size—I realize that even if I spent a fortune I could never look as good as he does or behave with such consummate finish. Of course, I am much taller than almost all Italians so that when he does find one it's more mid-knee than mid-calf. Still, it is very fine.

And then I see the price and start to give it back. But Maggie will have none of that. She pays with her credit card.

Figlio Veschi assures me: "Professore, not only will you wear this coat for the rest of your life but you will leave it to your grandson and it will be as beautiful on that day as it is today."

I believe him.

But I can also see in Veschi's glass that the coat does not make me look Florentine, or even European. It does not change me.

That will take more than a coat.

Maggie is right, as usual. I also need a change, a big change. But not the kind of change we made after our last stay here. Then I came, as Auden says in the great "Good-bye" poem, "In middle-age hoping to twig from/ What we are not what we might be next." And it worked. After Italy, Maggie and I set out deliberately to live differently, to pursue what the poem is wrong to dismiss as "the Myth of an Open Road,/ Which runs past he orchard gate and beckons/ Three brothers in turn to set out over the hills/And far away." Or in this case two parents, a son, and a daughter. It's not a myth. The road was open and it did lead us, in our different ways, far away. And it has been a marvel.

But this time, after our brush with death, with the children gone, even with this bizarre election that will not end, everything feels different, unsettled, unpredictable. What I see in Veschi's mirror now is not a man moving into middle age but a man moving past the meridian, the midpoint, moving from that time in life when you take control to a time when it is wiser to be open, to make the most of what comes. Pay attention and prize what's on offer.

I see what Maggie meant back there at Rivoire. It is time to stop insisting that life function like a plot with a through-line you manage, like a course you plan in a syllabus you invent. It is time to let life come not from me, but through, and to me.

What will this coat and I see and do in all the coming years, before—at a date far off, I hope—it passes to that grandson Signor Veschi was so sure of? I don't even have a grandson yet. But I think I will, and I think life itself will come crowding in with a whole new cast of characters, an entirely new set of possibilities. I'm fine with that. I have my coat, and my ticket home.

"Go I must," Auden writes, "but I go grateful."

Finale Ultimo
December 6-7

Gli studenti are gone. Not back to the States. All their friends at home are still in class. So our guys have just moved on to Paris and London to join up with all the other now-released Students Abroad, for a few final weeks of Euro revelry.

Mary Jo has flown off to Scotland.

Now Maggie is going also.

Last summer, as we planned our Italian sojourn, we thought it would be a good idea for her to go back first and reclaim the house. I would stay on here for a bit and nudge these chapters into a coherent first draft. But now we both regret this choice. She dreads going back to the empty house, and all alone restoring it to order after a three month sublet. And I dread even more staying on at Le Balze by myself. When I return from the Milan airport to Fiesole, even the indoor staff will be gone. One of the gardeners will come by each day, to make sure nothing is awry. But that will be it. Le Balze will be all and entirely mine. And I shudder at the prospect. Not absence-in-presence. Just absence.

Of all my many blunders this one seems the worst

Maggie is flying out of Malpensa. Dreaded Malpensa, where Cecilia and Doug were so shabbily treated just two weeks back. Her flight leaves very early tomorrow morning. We have decided to spend the night in a hotel near the airport, rather than in Milan, to make it easier on her. We take an early train from Florence, promising ourselves a last shopping expedition (it is, after all, Milan) and a final coffee with Pietro who lives there during the week. Then we'll make our way into the countryside, and the hotel. After she's left, I'll go overnight to Venice for a day to soften the separation. And then return to the vacated villa.

We do have a marvelous afternoon in Milan with Pietro. Tomorrow is the *Notte di Sant'Ambrogio*, the night the La Scala opera season opens, and you can feel the buzz already as the city revs up for its brightest moment. We have coffee in the famed Galleria and Maggie finds a lovely red leather purse, her final souvenir. Then, after dinner near the Duomo, in the foggy dark we take the long, dreary bus ride out to Malpensa, which like Dulles is far into the countryside. It's an interminable landscape of car dealerships and light industry alternating with long stretches of misty vacancy. Un-utterably bleak, entirely uninviting, completely unTuscan.

At the empty airport we leave the bus and find a cab whose driver claims to know exactly where our hotel is.

He doesn't.

We drive for an hour, his meter ticking the entire time. It turns out he knows where the hotel's little town is but not the hotel. He only knew where he thought it *normale*, proper, for such a hotel to be. And he doesn't concede even that much until Maggie insists he stop the cab and let us out. He then admits he is a Milanese driver, who found his cab empty after he took his fare to the airport. He was back on the road before he realized that we were not going into Milan also.

Twice he stops by a pay phone. Apparently, he is the only cab-driver, no, the only person, in Italy without a *telefonino*. Twice he gets directions for the hotel from the hotel. He continues neverthe-less to get lost, going in what seem to us to be circles. We actually spot the hotel several times. *Ecco là, ecco là.* But there is no way to get there from any kind of here.

He's not faking. He's not kidnapping us. He's not running up the meter. It's a matter of time and space: you just can't get there from here.

At last, by first breaking into a closed construction site, crossing several areas marked *Vietato* (Forbidden), and finally violating the driveway and backyard of a private house—we actually have to drive through its carport—we arrive at the hotel.

The cab rushes off as soon as *lire* change hands.

There's one bored young woman at the desk. We appear to be the only guests. Soon we learn why. At registration, the clerk tells us that it is not yet the full season and they are only partially open, as though we are intruders, imposing. We have reservations, I in-sist. Icily, she confirms that with a nod. *The more fools you.*

She gives us a key and directions to a distant room. On the sec-ond floor. There is no elevator. We have all of Maggie's luggage from three months here to lug upstairs in multiple stages. Eventually we locate the room. The room turns out to be even worse than the ride. The windows are covered by floor to ceiling iron shutters locked into the surbase. When I call down to the desk clerk to ask to have them unlocked, she explains that is *vietato* until the season properly begins. The heat, however, has been on at full blast. (I would guess at least since August.) It cannot be adjusted. Until the season properly begins. Unlocking the shutters and altering the thermostat require an *Ingegnere*, an engineer, who starts with the full season. There is one forty-watt bulb in one lamp. That's it for illumination. And the bed is sheeted in cellophane.

Exhausted, we don't sleep. We merely swelter.

The next morning we are not in the best of moods as we begin to say our unwelcome goodbyes. It is bad enough that Maggie has to go first, but to go after a sleepless night in a cinder block sauna, without breakfast (of course the hotel had no restaurant, no snack bar, no snack machine), this seems too much, excessively unfair even for Italy.

Even the briefest parting from Maggie makes me unbearably blue. But not this time. Somehow this time I can talk myself out of my habitual pessimism. The separation is only going to be for two weeks. There was a plane crash the other day. That infinitely multiplies the odds against her plane going down today. I find to my surprise that I can fight off my demons.

And then it's time to go. She gives me a bottle of whiskey she just covertly bought in a kiosk and tells me to use it. Not drink it. *Use it.* Then I watch her disappear through the first security check.

I wait for a moment but it's too much. I turn and race down a set of outside steps while she moves along the crowded interior ramps. A couple of spirals down I spot her, though she has no idea I'm out here. She's wearing her new Italian gloves, and a new Italian scarf, and new Italian shoes, and carrying her brand-new Milanese purse. She's also got that damned five-liter jug of the new olive oil from Volpaia. And somehow also—why isn't it packed?—she's carrying a bottle of *Brunello* that the headwaiter from 145 Piazza Mino insisted she take home with her when he heard that it was our final dinner in Fiesole. He even inscribed it. *Auguri.* Good luck.

She's like a moving pageant of Italy's generous bounty.

I can't believe it but despite the crowd of surging travelers, she remains unmistakable. She is fumbling with her passport. Her boarding pass must have gotten mixed up with her customs declarations. She is frowning, trying to keep everything in order, trying not to drop the oil or the wine. She is not going to look up or back. Why should she? She thinks I'm already several stories away and headed in the opposite direction toward the train. She just wants to make her way through the mob at the gate.

In my head I begin to hear the great aria from *Orfeo*: *"che farò senza Euridice?"* What will I do without Eurydice? But this isn't tragedy. Far from it. She turns, and spots me, and smiles. This is the opera *Orfeo* not the myth. Euridice returns to life. Despite the crowds, and the noise, and the difficulties of hanging on to tickets, passport, gloves, purse, olive oil and wine, she is glowing.

It has worked.

While week after week I let myself become more and more self-absorbed, Maggie came back. While she sat in the garden alone, and painted or read, and thought and looked, Italy did its best, quiet work. The Italy that can preserve sublime Sant'Antimo for a thousand years. The Italy that waits until *Ventuno* to press the olives. Not a day before or a day after, even if it rains. The Italy that grows the flawless pear, and plucks it only when perfect. The deepest, truest presence in all the absence. That Italy.

She's sad to go. I see that. She'd prefer we were going together. But deep down, I see this also, clearly, so would anyone who looks at her, even strangers, she's at peace, and glad.

And so, I find, am I.

We didn't find, Maggie and I, the magical Italy we left behind a decade and a half before. We found instead a decidedly imperfect, deeply flawed and dangerous Italy. An Italy Shakespeare showed me how to understand. And this new Italy found for us in turn the Maggie who had been, like the heroine in a late Shakespeare play, not lost, but clouded over, obscured, sent some distance away, and kept there for a while under wraps. Found her and restored her, so that now, even as I watch her disappear though the gates, swallowed up finally in the crowd, I know that Italy has done what we hoped for: returned Maggie to me. Exactly as she was. Is.

Yes, *Stefano, Italy is terrible but this is Italy also. The good new.*

Afterword 2017

In recreating this indelibly memorable autumn, I have also been conscious of the need to maintain the anonymity, not only of *gli studenti*, but of other individuals we encountered. I have changed the names of some persons and places, and I've also altered some identifying characteristics. But the essential truth, I think, and believe, remains.

The experience recorded in these pages is literally impossible now. Two years after we left Le Balze Georgetown gutted the villino to create more rooms for students and offices for faculty. Now the visiting faculty member and family live in a rented apartment somewhere up in the hills of Fiesole, quite apart from the life of Le Balze.

But of course that is not all that has changed.

In many ways the twentieth century has turned out to be as different from the twenty-first as the nineteenth was from the twentieth. Indeed, in some ways the experience recounted in these pages feels closer to the nineteenth century than to the way we live now. Even though it has not even been two full decades since our Le Balze stay, September 2001 has marked a pivotal point that I could only begin to sense in November 2000, and not just because of the rise of terrorism. President Clinton (still in office in the autumn of these chapters) used to talk a lot about building a bridge to the twenty-first century, but it would seem that where we once expected a bridge we now find a canyon.

When I first returned to the manuscript I thought I needed to update it. But now I see that its best claim on a reader's attention may come from the way it can serve as a time capsule.

Still some updating does seem in order.

Jane Harvey's prediction did not come true and, as of this writing, the walls of San Girolamo remain reliably in place. As do the walls of Le Balze. Readers will also, I hope, be glad to know that Cecilia did indeed marry Douglas Gordon, almost exactly three years after that difficult Thanksgiving visit. And the man at Veschi was right in his prediction. Maggie and I do have a grandson, in fact we have four, and a granddaughter.

And I am happy to make the last words of our still unfinished story their beloved names: Cooper Glavin, Holden Glavin, James Gordon, Sam Gordon, Genevieve Glavin.

CPSIA information can be obtained
at www.ICGtesting.com
Printed in the USA
LVOW12*0027281117

557775LV00001B/6/P